Love and the Politics of Care

Love and the Politics of Care

Methods, Pedagogies, Institutions

Edited by
Stanislava Dikova, Wendy McMahon and
Jordan Savage

BLOOMSBURY ACADEMIC
NEW YORK • LONDON • OXFORD • NEW DELHI • SYDNEY

BLOOMSBURY ACADEMIC
Bloomsbury Publishing Inc
1385 Broadway, New York, NY 10018, USA
50 Bedford Square, London, WC1B 3DP, UK
29 Earlsfort Terrace, Dublin 2, Ireland

BLOOMSBURY, BLOOMSBURY ACADEMIC and the Diana logo are
trademarks of Bloomsbury Publishing Plc

First published in the United States of America 2022
Paperback edition published 2024

Copyright © Stanislava Dikova, Wendy McMahon and Jordan Savage, 2022
Each chapter © of Contributors

For legal purposes the Acknowledgements on p. xvi constitute an
extension of this copyright page.

Cover design by Eleanor Rose
Cover image © Getty Images

All rights reserved. No part of this publication may be reproduced or transmitted in any form or by any means, electronic or mechanical, including photocopying, recording, or any information storage or retrieval system, without prior permission in writing from the publishers.

Bloomsbury Publishing Inc does not have any control over, or responsibility for, any third-party websites referred to or in this book. All internet addresses given in this book were correct at the time of going to press. The author and publisher regret any inconvenience caused if addresses have changed or sites have ceased to exist, but can accept no responsibility for any such changes.

Library of Congress Cataloging-in-Publication Data
Names: Dikova, Stanislava, editor. | McMahon, Wendy, editor. | Savage, Jordan, editor.
Title: Love and the politics of care : methods, pedagogies, institutions /
edited by Stanislava Dikova, Wendy McMahon and Jordan Savage.
Description: New York, NY : Bloomsbury Academic, 2022. | Includes bibliographical references and index. | Summary: "Interdisciplinary studies on the position of love in contemporary global thought and literature that address love and care work within social structures and institutions"– Provided by publisher.
Identifiers: LCCN 2022022591 (print) | LCCN 2022022592 (ebook) |
ISBN 9781501387647 (hardback) | ISBN 9781501387685 (paperback) |
ISBN 9781501387654 (epub) | ISBN 9781501387661 (pdf) | ISBN 9781501387678
Subjects: LCSH: Love–Social aspects. | Interpersonal attraction. |
Interpersonal relations. | Caring.
Classification: LCC HM1151. L68 2022 (print) | LCC HM1151 (ebook) |
DDC 302–dc23/eng/20220613
LC record available at https://lccn.loc.gov/2022022591
LC ebook record available at https://lccn.loc.gov/2022022592

ISBN: HB: 978-1-5013-8764-7
PB: 978-1-5013-8768-5
ePDF: 978-1-5013-8766-1
eBook: 978-1-5013-876-54

Typeset by Newgen KnowledgeWorks Pvt. Ltd., Chennai, India

To find out more about our authors and books visit www.bloomsbury.com
and sign up for our newsletters.

To Amy May

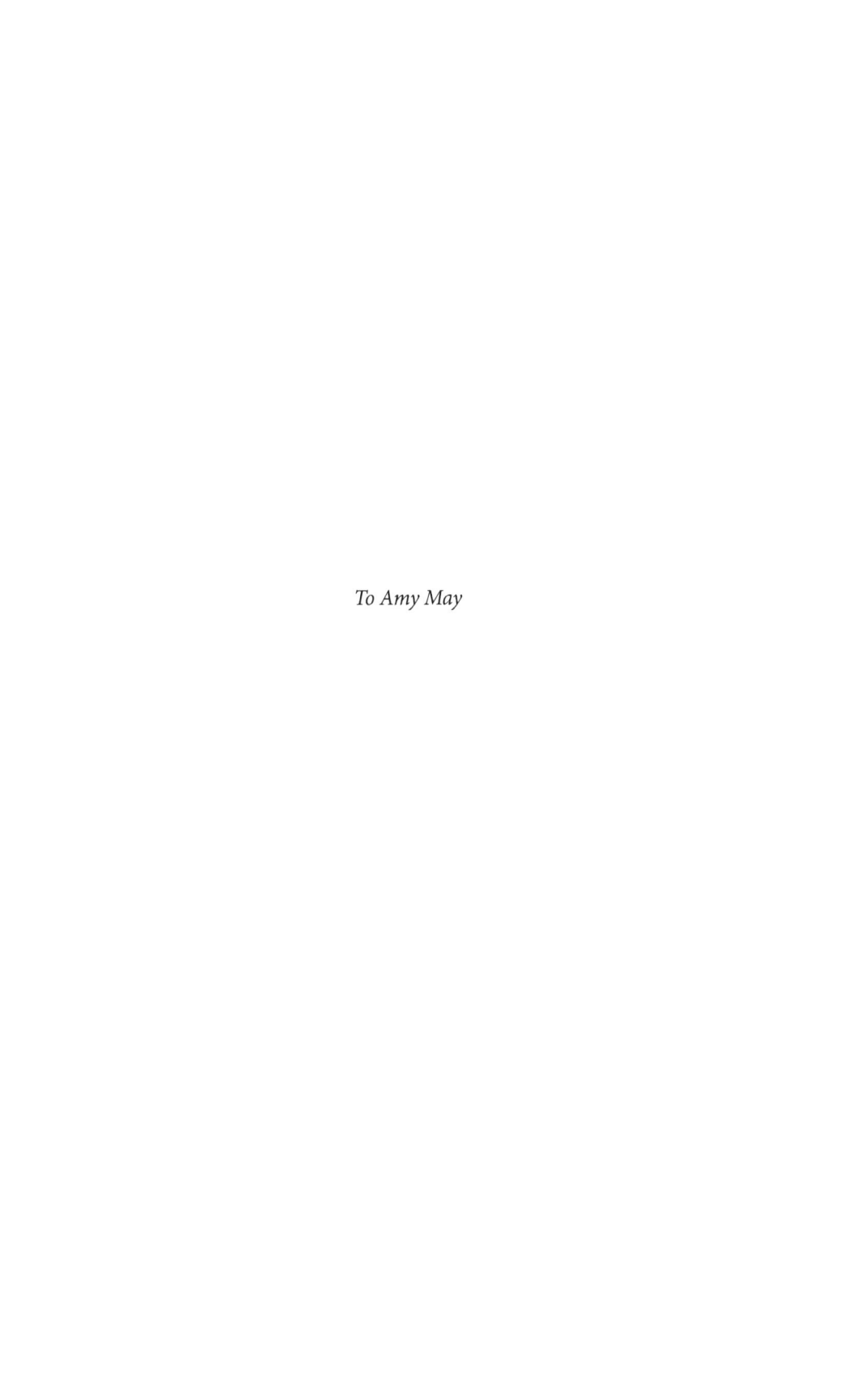

Contents

List of Figures	ix
Notes on Contributors	x
Preface	xiii
Acknowledgements	xvi

Introduction   1
Stanislava Dikova, Wendy McMahon and Jordan Savage

Part 1   Love and cultures of marriage

1. Public romance in India and its transgressive potential   15
   Meghna Bohidar
2. Gratitude's compulsion   35
   Lan Kieu
3. The *Beatitudes of Love*: Revisiting Stanley Spencer's ways of seeing   53
   Racheal Harris

Part 2   Love and communal pedagogies of care

4. Symbiosis masquerades as love in the (post-)apartheid world of Marlene van Niekerk's *Agaat*   73
   Shekufeh Owlia
5. Parenting as a political pedagogy: Love as methodology, parenting as praxis   89
   Shelley Maddox
6. *Caring with*, voice and under-represented expressions of love in and through *The Undefinable* by She Goat: An artist-researcher's perspective   107
   Eugénie Pastor, with Shamira Turner

Part 3 Love and neoliberal care

7   Not in the mood: Reading love in the contemporary university   129
    Karen Schaller
8   Should I be scared when you say that you love me? Youth work
    practice and the power of *professional love*   149
    Martin E. Purcell
9   Reciprocity, love and market in Brazilian care work for the elderly   169
    Anna Bárbara Araujo
10 Love, power and justice in the shadow of the contemporary
    English prison   185
    Christina Straub

Index   203

Figures

1.1 Wall painting (Translation: *Anarkali*) in Mumbai, India, by the Bollywood Art Project, 2012   16
1.2 Photograph of a wall of the *bada gumbad* (big dome) in Lodhi Garden, a park in New Delhi, 2019   27
6.1 The Undefinable by She Goat. Picture by James Allan, 2018   110

Contributors

Anna Bárbara Araujo is a professor at Federal University of Rio Grande do Norte, Brazil. She holds a PhD (2019) and a master's degree (2015) in sociology from the Federal University of Rio de Janeiro, Brazil. She was a consultant for UN Women researching the political organization of domestic workers in Brazil. Her research interests include care, domestic work, intersectionality, inequalities and emotions.

Meghna Bohidar is a PhD student in the Department of Sociology at the University of Delhi, India. For her dissertation, she is working on the experiences of public intimacy in urban spaces. Her research interests focus on the sociology of emotions, gender and sexuality, popular cinema and public space. Her recent publications include the chapter 'Performances of "Reel" and "Real" Lives: Negotiating Public Romance in Urban India' in *The Routledge Companion to Romantic Love* (2021).

Stanislava Dikova is a postdoctoral researcher and a visiting fellow in the Department of Literature, Film, and Theatre Studies at the University of Essex, UK. Her research interests revolve around twentieth-century literature and thought, writing by women, histories of knowledge and feminist social theory. Stanislava's writing has appeared in the *Modernist Review*, the *LSE Review of Books* and *Feminist Modernist Studies*. She is currently working on her first monograph.

Racheal Harris is a PhD candidate in sociology and religious anthropology at Deakin University, Australia. Her research is focused on spiritualism, death rituals and afterlife beliefs relating to companion animals. She is a qualified end-of-life doula, apprentice taxidermist and medium. Her latest book *Photography and Death: Framing Death throughout History* was published in 2020.

Lan Kieu has defended a PhD in gender studies at Umeå University, Sweden. Her chapter is drawn from this research, which has received full funding from Umeå University. Her research interests include postcolonial critique, feminist and political theory, ethics, subjectivity and resistance.

Shelley Maddox is a doctoral student in cultural and educational policy studies at Loyola University Chicago, USA. A mother, a lover and a philosopher, her work in philosophy of education lies at the intersections of educational, feminist and political theories and asks questions about the family as the site wherein children simultaneously learn about love, power and domination. Her research interests broadly seek to transform understandings of power within adult–child relationships, explore the legitimacy of authority in struggles for freedom and expand paradigms of possibility towards wholeness and abundance in a variety of contexts.

Wendy McMahon is Associate Professor in American Studies at the University of East Anglia, UK. Her research interests centre around contemporary literatures of the American hemisphere and their intersections with disaster studies, human rights, law, capitalism and globalization, conflict and security, migration and exile, place, belonging and citizenship. Wendy has a particular interest in the relationship between Caribbean and US topographies, colonialism, and decolonial emancipatory art, activism and writing. Wendy has published on Cuban exile writing, Caribbean literature and masculinity, African American literature and human rights, as well as the relationship between landscape and history in literature.

Shekufeh Owlia is a PhD candidate at the University of Tehran, Iran, working on post-apartheid South African fiction. She has served as an editorial member of *La Revue de Téhéran*, a journal published in French devoted to issues pertaining to Persian literature and culture for over a decade. She is the author of 'The New Woman and the Oriental Tropes as Portrayed in the Iranian Film *Tardid* Based on *Hamlet*' (2016), a chapter published in *Culture-Blind Shakespeare: Multiculturalism and Diversity*. Her areas of interest include postcolonialism, discard studies, orientalism and comparative literature.

Eugénie Pastor is a lecturer in the Department of Acting and Performance at London South Bank University, UK. Her research focuses on intimacy and embodied knowledge in performance, one-to-one performance, feminism, music-making and collaboration. Recent publications include the chapter 'Time, Friendship and "Collective Intimacy": The Point of View of a Co-Devisor from within Little Bulb Theatre' in *Time and Performer Training* (2019). She is also an artist who works in performance, theatre and music. She is one half of the experimental performance company She Goat, a member of Little Bulb Theatre as well as an independent performance-maker, whose work has been shown in the UK and internationally.

Martin E. Purcell is Lecturer in Community Education at the University of Dundee, UK. His research addresses the translation of professional values into practice, focusing in particular on the embodiment of professionally loving practice in work with marginalized and vulnerable young people and in community development. Martin has published on public participation in decision-making, pedagogy in higher education as well as *professional love* in radical community development and youth work.

Jordan Savage is Lecturer in US Literature at the University of Essex, UK. Her research centres on literary and cinematic constructions of US nationalism and national identity. She is interested in the iconography of dirt in the Western poetry, especially Native poetry, offering counter-narratives to US nationalism; and the myth structure of American exceptionalism. Jordan has published on contemporary poetry from Britain and the United States, modern poetics and Western generic studies.

Karen Schaller is Lecturer in Literature at the University of East Anglia, UK. Her research interests focus on feeling, feminism and affective economies with an attention to twentieth- and twenty-first-century English literature, film and art. She has published on the critical recuperation of mid-century writers such as Elizabeth Bowen and Sylvia Townsend Warner, political uses of feeling in mid-century literature as well as the domestic in the contemporary feminist imaginations of Miranda July, Zadie Smith and Deborah Levy. She is currently writing a book about feeling and feminist practice in the contemporary university.

Christina Straub is a researcher in the Department of Sociology at Durham University, UK, where she works together with Kate O'Brien to evaluate the *Early Days in Custody* support programme delivered by NEPACS. She is also involved in research conducted at HMP Long Lartin by Kate Gooch (Bath University) on the dynamics and pressures of life in a high-security prison. In October 2021, she took up a part-time role as research associate at the University of Manchester's Division of Nursing, Midwifery and Social Work, looking into support and assessment needs of older adults (and their families).

Shamira Turner is an artist and performance-maker with a focus on devised work that plays with gender expectations, integrates music in innovative ways and promotes kindness and curiosity. She is the producer and co-director of experimental duo She Goat, and a co-founder and associate artist of award-winning Little Bulb, with whom she has devised and performed since 2008. Shamira has collaborated with 1927, Theatre Ad Infinitum, Camden People's Theatre, Extant, Pilot Theatre; as music director on 'More Than Two' (Barbican); and she was part of Fuel Theatre's 'Creative Freelancers: Shaping London's Recovery' research project supported by the mayor of London.

Preface

This collection of essays, and its companion volume *Love and the Politics of Intimacy*, present an interdisciplinary, global study of love, drawing on sociology, philosophy, social care work, literary studies, film, the performing arts, the digital and medical humanities as well as creative writing practice. The case studies discussed in each chapter are situated in various locations across Europe, Africa, Asia and the Americas and provide a comprehensive coverage of love, both conceptually and practically, as an essential aspect of personal and public life. The temporal reach spans from the Enlightenment period, when most current forms of political, financial and institutional organization were elaborated, to the present day.

Every featured essay or creative piece has something to say about love and the various forms of difficulty encountered while trying to lead a loving life. The locations of love explored through these studies range from the deeply intimate space of a sexual encounter to the transnational arena of the global care work industry. This broad landscape demonstrates the foundational role love plays in the very fabric of our individual and social lives. The body, the family, the workplace, the home, the digital, the institutional and the global are all enclosures in which love meets with restrictions and which condition the lives of those who experience it. From racial and class barriers to physical borders between nations, love's boundaries are drawn by discourses of power, institutional and systemic practices of control and the forces of the marketplace. The intended consequences of this demarcation reach far into the lives of those individuals who love and wish to be loved, intimately, deeply, protectively and freely. All contributions across the two volumes work with these ideas and ask the following questions: who is allowed to love, and in what ways? What discourses of love do we feel obliged to participate in or are excluded from? How do national and international superstructures alter or instrumentalize love, and what are the effects of this? Questions of gender and sexuality, race, nation, faith and disability are all addressed. The guiding aim of this approach has been to provide a conceptual and genealogical overview of the existing tension between love and the lived conditions within which it is practised. In doing so, these volumes present an alternative history of love that, though not exhaustive, goes beyond its traditionally discussed theological and moral manifestations, focusing instead on its presence in everyday life. Talking about love across the disciplinary divide provides a further impetus for renewed investigation of a set of ideas all too often confined within the history of Western thought. Our two collections also look at the present and future moments in search of an inspiration for transforming and recharting the pathways of love in such a way as to lead us to a more diverse and emancipatory model of social life. The present volume addresses the politicization of love through practices of care that stretch from the familial to the institutional, and it looks at forms of regulation exercised over them within the context of the neoliberal ideological framework. Its companion volume, *Love and the Politics of Intimacy*, transposes these concerns to the construction of intimacy as a practice that occurs *between*, *through*, *within* and, increasingly, *beyond* bodies, asking questions about the norms and contexts in which they operate.

The emergence of this project was rooted in our experiences of the contemporary university in the UK, where ideas of love and care are often weaponized by government and management against staff in order to extract additional work and further erode working conditions.[1] This rhetoric is also commonly used to diminish resolve for industrial action and weaken union influence within the UK higher education sector. We wondered whether this power dynamic was in operation in other sectors of the economy, and by extension, in the homes and personal lives of those who labour in them, particularly in situations where there is an expectation of care. Our call for submissions generated a strong response, which convinced us that scholars and practitioners from many disciplines are interested in asking similar questions and that our collection could contribute to the burgeoning field of 'Love Studies' identified by Anna G. Jónasdóttir and Ann Ferguson as an emerging 'historically specific field of knowledge interests' that is both 'heterogeneous' and 'conflicted'.[2] The two volumes were conceived together and we hope that they will continue their joined existence by being read together, but this is by no means a requirement for productive engagement with either.

Notes

1 See Amelia Horgan, *Lost in Work: Escaping Capitalism* (London: Pluto Press, 2021), 58; 132-4. According to data provided by the University and College Union (UCU),

46 per cent of universities use precarious labour in the form of zero hours contracts to deliver their teaching and 68 per cent of research staff are on fixed-term contracts (UCU, 'Stamp Out Casual Contracts', https://www.ucu.org.uk/stampout [accessed 11 January 2022]).

2 Anna G. Jónasdóttir and Ann Ferguson, 'Introduction', in *Love: A Question for Feminism in the Twenty-First Century*, ed. Anna G. Jónasdóttir and Ann Ferguson (London: Routledge, 2014), 2.

Acknowledgements

We, the editors, would like to convey our immense gratitude and appreciation to all contributors to the volume for sharing their work with us at the most turbulent of times. This project began to take shape in the spring of 2019, before any of us knew that a global pandemic was about to alter the course of our professional and personal lives. Despite this, our contributors persisted with their searching inquiries and presented us with a selection of chapters, which we are honoured to present in this collection. We also wish to extend our gratitude to our commissioning editor at Bloomsbury, Amy Martin, whose faith in the project kept us on track throughout the process, and to the three anonymous readers, who gave us their time and generously provided thoughtful feedback.

A very special thanks is due to James Allan who kindly gave us permission to reproduce a photograph of She Goat and to Meghna Bohidar for supplying the images that illustrate her chapter in this volume. A further thanks is also due to all the anonymous participants who have taken part in the research interviews and questionnaires that have informed the research insights developed in several chapters. They are part of the larger global networks of care, which provide the backbone of the work presented here.

We acknowledge the support of our colleagues at the University of Essex, the University of East Anglia and Keele University. We are also grateful for the support and loving inspiration of our families, especially Ian, Russel and Andy.

Introduction

Stanislava Dikova, Wendy McMahon and Jordan Savage

Audre Lorde starts her famous essay 'The Uses of the Erotic: The Erotic as Power' with the simple declaration that 'there are many kinds of power, used and unused, acknowledged and otherwise'.[1] She continues to make the argument that the purpose of every act of oppression is the stifling of the impulse for change, focusing specifically on the patriarchal distortion and capitalist misappropriation of the discourse around erotic desire and its resulting usage to further subordinate women to conditions of domination. Lorde aims to reclaim the erotic power women have lost or confused for something else in order to offer a new model of political and ethical life, which is nourishing instead of harmful. 'The principal horror of any system', she writes:

> which defines the good in terms of profit rather than in terms of human need, or which defines human need to the exclusion of the psychic and emotional components of the need – the principal horror of such system is that it robs our work of its … life appeal and fulfilment. Such a system reduces work to a travesty of necessities, a duty by which we earn bread or oblivion for ourselves and those we love. But this is … not only next to impossible, it is also profoundly cruel.[2]

We recognize in this description a model of our contemporary society, its operational value systems and its governing modes of judgement. This volume has set itself a task similar to that of Lorde's essay – instead of the erotic, it looks at the practice of care and the psychic, familial, historical and institutional distortions it has sustained in the context of a global neoliberal order. Expanding on bell hooks's concern that 'we are never loved in a context where there is abuse', the Care Collective, a radical thought group of academics based in the UK, has asked in their recently published book whether care can be practiced at all in the context of neoliberalism.[3] Developing their discussion in hooks's tradition, *The Care Manifesto* diagnoses our current society as suffering from a 'crisis of care', stemming partly from the historical devaluing of care work, due to its 'association with women, the feminine and what have been seen as the "unproductive" caring professions', and partly from the expansion of neoliberal political and financial interests aiming to marketize and extract maximum value from insufficiently funded care services, which typically rely on precarious workers.[4] Care as a form of work is one of the central lines of inquiry that runs through this volume, and while some of the contributors position it in its professional contexts (Purcell, Araujo, Schaller), others expand these boundaries to examine the larger institutional conditions within which care functions, often unnoticed, in spaces such as the theatre hall (Pastor), the prison complex (Straub), the canvas (Harris), the urban landscape (Bohidar) and the family home (Kieu, Maddox, Owlia). In doing so, this volume joins *The Care Manifesto* in taking an approach to care that understands it as a wider social phenomenon, a 'capacity and a practice' that involves 'the nurturing of all that is necessary for the welfare and flourishing of life'.[5]

Under neoliberalism, governments and corporations often promote the idea that care is a matter of individual responsibility and refuse to 'recognise our shared vulnerabilities and interconnectedness'.[6] In doing so, they rely on a notion of the ideal neoliberal citizen, who is a 'self-sufficient figure' and does not require external, be it communally or state-provided, support to conduct their life.[7] This way of thinking has infiltrated feminist discourses too. As Catherine Rottenberg has argued, the convergence between liberal feminism and neoliberalism has resulted precisely in 'producing an individuated feminist subject whose identity is informed by a cost-benefit calculus'.[8] The operational logic in this process, as developed by Wendy Brown, is that 'neoliberal rationality has disseminated the market model to more and more domains and activities' which now have come to include reproductive work, domestic labour, education and various other forms of giving and receiving care.[9] One of Rottenberg's concerns regarding the production of this new form of neoliberal subjectivity is that it 'aims to transform women into neoliberal human capital', while at the same time attenuating 'the links between these women and reproduction and care work'.[10] As it is often women, historically and presently, who suffer under this ideological construction of care as something required for those and from those who cannot serve a better economic purpose in society, it is not surprising that ideas of oppression and coercion lurk by in most feminist discussion of care.

In an influential account, Marilyn Frye defines oppression as a 'system of interrelated barriers and forces which reduce, immobilize and mold people who belong to a certain group, and effect their subordination to another group'.[11] On this basis, the term is often used in connection to practices of 'marginalization, exploitation, and powerlessness' that go beyond 'economic and political forces to include psychological barriers'.[12] According to Ann Cudd, oppression is 'an institutionally structured harm perpetrated on groups by other groups'.[13] What such definitions have in common is that they understand oppression as a structure of domination which pervades every part of our social and private lives, from the most deeply psychological aspects of our self-relation to the farthest recesses of the global neoliberal economy. While the essays in this collection do not specifically identify singular groups or populations which are directly implicated in this bilateral political exchange and do not aim to construct a theoretical account of the exact processes at play in their respective areas of interest, their combined contributions clearly highlight oppression's deeply rooted presence in the practices of care they examine. That care and oppression can be so closely linked might seem odd at first, especially as care work is often understood in the strictest sense as being in direct relation to looking after those who are not able to do so for themselves. Wendy Brown even goes as far as to call it the 'invisible infrastructure for all developing, mature, and worn-out human capital, children, adults, disabled, and elderly'.[14] Often occurring behind closed doors and within tightly controlled institutional settings, such as people's homes, the prison system or the youth worker's meeting room, the heavily corporatized standards and practices which guide the delivery of care are left to be experienced by those in need of care, who in many cases are too vulnerable to speak up and advocate for themselves and their families. Due to this invisibility and its implied associations with ideas of love, goodness and moral duty, many forms of ongoing care work escape scrutiny, especially within a densely marketized neoliberal political landscape, where direct, hands-on care work is often outsourced to and provided by the so-called care industry. This kind of pigeonholing strategy aims to provide legitimacy for the industry and all its beneficiaries, including governments, who can pass on the regulatory responsibility and delegate it to the purported sophistication of the market. Whether within the context of underfunded state services, such as the youth work and prison provisions in the UK, or of market-driven industries oriented towards profit making, such as privatized care for the elderly in Brazil, capital emerges as another significant aspect in the delivery of care that seems to disrupt the long-established association between care, love and moral action.

As Andrea C. Westlund argues, the recent philosophical literature on care can be broadly separated in two different categories: a moral strand that focuses on 'care as an attitude toward other persons' and a human agency strand that engages with 'care as an attitude toward objects, places, ideals, and so forth in addition to persons'.[15] These definitions question the moral foundations of the principles of care, both within the sphere of interpersonal relations, as they apply to those who need and receive care, those who provide it, their agential status, and the epistemic conditions under which they operate, and the larger realm of care as a form of orientation towards the wider world, with its animate and inanimate objects, forms and ideas. Joan Tronto's work in the early 1990s radically expanded the ways in which care of the first kind was conceptualized to extend beyond the domestic, medical, professional and social care settings. In her ground-breaking paper 'An Ethic of Care', she introduces 'a way of thinking about caring that expands our notions of the "ethical" to include many of the everyday judgements involved in activities of caring for ourselves and others'.[16] Linking this to the ancient origin of ethics as a form of knowledge related to living the 'good life' and building on existing feminist work on the issue, she argues that an expanded understanding of care will 'enrich' our 'moral sensibilities' and thus offer enormous benefit in terms of helping us develop novel modes of relation to ourselves and others.[17] The problem with care, Tronto argues, is that partly due to the nature of its double meaning (care as attending to another's needs and care as an object, feeling or occasion of concern), its actual relation to work, and to contemporary neoliberal work, we must add, has remained misunderstood: 'much of the current discussion of care either overemphasizes the emotional and intellectual qualities and ignores its reference to actual work, or overemphasizes care as work at the expense of understanding the deeper intellectual and emotional qualities'.[18] In this sense, *Love and the Politics of Care* offers an attempt to redress this balance by combining contributions emerging from several disciplines within the humanities and social sciences, including literature, sociology, cultural and media studies, philosophy, education and art history, motivated by a commitment to understanding how care functions in a global context. The chapters in this volume treat care through its association with love, as a form of labour, which is entrenched in the affective and intellectual forces that shape our individual and collective existence and which is structured by the systematic politics of neoliberal organization. These inquiries make use of a variety of conceptual tools and research methods, ranging from data analysis to psychoanalytic reading, to performance, with the aim of offering a contemporary assessment of the state of care within our intimate lives, families, places of learning and institutions. In doing so they engage with various instances of misconception, misplacement or misuse of care, with occasions in which care can misbehave or produce harm, and with practices in which care becomes synonymous with oppression. However, they also offer glimpses of more positive and fulfilling experiences of caring and being cared for, of 'caring with', and 'caring about', proposing visions for the future, often positioned at the generative intersection between love and care, which could provide the 'necessary social infrastructure' to transform our contemporary politics of care.[19]

* * *

The volume consists of three parts, each dealing with the contemporary politics of care through interdisciplinary case studies drawn from locations situated across the globe.

Part 1, 'Love and cultures of marriage', explores the economies of marriage through the spousal relationship and the wider nuclear family. The 'nuclear family still provides the prototype for care and for contemporary notions of kinship' despite the various challenges it has encountered from feminist and queer scholarship and histories of descent.[20] Our contributors interrogate the norms that constitute this paradigm, and specifically those associated with the maintenance of marriage as an institution and a model of care across different cultural settings, using analytical tools provided by cultural history, sociology, feminist theory, art history and postcolonial literature. In Chapter 1, Meghna Bohidar examines the commodification of romance in contemporary India through an analysis of the visual and spatial arrangements occupied by the forbidden love trope. The essay interrogates how public and marketized spaces are used by couples, especially in cases, such as in inter-caste or inter-religious relationships, where they may want or need to escape the confines of the traditional home. Bohidar takes the notion of transgression, associated with experiences of romantic love, considered illicit by recalcitrant patriarchal standards, and works to destabilize the ease with which transgression often becomes synonymous with a movement of radical change, especially within current regimes of global inequality.

Lan Kieu's sociological study in Chapter 2 continues to develop themes of inequality and oppression by examining interracial marriages between Swedish men and Vietnamese women through the framework of gratitude and indebtedness. As Kieu's essay reveals, the women who participated in her study often felt an overwhelming sense of gratitude towards the men they married. These marriages lifted them out of conditions of extreme poverty and provided an immigration route to Western Europe, a much needed lifeline not only for themselves but for their extended families. The essay makes extensive use of interviews with women whose lives have been changed and shaped by their decisions to enter into such relationships, exposing the various forms of interdependence and vulnerability they are subjected to as participants in global currents of capital and migration. In Chapter 3, Racheal Harris offers an art historical perspective on love, desire and exchange within the construct of a cisgender, heterosexual marriage. Harris's enquiry focuses on the work of twentieth-century British painter Stanley Spencer (1891–1951) and his series of paintings of grotesque and 'ugly' bodies entitled the *Beatitudes of Love*. These works received a negative response both from public and critics alike, which Harris argues is linked to certain problematic preconceptions about the nature of erotic and romantic love and the kinds of bodies that are seen as deserving of receiving it. The essay also offers an illuminating biographical background of Spencer's unhappy marriage and lifelong relationship with fellow artist Hilda Carline (1889–1950), positioning their partnership in a long line of difficult creative collaborations which challenge the confines of the traditional marriage establishment.

The volume's second part, 'Love and communal pedagogies of care', moves the conversation from practices of spousal care to consider the types of care undertaken within families and communities, particularly through experiences of learning. Shekufeh Owlia's essay, Chapter 4, looks at the impact a violent and dysfunctional marriage can have on the wider domestic structure, focusing specifically on the types of learning that take place under such conditions. Through a psychoanalytic reading of personal and historical trauma in Marlene van Niekerk's family saga, *Agaat* (The Way of the Woman) (2006), Owlia utilizes Erich Fromm's theory of love to lay bare the psychical and physical scars left on van Niekerk's women by the brutal apartheid regime in South Africa. Locked in a sado-masochistic mother–daughter relationship, Milla and Agaat struggle to find a way to love each other without resorting to the realities of torture and instrumentalization they have become accustomed to, a relational dynamic that transforms love into something monstrous. In Chapter 5, philosophy of education scholar Shelley Maddox considers the multigenerational experiences of education that develop within the home as a place of discovery, which furnishes children with the basic rulebook for conducting their future personal and social lives. Maddox engages us in a deeply personal yet fundamentally political meditation on the ways in which love functions within traditional (patriarchal, heteronormative) family settings: the place where children learn about social hierarchies, domination and love. Referring to Paulo Freire's *Pedagogy of the Oppressed* and bell hooks's foundational work on love and teaching, the essay reimagines parenting as a political pedagogy which centres the ethics of love and offers a transformative model with the power to restructure existing social hierarchies. In Chapter 6, Eugénie Pastor explores her relationship with collaborator Shamira Turner in their work with the theatre company She Goat. Pastor uses the concept of 'queer platonics' to talk about the blending of individual identity which occurs in the process of creating collaborative work, referring to instances of the two creators being mistaken for one another. The essay, based on the collaborators' creative practice and performances of their theatre piece *The Undefinable*, ruminates over experiences of fluidity, ambiguity and indeterminateness, asking what they might mean in terms of the plasticity of their *métier* as creators, humans and social actors. In doing so, Pastor offers a vision of the theatre as place of learning, a truly caring and accessible space that steps beyond a normative understanding of the theatregoer's (able) body.

The essays collected in Part 3, 'Love and neoliberal care', explore the relationship between care and love in contexts of institutional direction and control. Cumulatively, these discussions demonstrate the dissociative role of neoliberalism, an ideology that constructs forms of social enclosure in which we are encouraged to think of professionalism and care as antithetical to love. In Chapter 7, Karen Schaller invites us to 'imagine a scholar' in order to think through the role of love in the contemporary university. By way of the critical studies of love, Schaller reframes the arguments that love can counter the neoliberal university and shows that the rhetoric of affect and emotion and the subject position of the devoted academic is central to neoliberal institutions. Love here is injurious rather than transformative. Schaller elaborates her argument through close readings of two historically located 'love scenes' and an examination of academics in love: the 1990s, through Donna Tartt's *The Secret History* (1992) and A. S. Byatt's *Possession: A Romance* (1990), and the early 2000s, though Zadie Smith's 2005 novel *On Beauty* and Luca Guadagnino's 2017 film *Call Me By Your Name*. Love remains difficult to navigate and acquires even more problematic qualities in the context of work that involves providing care for vulnerable individuals, as in social work with young people or the elderly, or within the prison system, where institutional forms of care operate with little consideration of discourses relating to love. Purcell's attention to the care system in particular encourages us to look at the impact of this separation between love and work on the lived experiences of young people in Chapter 8. Having conducted his research during the Covid-19 pandemic, Purcell outlines the existing operational and ethical frameworks for practicing youth work in Britain, and using a sample of international youth work practitioners, he investigates professional attitudes towards constructing a more compassionate model, built around an explicitly loving practice. Anna Araujo's essay, Chapter 9, alerts us to the potential dangers of utilizing love as a model for practicing care. Araujo considers professional care work as an occupation driven and controlled by market forces and related experiences of race, class and migration in contemporary Brazilian society. Using interviews with workers who care for the elderly, Araujo identifies three different models of practicing care work in this context and evaluates their relationship to ideas of love, duty and the family. Araujo's analysis highlights the potential dangers of letting the market co-opt love as a core value and requirement of the workforce, which can lead to further emotional and financial exploitation of workers who are already precariously employed. Christina Straub's contribution, based on original research with participants, takes a more broadly historical and theoretical tone. In Chapter 10, Straub traces the transition from capital punishment to the penal justice model in operation today in the UK and considers its moral legitimacy in the face of scholarly and societal criticism over its outdated treatment of inmates. Straub considers love as a relational practice that, if introduced into the organizational channels of the prison, would aid the overall development, education and human flourishing of those deprived of freedom, and would potentially have further beneficial effects on their preparedness for re-entering the social world, following their sentence.

The intention behind *Love and the Politics of* Care and its accompanying volume *Love and the Politics of Intimacy* is simple. It is to offer an interdisciplinary survey of the field that reveals where love is useful, where love is difficult, what stands in the way of love. We hope that the essays presented here help to bring loving practices more readily to hand for all of our readers.

Notes

1. Audre Lorde, 'The Uses of the Erotic: The Erotic as Power', in *Sister Outsider: Essays and Speeches* (Berkeley: Crossing Press, 1984), 87.
2. Ibid., 89.
3. bell hooks, *All about Love: New Visions* (New York: Harper Perennial, 2000), 9.
4. Andreas Chatzidakis et al. (The Care Collective), *The Care Manifesto: The Politics of Interdependence* (London: Verso, 2020), 2–3.
5. Ibid., 5.
6. Ibid., 13.
7. Ibid., 12.
8. Catherine Rottenberg, 'Neoliberal Feminism and the Future of Human Capital', *Signs: Journal of Women in Culture and Society* 42, no. 2 (2017): 332
9. Ibid., 339. See also Wendy Brown, *Undoing the Demos: Neoliberalism's State Revolution* (New York: Zone, 2015), 22.
10. Rottenberg, 'Neoliberal Feminism', 332.
11. Marilyn Frye, *The Politics of Reality: Essays in Feminist Theory* (Freedom, CA: Crossing Press, 1993), 33.
12. Andrea Veltman and Mark Piper, 'Introduction', in *Autonomy, Oppression and Gender*, ed. Andrea Veltman and Mark Piper (Oxford: Oxford University Press, 2014), 3.
13. Ann Cudd, *Analyzing Oppression* (New York: Oxford University Press, 2006), 26, cf. 23-7. For further recent work on oppression, see Sandra Bartky, 'On Psychological Oppression', in *Feminist Theory: A Philosophical Anthology*, ed. Ann Cudd and Robin Andreasen (Malden: Blackwell, 2005), 105–12; Diana Tietjens Meyers, *Gender in the Mirror: Cultural Imagery and Women's Agency* (New York: Oxford University Press, 2002).
14. Brown, *Undoing the Demos*, 105.
15. Andrea C. Westlund, 'Autonomy and Self-Care', in *Autonomy, Oppression and Gender*, ed. Andrea Veltman and Mark Piper (Oxford: Oxford University Press, 2014), 182. See also Nancy Fraser, *Fortunes of Feminism: From State-Managed Capitalism to Neoliberal Crisis* (London: Verso, 2013); Ann Orloff and Talia Schiff, 'Feminism/s in Power: Rethinking Gender Equality after the Second Wave', *Political Power and Social History* 30 (2016): 109–34; Elisabeth Prügl, 'Neoliberalising Feminism', *New Political Economy* 20, no. 4 (2015): 614–31.
16. Joan Tronto, 'An Ethic of Care', *Generations: Journal of the American Society on Ageing* 22, no. 3 (1998): 15.
17. Ibid., 16.
18. Ibid.

19 Chatzidakis et al., *The Care Manifesto*, 21, 28. For a full discussion of the difference between 'care for', 'care with' and 'care about', see Joan Tronto, *Caring Democracy: Markets, Equality, and Justice* (New York: New York University Press, 2013).
20 Chatzidakis et al., *The Care Manifesto*, 17.

Bibliography

Bartky, Sandra. 'On Psychological Oppression'. In *Feminist Theory: A Philosophical Anthology*, edited by Ann Cudd and Robin Andreasen, 105–12. Malden: Blackwell, 2005.

Brown, Wendy. *Undoing the Demos: Neoliberalism's State Revolution*. New York: Zone, 2015.

Chatzidakis, Andreas et al. (The Care Collective). *The Care Manifesto: The Politics of Interdependence*. London: Verso, 2020.

Cudd, Ann. *Analyzing Oppression*. New York: Oxford University Press, 2006.

Fraser, Nancy. *Fortunes of Feminism: From State-Managed Capitalism to Neoliberal Crisis*. London: Verso, 2013.

Frye, Marilyn. *The Politics of Reality: Essays in Feminist Theory*. Freedom, CA: Crossing Press, 1993.

hooks, bell. *All about Love: New Visions*. New York: Harper Perennial, 2000.

Horgan, Amelia. *Lost in Work: Escaping Capitalism*. London: Pluto Press, 2021.

Jónasdóttir, Anna G., and Ann Ferguson, eds. *Love: A Question for Feminism in the Twenty-First Century*. London: Routledge, 2014.

Lorde, Audre. 'The Uses of the Erotic: The Erotic as Power'. In *Sister Outsider: Essays and Speeches*, 87–91. Berkeley: Crossing Press, 1984.

Meyers, Diana Tietjens. *Gender in the Mirror: Cultural Imagery and Women's Agency*. New York: Oxford University Press, 2002.

Orloff, Ann, and Talia Shiff. 'Feminism/s in Power: Rethinking Gender Equality after the Second Wave'. *Political Power and Social Theory* 30 (2016): 109–34.

Prügl, Elisabeth. 'Neoliberalising Feminism'. *New Political Economy* 20, no. 4 (2015): 614–31.

Rottenberg, Catherine. 'Neoliberal Feminism and the Future of Human Capital'. *Signs: Journal of Women in Culture and Society* 42, no. 2 (2017): 329–48.

Tronto, Joan. 'An Ethic of Care'. *Generations: Journal of the American Society on Ageing* 22, no. 3 (1998): 15–20.

Tronto, Joan. *Caring Democracy: Markets, Equality, and Justice*. New York: New York University Press, 2013.

Veltman, Andrea, and Mark Piper. 'Introduction'. In *Autonomy, Oppression and Gender*, edited by Andrea Veltman and Mark Piper, 1–12. Oxford: Oxford University Press, 2014.

Westlund, Andrea C. 'Autonomy and Self-Care'. In *Autonomy, Oppression and Gender*, edited by Andrea Veltman and Mark Piper, 181–98. Oxford: Oxford University Press, 2014.

Part 1

Love and cultures of marriage

1

Public romance in India and its transgressive potential

Meghna Bohidar

Introduction

The Bollywood Art Project (BAP), started by artist Ranjit Dahiya in 2012, is an urban renewal project intended to beautify the dilapidated streets of Mumbai, home to the Bollywood industry. Their first wall painting was a still from the film *Anarkali*,[1] a testament to one of the greatest love stories, different versions of which have been in circulation in the Indian subcontinent since the Mughal era. The most well known of these versions is the blockbuster film *Mughal-e-Azam*.[2] Both *Anarkali* and *Mughal-e-Azam* are historical dramas and portray the love story of Anarkali, a courtesan in the Mughal Emperor Akbar's court, and Prince Salim, heir to the throne. On discovering their secret love, the emperor vehemently opposes it, alluding to Anarkali's unsuitability for marriage into the royal lineage. Prince Salim revolts and wages a battle against his father, which he loses, not having the resources to bring down an emperor. Knowing that the consequence of defeat would mean death for Salim, Anarkali offers her life in his stead. Akbar orders her entombment in the walls of the palace. At the final moment, however, he has a change of heart and arranges for Anarkali to secretly escape on the condition that she would never meet Salim again.

This story represents one of the most common tropes associated with passionate love in many parts of Southeast Asia, represented as forbidden love thwarted by familial and patriarchal structures. Similar tales such as that of Heer–Ranjha, Layla–Majnun, Sohni–Mahiwal and Radha–Krishna narrate stories of secret love, distant and unattainable. Bollywood cinema has hitherto capitalized on this ethos and recycled such stories. Apart from being phantasmic in which self-sacrifice, passion and madness are presented as sublime, these tales

Figure 1.1 Wall painting (Translation: *Anarkali*) in Mumbai, India, by the Bollywood Art Project, 2012. Courtesy of Meghna Bohidar.

are cautionary. The wall painting's historical romantic significance then occupies a liminal space where the possibility of the fantasy being realized is exhilarating yet frightening, as it would disrupt the social system of family-arranged and endogamous marriage. Therefore, in the Indian context, the possibility of romantic choice itself holds transgressive potential.

This chapter is organized in three sections: first, it situates how 'erosic love'[3] is devalued in practice but idealized in representations; it then considers the complexities of public intimacy/romance, which is constructed as 'out-of-place'; and finally, by juxtaposing varying transgressive moments, it attempts to destabilize the idea of transgression itself by locating it spatially and examining it as fluid and processual rather than final.

Idealization and devaluation of eros

Before delving into the complexities of passionate love in the Indian context, it would be worth asserting that disaffection towards it is not unique to India. From early Greek philosophers to the advocates of the Enlightenment, Western philosophy has hitherto been largely sceptical towards disorderliness and chaos associated with passionate love. The Grecian model of the horse (body) and charioteer (mind), furthered with modern science and the Cartesian principle of *cogito ergo sum*, rendered the body as an inferior space, to be controlled and subdued by the mind. Consequently, emotions were subordinated to thought and reason in praxis too. Charles Lindholm[4] notes that there was no term for 'emotion' in Latin until the late eighteenth century, and instead *passus* was used to describe passions, which were uncontrollable and capable of enslaving human beings. The words 'passion' and 'passive' also share the same root in Latin, *passio*, which means 'suffering'.[5]

In Indian folktales, yearning and suffering are not inferior qualities; rather they signify the highest form of passion towards an elusive lover. In practice, theistic movements such as the Bhakti and Sufi (twelfth–fourteenth centuries) foregrounded erosic love for the beloved. The *bhajans* (devotional songs) of Mira Bai, a Rajput princess who pursued her love for Lord Krishna in disregard of her marital responsibilities, convey her desire for becoming one with the Lord. In Sufi literature, *ishq* (passionate love) was considered the highest form of love that led to ultimate surrender and *fanaa* (annihilation). This love refers to a union with God, wherein boundaries between the self and other are dissolved. *Ishq* is thus almost impossible to attain, only accomplished by the most faithful servants of God.[6] This valorization of erosic love, represented as an end in itself rather than a means to an end (such as marriage/sexual fulfilment), finds resonance in the linguistic and cultural repertoire of the Indian subcontinent even today. Renditions of the *bhajans* of that era echo in Bollywood songs, declaring undying love towards a human lover in place of God. Erosic love then acquires meaning through emotions and bodily expressions such as singing and dancing, which are not subordinated to rationality.

The Eurocentric vision of the interconnectedness of love–marriage–sex finds no place in these tales where passions do not require marriage. Madhavi Menon uses examples of Sufi *pirs* (saints) who were buried with their male disciples, like husbands and wives, to demonstrate the fluidity of desire in precolonial 'India'.[7] This confused European colonizers, for whom sexual desire automatically translated into concrete and fixed sexual identities.[8] This ridge between sexual identity and behaviour is also exemplified in Jeremy Seabrook's study[9] of single or married men engaging in same-sex relationships in India without necessarily identifying themselves as homosexual or bisexual. However, one must be careful not to conclude that sexual and romantic passions were free in precolonial India. Menon asserts that both 'desire' and 'India' are unstable and uncodified categories, requiring complex examination.[10] The Bhakti and Sufi movements, albeit significant in instilling the ideal template of passionate love, were limited when it came to practice. In the social realm, the dominant Brahminical/patriarchal ideology (prior to colonization) emphasized the purity of bloodlines and marriage within appropriate kinship networks and closely monitored heterosexuality. However, with colonial ideas of modernity, romance was integrated into the system of arranged marriage, wherein the *dharma* (duty) of the ideal wife was reconfigured towards the husband rather than the entire family.

This practice is still predominant in contemporary India where more than 90 per cent of all marriages are arranged. It is routine to come across reports of 'honour killings' wherein the older male members of the family kill lovers, especially when love transgresses boundaries of acceptable marriage, that is, in cases of inter-caste and interfaith marriages. For example, romance involving a Muslim man and Hindu woman has been labelled 'Love Jihad', an Islamophobic conspiracy theory by right-wing groups, connoting deliberate seduction aimed at religious conversion.

The case of Hadiya, a Hindu woman who converted to Islam and married a Muslim man by choice, received national media attention in 2017. Her father challenged her elopement and marriage on grounds of 'Love Jihad'. The Kerala High Court annulled the marriage even though it was consensual. This was overturned by the Supreme Court a year later, which ruled that marriages cannot be annulled without the consent of the couple. Yet, the dominant media discourse was that of a 'gullible' woman brainwashed by a Muslim man. This discourse highlights two things: one, the othering of a community, be it Muslim or lower caste men, who supposedly destroy the sanctioned social structure of an imagined Hindu India; and two, that the sexuality of a naïve woman, incapable of choosing their own lover/husband, ought to be controlled. Thus, the issue with romantic love is inherently gendered: that is, it is immoral for women to find partners for themselves. Men have always had the leeway for having 'affairs', provided they marry appropriately.

Frameworks of love and transgression

Simone de Beauvoir critiques this asymmetry underlying romantic relationships wherein the master–slave dialectic described by Hegel is reproduced.[11] Wendy Langford advances this framework to discredit the popular thesis of 'democratisation of love' by Anthony Giddens and suggests that confluent love relationships are far from being egalitarian.[12] Instead, women engage in self-silencing, which creates hierarchical relationships, thereby making love a 'misguided revolution'.[13] Even bell hooks critiques the fact that love has become a slave to capitalism and that abuse in the name of love is normalized.[14] These works are invaluable to understand *how* romantic love is framed and experienced in varied sociocultural contexts; however, they often consider romantic love *as it exists* as false consciousness. For example, hooks outlines her theory of 'true love' as one that does not conflate love and abuse, but rather thrives on mutual recognition.[15] These analyses therefore tend to either glorify a purer form of love existing in primitive cultures or seek a transformation of love in a utopian, likely post-capitalist world.

Another issue with this conceptualization is that it necessitates an idealization and subsequent revival of an *a priori* love. By positing a total transformation and revolutionizing love, this theoretical stance overlooks smaller, everyday forms of resistance. For instance, Langford argues that women 'write themselves'[16] into their love stories to gain control but remain 'deluded'.[17] Her reading of it as false consciousness comes in the way of such actions being agentic. The problem with this way of thinking is twofold: first, although they look for alternate meanings of love, they inevitably ignore the multiplicity of meanings it already holds and argue for a fixed (although well-intentioned) meaning; and second, they reinforce the disembodied, rational, egoist subject intent on mastering the world through knowledge and ontology, as valorized by Western philosophy.

The overemphasis on knowledge or meaning-making in this episteme makes knowledge available only to conscious and rational subjects.

I borrow from these theorists only to explore *how* erosic love can be transgressive in the Indian cultural context, rather than defining *what* love *is* or how it *could be*. I turn to feminist literature in non-Western contexts, such as that in the Middle East, by Leila Abu-Lughod and Saba Mahmood who critique the undue emphasis on intentionality and knowing in feminist theory. Mahmood asks: 'does the category of resistance impose a teleology of progressive politics on the analytics of power – a teleology that makes it hard for us to see and understand forms of being and action that are not necessarily encapsulated by the narrative of subversion and re-inscription of norms?'[18] She attempts to disentangle the analytic category of agency from resistance and suggests that agential capacity is entailed not only in those acts that resist norms but also in the multiple ways in which one inhabits them.[19]

Using this framework, I demonstrate how erosic love is considered 'out-of-place' in India because it disrupts traditional moral structures while rejecting containment in hypermarketized spaces. I discuss how this 'out-of-placeness' captures both the social and the spatial, focusing on public romance to elucidate this point. Finally, I use Tim Creswell's[20] formulation to understand how transgression is geographically different from resistance and subversion. The former simply refers to crossing a boundary, which could be unintentional, but carries subversive value, unlike resistance, which is always intentional.

It is in this context of plural desires and the transgressive space they occupy that the *Anarkali* wall painting becomes important. It subverts the secrecy associated with tarnished/inappropriate romance by visibilizing it. It is worth asking: what happens when a woman who was buried inside a wall for her transgression is replaced *on* a wall for public display and consumption? What are the symbolic meanings of such a representation and how do they affect the meanings that were previously associated with that space?

Spaces for romantic consumption

Globalization and economic liberalization have had unintended consequences for the family with the weakening of control over women's sexuality. For example, the access to literacy enabled love-letter writing,[21] cell-phone technology offered avenues for sexting and romantic chatting and increased mobility for work/

education allowed women to engage in cross-sex interactions.[22] These changes aimed at economic development had the unintended consequence of enabling romantic encounters that challenged the traditional structures in India. Hadiya's case shows us that although structures that 'prevent' passion are in place, there are ways in which individuals transgress them. She met her lover at an educational institution; such 'away-from-home' spaces[23] are significant arenas for women to make romantic choices relatively freely.

Rapid urbanization in the 1990s also meant the redevelopment of public places and cafes, malls and other spaces were set up to encourage consumption. When multiplex theatres and five-star hotels were built, 'going out' culture was promoted, and families encouraged to dine out or watch movies together. These became avenues where couples could 'date' outside private, familial spaces. This performance of love as always public begins to unravel the Eurocentric discourse where romantic love is often considered as private and separate from the public sphere.

Celebration of global festivals like Valentine's Day became a popular cultural practice from 2000 onwards. Christiane Brosius's study[24] of Valentine's Day greeting cards demonstrates how romance was redefined through practices of celebrating love and gifting. She notes that most of the greeting cards produced earlier depicted foreign (white-skinned), heterosexual couples rather than Indian ones. This allowed couples participating in gifting practices to both relate to and disavow themselves from global practices, thus retaining 'Indian-ness' while celebrating a global festival. It also provided an opportunity for couples to publicly display romantic affection, which could previously be enjoyed only vicariously in movies. Further, a sense of 'fun' is evoked, and there is separation of sexuality from reproduction, religion and caste.[25]

Conservative groups annually declare war on Valentine's Day by threatening to attack couples 'found' in public spaces. These celebrations are portrayed by them as frivolous, hedonistic and associated with 'Westernization' where individual rights are privileged over familial values. Several such groups celebrate '*Matra–Pita Diwas*' (Mother–Father Day) on 14 February, attempting to re-signify and appropriate the meanings associated with love.

Public romance has become entangled with a desire to access neoliberalism and is a contested space for visibility and recognition for urban middle-class India. Popular cinema's representation of romance as the epitome of individualism, free from the constraints of family-arranged marriages, resonates with many. Privatized public spaces such as malls and cafes have become significant for performing consumption-based romance, albeit offering limited access to those with sociocultural capital. Therefore, while the processes of globalization and urbanization enable couples to challenge traditional meanings of love, they are far from being a revolutionary space for romance because they are profit-oriented and exclusionary.[26]

Politics of public romance

Couples who cannot afford the luxury of privatized public spaces take to heterogenous public spaces such as parks, promenades and monuments where accessibility is not based on consumption. If one were to visit these spaces in cities today, it would be hard to miss the sea of heterosexual couples. Seabrook describes parks as spaces that are 'forced open by the urgency of desires that can no longer be suppressed'.[27] However, these spaces are fraught with varying degrees of violence towards couples: from mild rebuking to physical beatings. Sneha Annavarapu[28] notes how, concurrent to love's marketization, India witnessed its politicization. She suggests that with the redevelopment of previously 'open spaces' such as parks, abandoned houses and promenades into 'public spaces', the norms of occupying these spaces changed significantly. This was most notable in the enforcement of the obscenity law, which was applied to couples engaging in public kissing/hugging. When 'publics' came to be defined, the meanings and behaviours appropriate in that space became fixed. In many parks and autorickshaws, one can find 'No Kissing' stickers as a determent to inappropriate behaviour.

This fixity in the meanings of what constitutes 'appropriate' behaviour effaces the multifarious uses of the city's spaces. For example, railway stations are meant for transit and not spaces appropriate for homeless persons or lovers locking lips. Similarly, there are written or unwritten rules of behaviour such as silence in the library. However, these spatial orders that appear to be controlled by 'objective' or 'natural' laws over time are severed from the idea of social production.[29] These norms are only conceived by certain dominant groups that organize spaces with singular (or fixed) meanings to be experienced homogenously. The standards of homogeneity are of course that of the 'normal, able-bodied, heterosexual, upper-middle class, male'.[30]

Thus, even if we think of the right-wing groups as antagonists of romantic love, their actions are not aberrant but exist in a continuum, in which we must also place 'concerned' neighbourhood residential groups that seek to remove couples from parks and bus stops to restore familial ethos. In Mumbai, for instance, the local civic body installed single-seater benches in parks to discourage couples from sitting close together after receiving complaints that parks for the elderly had become prime spots for hooligans and lovers.[31]

Elite groups often visit and participate in events like Valentine's week in privatized public spaces where public romance is tolerated or even encouraged. Pleasure is organized as a display of 'talent' (such as dance shows or competitions for couples like compatibility quizzes) in these spaces. In contrast, romance/intimacy in heterogenous public spaces is seen as transgressive and offensive. If romantic love suggests access to freedom, hypermarketization has resulted in unequal access to romance as a commodity. Katherine Twamley's[32] work indicates that couples who visit privatized public spaces distance themselves from 'others' who occupy parks by expressing disgust, thus revealing a politics of taste. Pierre Bourdieu explains that this visceral disgust towards behaviours not part of one's habitus is naturalized over time, making certain strata appear more 'cultured' than others.[33] Hypermarketization has indeed enabled only 'Westernized' elite bodies to perform resistance through romantic consumption. Certain acts are considered aesthetic only when performed by particular bodies consonant with ideals of hypermaketization (i.e. beauty and class). Cinematic representations of public romance are therefore viewed as tasteful or erotic whereas the same act when performed in a heterogenous public space is charged with obscenity.

Thus, the claim of aesthetic-based resistance to romance is not so much that it is morally incorrect but that it disrupts normative ideals of order and beauty. Daniella Gandalfo describes how the cleanliness drives in Lima extended to moral cleanliness, where vagrants were considered a potential threat to the city because they personified lack of productivity, filth and idleness.[34] The crime of the couple then, much like hawkers and sex workers, is not only that they are illegal, but also that they threaten modernist ideas of development by visibilizing disorder and chaos.

Right to the city

Returning to the *Anarkali* wall painting, let us nuance the analysis. The rationale of painting it, to begin with, was to beautify the city. By representing a popular love story, it ascribes a certain value to erosic love in a public place.

However, the artist has stated on several fora that he would like his artwork to be legitimized by art galleries and museums. Creswell's[35] examination of graffiti raises important questions around what constitutes subversion and how it needs to be understood contextually. On the surface, graffiti challenges the dichotomy between private and public space – it assumes that everywhere is free space and challenges dominant divisions of spatial meanings. However, graffiti underwent a metamorphosis from crime to art with its displacement from the street to the gallery. He writes that in the gallery the graffiti is in its 'proper' place and is no longer the tactic of the marginalized, but part of the strategy of the establishment. In his words, 'the ordination of graffiti as art, consciously or not, subverted the subversive'.[36] The *Anarkali* wall painting can be juxtaposed with the work of an anonymous group, 'Limits Within', who put up posters of kissing couples on the streets of Mumbai. The first significant difference here is that Limits Within, in contrast to BAP, did not acquire permission from the local authorities to put up the posters and did so secretly at night. Second, the group's intention was to test what was permitted or forbidden in public spaces. The artist claimed:[37] 'people say that this is wrong because kids, women and old people will see it. So, at male-dominated places like chai and cigarette shops or lavatories, the posters remained for longer [without being ripped down]. At bus stops where there aren't only men, they were removed much faster. That might be because men control those spaces.'

The motive changes the context: while the wall painting attempts to restore beauty through forms of media deemed acceptable by dominant groups, the posters challenge prevailing norms of occupying public spaces. This intentional resistance to normative romantic behaviour can be grouped with similar protests such as 'The Kiss of Love'. Beginning in response to the attack by a right-wing group on a couple kissing in a café, the protest gained nationwide recognition in 2014. It borrowed its name from a popular Bollywood song and asserted the right to kiss publicly. Another popular protest was organized in Delhi after a political party declared that interfaith couples found on Valentine's Day would be forced to undergo a *Shuddhikaran* (purification ritual) and Hindu couples would be married off. A protest in the form of a marriage procession was organized in front of a police station in response, in which homosexual couples, non-couples and others insisted on getting married. Although marriage has been a point of contention for feminists, this act subverted patriarchal notions of love and marriage as connected, especially since homosexuality was criminalized at the time. Another nationwide online and offline protest 'Park *mein* PDA' (Public

Display of Affection in the Park) invited couples to share pictures of themselves holding hands, hugging or kissing. These movements 'challenge the dominant order and territorialisation of urban spaces through presencing of the bodily subject that appears on the squares and streets, thereby reclaiming right to city'.[38]

While these movements subvert traditional norms, they have several limitations. A common criticism is that they are restricted to upper-middle class, educated groups who are privileged enough to demand the right to risk and pleasure, which is considered frivolous compared to more pressing issues such as poverty, unemployment and rape.[39] However, the right to pleasure is significant, even if it only matters to a small section of society. Instead, for me, the more significant limitations are as follows: first, what is the politics of what is worthy of outrage? In other words, which bodies matter? This form of organized outrage against the beating of an upper-middle class couple in a café (considered a 'safe' space) is hardly ever seen against the more pervasive violence faced by couples who are unable to access privatized public spaces. Second, who participates in these protests? Are they people who regularly occupy the heterogenous public spaces that they seek to reclaim? Or are they using these spaces to assert their right to pleasure when they have the choice of when and when not to be there? Third, these groups often use the discourse of modernity to challenge right-wing Hindu groups, who are then constituted as the 'regressive' other that needs disciplining. In reifying the regressive-progressive divide, their language of articulating protest is paradoxically akin to that of the same right-wing groups that they oppose. Both groups seemingly speak for 'love' – albeit different forms. Conservative groups base their oppositions on the love for the nation, for being 'Indian' and restoring India's culture to its former glory by reversing the 'colonial hangover'. They do not position themselves as anti-love but as lovers of a precolonial Indian culture that was purer. Liberal groups tend to speak in the name of a love that is permissive, modern and synonymous to freedom.

I would pause to ask the question that Sara Ahmed so eloquently poses:[40] 'What are we doing when we do something *in the name of love?* Why is it assumed to be better to do the same thing if it is done *out of love?*' She uses the Freudian concept of 'introjection' to understand how the ego takes on the characteristic of the lost object of love. Both liberal and conservative groups therefore generate a 'we-feeling', thus demonstrating that who we love is a reflection of what we want to be – that is, love is the extension of one's self, and it orients the subject towards some others (and away from 'other others'). If persons are imagined as 'could have been me', then their loss is considered a loss. Judith Butler too makes this connection between lives that are grieveable and those that are imagined as liveable and loveable.[41] In this case, when violence is imagined as being a possibility, even in safe spaces, it is organized into movements. The issue then is not that these movements are frivolous, but that they can be exclusionary. Finally, they reify the centrality of intention to subversion/resistance – thus distancing themselves from the 'false consciousness' of the masses. Although they seek to assert the right to 'purposeless pleasure' such as loitering, kissing and sleeping in public spaces, they are eventually intentional. Sending out invitations and soliciting participation ironically renders them 'purposeful'.

Loving in the city

Previously, I juxtaposed the *Anarkali* wall painting and the posters by Limits Within to discuss how they differ in intent, reception and aesthetics and how they were able to subvert or inhabit dominant meanings of space. Now I introduce a third aspect – one which is treated as vandalism. As mentioned earlier, it is common to see couples crowding in heterogenous public spaces in India. This is about their habitat and everyday experiences in the city spaces. Inscriptions on walls/trees/any available surface offer visually striking evidence of their presence. Although couples do not write on the walls to assert the right to love publicly, like in the case of the organized social protests, this act transgresses traditional notions of how to occupy public spaces. News articles and online fora (e.g. Quora) most predominantly focus on how this 'vandalization' of historical monuments reduces its tourism value and hinders development. Another criticism is that it destroys a place that is a repository of historical knowledge. A careful examination of these criticisms reveals that these acts either undermine the commercial value of the space or render it unaesthetic.

Using Henri Lefebvre's[42] analysis of space, I argue that these inscriptions should be viewed as couples' embodiment and meaning-making of city spaces. This act, although not intended to subvert norms, could be seen as an urban encounter resisting both consumption-based romance (based on its location) and the 'conscious intellectualism of performance art'.[43] At the heart of Lefebvre's[44] work lay the emphasis on dismantling bureaucratically managed spaces where sexuality and sensuality are peripheral and engaging in a carnivalesque reclamation of market spaces and educational centres, reiterating a fundamental human desire of play/pleasure (as opposed to work). This 'restoration' of Eros

Figure 1.2 Photograph of a wall of the *bada gumbad* (big dome) in Lodhi Garden, a park in New Delhi, 2019. Courtesy of Meghna Bohidar.

is also elaborated by Herbert Marcuse who notes how, in advanced capitalist societies, the organism is transformed from a 'subject-object of pleasure into a subject-object of work'.[45] He further believes that the reality principle in modern civilization has taken the form of the 'performance principle'[46] with its goal as productivity and performativity and emphasis on the work ethic. The individual is required to work to fulfil his needs whether or not direct pleasure is obtained. The crux of his argument points to the irony that individuals must alienate themselves from their instincts or 'authentic' nature to experience freedom.

These inscriptions represent one of the many ways in which couples inhabit and make sense of the space around them. However, it is important to separate these acts from the wall painting and the intentional protests because they are everyday embodiments rather than spectacular performances of resistance. Instead, couples' lived experiences in public spaces are an unintended spectacle at best because they make efforts to be inconspicuous. Women especially perform anonymity and negotiate (in)visibility in public spaces by demonstrating purposiveness[47] (e.g. by pretending to talk on the phone). This is done to demonstrate respectability as any 'good woman' would not be loitering on the streets. Couples adopt tactics such as covering their faces with scarves, carrying umbrellas and visiting areas that are far from home. Eva Illouz suggests that couples find 'islands of privacy'[48] to be alone in public; I add to this the concept of 'islands of solidarity' where couples congregate near each other to ensure safety. Such spaces are known as 'couples' spaces' colloquially, often with negative connotations, and act as a heuristic among couples to guide them to relatively safer environments. These varied strategies indicate that while couples may be subverting some norms, they also choose to inhabit others such as appropriate dressing, demonstrating respectability in front of other publics and finding corners away from familial spaces. Even their presence in these spaces is more out of compulsion at not being able to afford a private space rather than out of choice.

Nevertheless, these strategies speak to the ways in which they make meaning while navigating public spaces, knowing well the risk of being caught. The transgressive potential here lies in the meanings produced by the act, regardless of their intention. The act of inscribing their names on walls might offer ways for couples to experience themselves as immemorial and forever united, not in death or marriage, but in writing. It may indicate a form of presencing the body, even when their physical bodies are not in that space. Furthermore, the visual of the sea of lower-middle class lovers in heterogenous public spaces in the middle of the afternoon on a working day disrupts the idea of economically productive and disciplined subjects who manage time and space efficiently. In these spaces then, there is no way to 'control' when and where leisure can be performed, like it can be in privatized urban spaces.

Conclusion

The locking of lips in a movie theatre or a café where Valentine's Day is celebrated and the locking of lips in a public ('family') park have substantially different meanings. While one is considered 'in-place' (although in India, this became in-place only in the late 2000s), the other is considered dirty and obscene. The question that needs to be asked is: if erosic love is devalued across civilizations and pleasure in public spaces is condemned, what does public romance do to the social and spatial organization of meanings? The point of demonstrating three such 'out-of-place' incidents with varying intents is not to suggest that one is more or less transgressive than the other. Rather, the aim has been to remove the undue importance on intentionality and knowing and to underline the significance of context while studying transgression. To recapitulate, while the symbolic value of the wall painting is transgressive, it reinscribes an aesthetic value that is socially acceptable. The kissing pictures and the social movements can be read together, as they both reimagine ways of occupying public spaces. Yet, the burden of intentionality and emphasis of an alternate, 'correct' meaning of occupying a space is disconcerting. Lovers' visibility in public spaces on an everyday basis challenges traditional and moral meanings associated with those spaces (parks are for families/elders/children) as well as the capitalist organization of leisure, time and space. They are not spectacular movements or temporally circumscribed 'events'; rather, they attempt to be as unspectacular as possible. Still, they are agentic ways of negotiating, inhabiting and subverting norms.

Instead of copiously trying to locate, as philosophers have for centuries, the truth of erosic love or resistance, it is perhaps worthwhile to look at both as processual and fluid. If love already exists as a multiplicity, resistance needs to be understood contextually rather than as a universal remedy. And we will do well to remember Creswell's words that what is transgressive now may or may not be so tomorrow:[49] 'The new social spaces that result from the transgression of old social spaces will themselves become old social spaces pregnant with the possibility of transgression.'

Notes

1. *Anarkali*, dir. Nandlal Jaswantlal (India: Filmistan, 1953).
2. *Mughal-e-Azam*, dir. K. Asif (India: Sterling Investment Corporation, 1960).
3. I use the term 'erosic' to describe the characteristic of 'eros' instead of 'erotic' to allow readers to distance themselves from its connotations as purely physical/sexual. Eros has a wider range of meanings attached to it in psychoanalytic literature which is not captured adequately by the term 'erotic'. For example, eros is read as life energy that is polymorphous (where erogenous pleasure is derived from the whole body and not just the genitals) and is sublimated for the 'good' of civilization/work ethic.

4 Charles Lindholm, 'An Anthropology of Emotion', in *A Companion to Psychological Anthropology: Modernity and Psychocultural Change*, ed. Conerly Casey and Robert B. Edgerton (London: Blackwell, 2005), 30–47.
5 Sara Ahmed, *The Cultural Politics of Emotion* (Edinburgh: Edinburgh University Press, 2004), 2–3.
6 Joseph E. B. Lumbard, 'From *Hubb* to *Ishq*: The Development of Love in Early Sufism', *Journal of Islamic Studies* 18, no. 3 (2007): 345–85.
7 Madhavi Menon, *A History of Desire in India* (New Delhi: Speaking Tiger, 2018), 44–5.
8 Ibid., 13.
9 Jeremy Seabrook, *Love in a Different Climate: Men Who Have Sex with Men in India* (London: Verso, 1999).
10 Menon, *History of Desire in India*, 25.
11 Simone de Beauvoir, *The Second Sex* (New York: Vintage Books, 1952), 645.
12 Wendy Langford, *Revolutions of the Heart* (London: Routledge, 1999), 9–10.
13 Ibid., 151.
14 bell hooks, *All about Love: New Visions* (New York: Harper Perennial, 2000), 22.
15 Ibid., 183.
16 Langford, *Revolutions of the Heart*, 142.
17 Ibid., 139–40.
18 Saba Mahmood, *The Politics of Piety* (Princeton, NJ: Princeton University Press, 2005), 9.
19 Ibid.
20 Tim Creswell, *In Place/Out of Place: Geography, Ideology, and Transgression* (London: University of Minnesota Press, 1996), 23.
21 Laura Ahearn, *Invitations to Love: Literacy, Love Letters, and Social Change in Nepal* (Ann Arbor: University of Michigan Press, 2001).
22 Caroline Osella and Filipo Osella, 'Friendship and Flirting: Micro-Politics in Kerala, South India', *Journal of the Royal Anthropological Institute* 4, no. 2 (1998): 189–206.
23 Parul Bhandari, 'Pre-Marital Relationships and the Family in Modern India', *South Asia Multidisciplinary Academic Journal* 16 (2017): 4, http://samaj.revues.org/4379.
24 Christiane Brosius, 'Love Attacks: Romance and Media Voyeurism in the Public Domain', in *Sexuality Studies*, ed. Sanjay Srivastava (New Delhi: Oxford University Press, 2013), 255.
25 Ibid., 269.
26 Although I use differential terms to describe conservative groups and the 'Westernized' market, their relationship is more complex. For example, when McDonald's entered India, it removed the cheeseburger from the menu so that the

Hindu community is not offended. Thus, the global market changes form with its audience and often remains as conservative as the population.

27 Seabrook, *Love in a Different Climate*, 6.
28 Sneha Annavarapu, '"Where Do All the Lovers Go?"– The Cultural Politics of Public Kissing in Mumbai, India (1950–2005)', *Journal of Historical Sociology* 31, no. 4 (2018): 7.
29 Rosalyn Deutsch, 'Uneven Development: Public Art in New York City', in *The City Cultures Reader*, 2nd edn, ed. Ian Borden, Tim Hall, and Malcom Miles (New York: Routledge, 2004), 422.
30 Shilpa Ranade, 'The Way She Moves: Mapping the Everyday Production of Gender-Space', *Economic and Political Weekly* 42, no. 17 (2007): 1522.
31 Anonymous, 'Nana Nani Park or Anti-Socials' Adda??', *Home Times*, 22 December 2019, http://www.hometimes.in/nana-nani-park-or-anti-socials-adda/.
32 Katherine Twamley, *Love, Marriage and Intimacy among Gujarati Indians: A Suitable Match* (New York: Palgrave Macmillan, 2014).
33 Pierre Bourdieu, *Distinction: A Social Critique of the Judgement of Taste* (Cambridge, MA: Harvard University Press, 1984).
34 Daniella Gandalfo, *The City at Its Limits: Taboo, Transgression, and Urban Renewal in Lima* (Chicago: University of Chicago Press, 2009).
35 Creswell, *In Place/Out of Place*, 47.
36 Ibid., 52.
37 Mridula Chari, 'Meet the Artist Who Has Riled Up Mumbai with Posters of Kissing Couples', *Scroll.in*, 28 August 2015, https://scroll.in/article/751527/meet-the-artist-who-has-riled-up-mumbai-with-posters-of-kissing-couples.
38 Mahima Taneja, 'Politicizing Right to City and Gendered Corporeality: Some Case Studies from Delhi', in *Living and Building the Right to the City: Experiences in the South*, ed. Amandine Spire and Marianne Morange (Paris: Paris Nanterre, 2020), 191.
39 Ibid.
40 Ahmed, *Cultural Politics of Emotion*, 124, italics in original.
41 Ibid.
42 Henri Lefebvre, 'The Right to the City', in *Writings on Cities*, ed. and trans. E. Kofman and E. Lebas (London: Blackwell, 1996), 150.
43 Steve Piles, *The Body and the City: Psychoanalysis, Space, and Subjectivity* (London: Routledge, 1996).
44 Lefebvre, *Writings on Cities*.
45 Herbert Marcuse, *Five Lectures: Psychoanalysis, Politics and Utopia* (New York: Beacon Press, 1970), 5.
46 Herbert Marcuse, *Eros and Civilization* (New York: Beacon Press, 1955), 44.

47 Shilpa Phadke, Shilpa Ranade and Sameera Khan, *Why Loiter? Radical Possibilities for Gendered Dissent* (New Delhi: Penguin, 2011).
48 Eva Illouz, *Consuming the Romantic Utopia: Love and the Cultural Contradictions of Capitalism* (Berkeley: University of California Press, 1997), 56.
49 Creswell, *In Place/Out of Place*, 176.

Bibliography

Ahearn, Laura. *Invitations to Love: Literacy, Love Letters, and Social Change in Nepal*. Ann Arbor: University of Michigan Press, 2001.

Ahmed, Sara. *The Cultural Politics of Emotion*. Edinburgh: Edinburgh University Press, 2004.

Anarkali. Directed by Nandlal Jaswantlal. India: Filmistan, 1953.

Annavarapu, Sneha. '"Where Do All the Lovers Go?"– The Cultural Politics of Public Kissing in Mumbai, India (1950–2005)'. *Journal of Historical Sociology* 31, no. 4 (2018): 1–15.

Anonymous. 'Nana Nani Park or Anti-Socials' Adda??' *Home Times*, 22 December 2019. http://www.hometimes.in/nana-nani-park-or-anti-socials-adda/.

Beauvoir, Simone de. *The Second Sex*. New York: Vintage Books, 1952.

Bhandari, Parul. 'Pre-Marital Relationships and the Family in Modern India'. *South Asia Multidisciplinary Academic Journal* 16 (2017): 1–15. http://samaj.revues.org/4379.

Bourdieu, Pierre. *Distinction: A Social Critique of the Judgement of Taste*. Cambridge, MA: Harvard University Press, 1984.

Brosius, Christiane. 'Love Attacks: Romance and Media Voyeurism in the Public Domain'. In *Sexuality Studies*, edited by Sanjay Srivastava, 255–86. New Delhi: Oxford University Press, 2013.

Chari, Mridula. 'Meet the Artist Who Has Riled Up Mumbai with Posters of Kissing Couples'. *Scroll.in*, 28 August 2015. https://scroll.in/article/751527/meet-the-artist-who-has-riled-up-mumbai-with-posters-of-kissing-couples.

Creswell, Tim. *In Place/Out of Place: Geography, Ideology, and Transgression*. London: University of Minnesota Press, 1996.

Deutsche, Rosalyn. 'Uneven Development: Public Art in New York City'. In *The City Cultures Reader*, 2nd edn, edited by Ian Borden, Tim Hall and Malcom Miles, 420–2. New York: Routledge, 2004.

Gandalfo, Daniella. *The City at Its Limits: Taboo, Transgression, and Urban Renewal in Lima*. Chicago: University of Chicago Press, 2009.

hooks, bell. *All about Love: New Visions*. New York: Harper Perennial, 2000.

Illouz, Eva. *Consuming the Romantic Utopia: Love and the Cultural Contradictions of Capitalism*. Berkeley: University of California Press, 1997.

Langford, Wendy. *Revolutions of the Heart*. London: Routledge, 1999.
Lefebvre, Henri. 'The Right to the City'. In *Writings on Cities*, edited and translated by E. Kofman and E. Lebas, 147–60. London: Blackwell, 1996.
Lindholm, Charles. 'An Anthropology of Emotion'. In *A Companion to Psychological Anthropology: Modernity and Psychocultural Change*, edited by Conerly Casey and Robert B. Edgerton, 30–47. London: Blackwell, 2005.
Lumbard, Joseph E. B. 'From *Hubb* to *Ishq*: The Development of Love in Early Sufism'. *Journal of Islamic Studies* 18, no. 3 (2005): 345–85.
Mahmood, Saba. *Politics of Piety*. Princeton, NJ: Princeton University Press, 2005.
Marcuse, Herbert. *Eros and Civilization*. New York: Beacon Press, 1955.
Marcuse, Herbert. *Freedom and Freud's Theory of Instincts*, Five Lectures: Psychoanalysis, Politics and Utopia. New York: Beacon Press, 1970.
Menon, Madhavi. *A History of Desire in India*. New Delhi: Speaking Tiger, 2018.
Mughal-e-Azam. Directed by K. Asif. India: Sterling Investment Corporation, 1960.
Osella, Caroline, and Filipo Osella. 'Friendship and Flirting: Micro-Politics in Kerala, South India'. *Journal of the Royal Anthropological Institute* 4, no. 2 (1998): 189–206.
Phadke, Shilpa, Shilpa Ranade and Sameera Khan. *Why Loiter? Radical Possibilities for Gendered Dissent*. New Delhi: Penguin, 2011.
Piles, Steve. *The Body and the City: Psychoanalysis, Space, and Subjectivity*. London: Routledge, 1996.
Ranade, Shilpa. 'The Way She Moves: Mapping the Everyday Production of Gender-Space'. *Economic and Political Weekly* 42, no. 17 (2007): 1519–26.
Seabrook, Jeremy. *Love in a Different Climate: Men Who Have Sex with Men in India*. London: Verso, 1999.
Taneja, Mahima. 'Politicizing Right to City and Gendered Corporeality: Some Case Studies from Delhi'. *Living and Building the Right to the City: Experiences in the South*, edited by Amandine Spire and Marianne Morange, 177–92. Paris: Paris Nanterre, 2020.
Twamley, Katherine. *Love, Marriage and Intimacy among Gujarati Indians: A Suitable Match*. New York: Palgrave Macmillan, 2014.

2

Gratitude's compulsion

Lan Kieu

Introduction

Contesting our feminist nostalgic reliance on the 1960s revolutionary motto's 'the personal is political', critical scholars have expressed concern about feminist complacency in the increasing public deployment of private stories and personal testimonies from disenfranchised groups.[1] As a 'relief from the political',[2] this proliferation of intimate stories for public consumption has willy-nilly been complicit with the regulatory power of knowing and controlling the marginalized other. Our current time of non-sovereignty, disciplinarity and self-governmentality, as Foucault diagnoses, has posed a critical challenge to the traditional understanding of subjugation and the subjugated subject when this subjugation is no longer simply imposed by the regulatory domination whereas the binary position between the subjugated and the subjugator is no longer stable.[3] The subject of subjugation, in a Foucauldian lens, is no longer simply subjected to an external force of exploitation and domination, but is ever tied to her own subjection in both senses of subjecting herself and being subjected to.[4] Yet, in the field of postcolonial feminist scholarship, little attention has been paid to examine the convoluted postcolonial structure of feeling gratitude as a violating and productive condition of power and subjection in the process of making the postcolonial subject.[5] Although postcolonial feminist critique has compellingly questioned Western narratives of saving the 'third-world' other, what critique might have left out is a thorough examination of how the need to 'save' the other has met a complicitous grateful response from the marginalized. Because of the consensual mood of 'righting wrongs',[6] Left critique has been unable to avow the ambivalent complexity of the enabling violation of the structure of domination and is reluctant to critically scrutinize the violence, complicity and susceptibility of the 'third-world' other within this structure.

Inspired by the Foucauldian critical revision of the subjugated subject and the mechanism of subjection, this chapter critically examines gratitude as an intimate self-coercive structure of feeling among Vietnamese migrant women in Sweden who have been in intimate relationship with Swedish men. My intention is to rearticulate the relations of exteriority by critically deconstructing the epistemic and moral privilege of the marginalized subject of feeling and to come to terms with the convoluted logic of postcolonial violence, complicity and susceptibility to the enabling violating structure of imperialism and colonialism. Unlike other 'progressive' postcolonial communities, scholars have pointed out that Vietnamese diasporas, though sharing their injurious suffering from the aftermath of colonialism, are not always politically progressive or radically resistant to their conditions of subjection.[7] Drawing from interview narratives with Vietnamese migrant women in Sweden,[8] my critical reading of their feeling of gratitude suggests that this feeling cannot be seen as an unmediated and uncontestable source of collective feminist truths, knowledges and powers,[9] but rather, gratitude – constituted by the convoluted working of power – produces while at the same time subjugates the migrant subjects. My concern is thus not simply to offer an anti-imperialist and anti-colonialist critique of the violence of the gift of gratitude bestowed by the empire, but rather a critical interrogation of the working mechanism of self-coercion and the formation of the self-coercive postcolonial subject, to which the sticky lure of the gift of gratitude is incessantly tied.

Gratitude as desiring the good object

This section shall start with Quyen's narrative, in which I will demonstrate that the self-coercive power of gratitude is unrelentingly produced and reproduced through the productive working of the subject's desire for the good object within the dynamic structure of rescuing and being rescued. Quyen, who has earned a master's degree from one of the top universities in Sweden and is currently working for a state company, moved to Sweden more than twenty years ago. Her love story could be read as another version of the Western Disney Cinderella, but this time, Cinderella is no longer a white girl. Quyen says she first met her Swedish husband, who at that time was a tourist in Vietnam, when she was a young woman in her early twenties, working in her father's souvenir shop in

Saigon after his business had not performed well and her family's properties had been confiscated. This Swedish man appeared in her life, at first, as a customer in the shop. He was a card-carrying socialist, empathetic, wealthy, well-educated, a qualified practising middle-aged doctor, who was touring Vietnam to learn about the socialist country and its people after its war-torn period. Quyen did not have any educational qualifications and barely spoke English when the two met. In addition, she always felt a lack of love and support from her own family, especially after her mother died in a traffic accident when Quyen was a teenager. The only source of warmth and comfort for her at that time, the only person with whom she could share her timid emotional life, was her Vietnamese boyfriend. But the two soon broke up, leaving Quyen to float in a state of loneliness and depression. Saturated in boredom and the sadness of life, she wanted to escape her situation, imagining herself running away to a far-away country barely known to her, becoming a stranger herself, in order to forget and to restart. She recalls:

> I didn't love him at first. But gradually I fell in love with him because he's a very good man. He works as a doctor, so he has a caring character. He cared for me and helped me learn English. I practised speaking English through going to evening English classes thanks to the money he sent me to pay for my tuition fees. I didn't know who I was or what I wanted to become before I met him. But he changed me for the better, and Sweden changed me for the better. Since arriving here, I've found out what I wanted to study, what I wanted to work at, and what I wanted to become. I'm very grateful for that.

'He has a good heart', she confirms. 'His generosity has inspired me and made me a better person.' As Melanie Klein reminds us, if there is such a thing as an absolute autonomy of the self, such autonomy must be spurious because the condition of life is predicated upon the primary ontological dependency, the dependency of an infant on the mother's breast.[10] Thriving on this primary dependency that one can never choose, one can gain autonomy only on the condition of such dependency.[11] Quyen's gratitude for having a better life and becoming 'a better person', as she acknowledges above, displays this violence of vulnerable dependency when the imperative goodness provided by her Swedish husband and his Swedish way of life is the condition of dependency that Quyen cannot turn against. She goes on:

> If I were in Vietnam, I would not have become who I am now; I would have struggled to make a daily living and still lived under heavy social pressure from a conservative, corrupt and money-oriented society. Here I have knowledge,

education and have become a better person. I'm happy I can be here. A couple of years ago I used to think I'll go back to Vietnam when I get old, but now, I don't want to go back anymore. It's fine to go back just for a short visit, but I don't want to live there permanently. Air pollution, food poisoning, poor healthcare services, an educational system in crisis – those things are not desirable there. Here, it's too quiet and sometimes lonely, but it's still better.

Because 'the need for a good object is universal',[12] and because the good object is what 'one cannot not want',[13] it is understandable that Quyen cannot imagine herself returning Vietnam and struggling 'to make a daily living … under heavy social pressure from a conservative, corrupt and money-oriented society' with 'air pollution, food poisoning, poor healthcare services', and 'an educational system in crisis'. Yet, this imperialist and civilizing discourse of white supremacy over the uncivilized other that Quyen employs is difficult to dismantle. Expecting Quyen to dismantle this 'civilizing' Swedish life, expecting her to be self-sufficient and free from the tie of dependency on the imperialist good life, is thus, paradoxically, no less violent to herself than the violence imposed by her vulnerable dependency on the Swedish life. This feeling of gratitude as feeling of vulnerable dependency cannot easily be contested, especially when the coercion of the good object has been tied to the existence of the postcolonial subject. Yet, as long as migrant subjects endlessly crave for the Western good life, gratitude for the good life can operate as a power of gratification and self-preservation for life while, simultaneously, limiting the type of 'life' that can be considered a 'life'. On the condition of this self-coercion for some certain ways of life, the capacity to reserve life is also the capacity to exclude life, since life is only predefined by some certain good objects and not others. The vulnerable fantasy of 'having a good object' (e.g. a good education, a good Swedish life) in Quyen's narrative thus becomes the violence of restricting what is meant by a 'life' to capitalistic and colonialist materialist possessions. In a Derridean conception, a gift can be considered a gift only if it does not demand anything in return.[14] Quyen's gratitude to the restrictive attribution towards some certain good objects and her indebtedness towards the Swedish good objects is, paradoxically, an annulment of the Swedish gift giving and its gift of gratitude.

Since imperialism is a 'social mission',[15] this alibi of rescue is not hard to find in Quyen's narrative of gratitude. Quyen's prior wounded feelings and her state of destitution – for example, lacking education, lacking money, lacking access to upgrade mobility when she was in Vietnam – could justify the Swedish man's feeling of entitlement to his mission, a beautiful and romantic mission in the name of love that imposes a lifetime of gratitude on her. Read in this way, Quyen's narrative and the gift of life that her Swedish man offers could still be understood within a traditional framework of the white man saving the brown woman from the brown man, as Spivak has criticized.[16] However, I believe that, under the postmodern tactics of imperialism, the impoverished binary understanding of the rescuer and the rescued might be challenged by a dynamic state of complicities and connections among relations of domination. Read in this sense, it is not simply that Quyen's story is about the white man saving the yellow woman, but that the yellow woman in Quyen's narrative is also actively participating in the process of saving herself. She is working out through herself, transcending herself, making herself 'a better person', which, simultaneously and unintentionally, is also saving the man by collaboratively fulfilling his task of saving. Within this dynamic of saving, the rescued subject is no longer a passive object, while the rescuer himself is also vulnerable in seeking a satisfactory fulfilment of his task. Quyen did not love her husband at first, but she let the man believe that he had been loved by her, because in this interdependent vulnerability and rhizomatic collaboration, he also needs her to save his conscience. In this sense, Quyen rescues his feelings and compensates for his mission in as much as she also needs him to feel good about herself. In a Foucauldian fashion, the Swedish loving and caring could be understood as exclusively intrinsic to Christian pastoral power of civilization.[17] Yet, this pastoral power is precisely an apparatus of security and population management against which one cannot revolt because one mutually benefits from and desires that power.[18] In Quyen's case, the Swedish pastoral power has activated her desire and accelerated her interests so that she came to know the truth about herself, about what she needs, what she wants to become, what she wants to study, where she wants to work and how to maximize herself. Interestingly, this individualization of conducting oneself based upon one's interests, one's desire, whether one is aware of its compulsion, has incorporated gratitude for the imperialist empire with gratitude for oneself so that Quyen's gratitude becomes a self-gratitude, a self-congratulation and a self-consolidation.

Reading Quyen's story, I believe that gratitude is not simply a manifestation of an interpellation, although one cannot deny this interpellation. And gratitude is not simply an internalization of the good object, although one cannot disavow this internalization. There might be a space for the deferral, for a 'grey' zone of the indeterminable in Quyen's feeling of gratitude when she tries to lay claim to her semi-autonomy that is different from Swedishness. She tells me:

> I'm always Vietnamese. I'm proud of being Vietnamese. The Vietnamese are hard-working, diligent, caring and self-sacrificing. No matter how many years I've been living in Sweden, the fact that I am Vietnamese cannot be washed away.

However, what Quyen is trying to convey is predicated on her fantasy of 'being Vietnamese', of being a 'cultural difference' – although this phantasmatic cultural difference proves to be insufficient for any claim to an ontological difference. Within this phantasmatic cultural difference, Quyen's identification of herself with another good object, a semi-good object, as Quyen's claim of semi-autonomy against the totalizing gratitude by referencing her culturalism ('I'm always Vietnamese', 'I'm proud of being Vietnamese', 'the fact that I am Vietnamese cannot be washed away') is problematic because failing to question this culturalism and allowing it to work as naturalism is to be complicit with a liberal tactics of multicultural management, in which gratitude for having a Swedish life must be decentred so that its working power becomes discreet. In a benevolent and uncritical enthusiasm of cultural difference within the imperialist calculus, Quyen's relative autonomy against the power of gratitude proves to be merely supplementary: a supplementary difference, a supplementary autonomy.

If gratitude is a moral imperative that compels one to pay tribute to the good object that one receives, then gratitude cannot be resisted. Perhaps one need not be grateful, if one is privileged enough to live independently, for an independence that might eventually turn out to be only relative and temporary. While completely permissible and stimulable within the culture of liberal imperialism, the anti-imperialist and anti-colonial sentiment from both Western and postcolonial progressives might create an easy assumption that resistance to gratitude is a matter of consciousness-raising about one's entitlement to compensation for the injurious past and the enduring unjust present. If gratitude is the satisfaction of a desire that seeks to be loved and accepted, even though feeding this craving might be toxic, a denial of gratitude might just prove to be the reverse: that one wants it more and more in order to be grateful enough. If gratitude is an expression of thanks for something that is not one's entitlement, then requesting an entitlement so that one does not need to thank will always already imply the thanks: the thanks for the request, the thanks for the entitlement of not having to thank, the thanks for overcoming the thanks, the thanks for not feeling thankful. In this sense, a postcolonial request of ingratitude is already an acknowledgement of gratitude. If gratitude is inseparable from envy,[19] then this postcolonial envy, negated in the forms of devaluing the good object and turning away from it, is an unacknowledged exaltation and idealization of it while insatiably wanting for it.

Foreclosed gratitude

'Everybody is all satisfied and happy here, you shouldn't be too pessimistic, too cynical!' – Nhan, a woman who is married to a Swedish man and has lived in Sweden for ten years, advises me. 'There are so many wealthy Vietnamese here, and they all have a comfortable life', she continues. 'But there are still those who are excluded and not that wealthy', I resist. 'No, even the poor are good here; even the poor have a good life here', she insists. 'If you're poor, but you're good, you're helpful, you're generous, you're hardworking, you will be fine. But if you're bad, you will have bad luck', she adds. 'If you're good to people, then people are good to you', she confirms. What can be read from Nhan's commentary is that gratitude is a phantasmatic condition of possibility ('everybody is all satisfied and happy here', and 'they all have a comfortable life') while, paradoxically, it is also a mechanism of negation between those migrants who deserve and those who do not. As a technology of biopower, gratitude categorizes human beings as living species whose hierarchy of difference between the 'good' migrants and the 'bad' migrants naturalizes the unequal selection and distribution of gratitude. Buying into this hierarchical logic of gratitude as a legitimate mechanism of exclusion, Nhan believes that

> a biological child and a foreign adopted child must not be treated in the same way. You will never love them the same way, although you can try to do so. It's normal. In Vietnam, in the place where you were born, you're not treated well, you're poisoned by pollution, by toxic food, by a bad government, so here, you should not blame [anyone] if you're not treated better because this is not your birth country. Among several hundreds of thousands of migrants arriving in this country, only a few being expelled won't make a big issue.

This binary differentiation between the good migrant that counts and the bad one 'being expelled [that] won't make a big issue', which the Vietnamese migrant woman purchases, works in tandem with the colonialist imperialist logic of binary classification between white as the first order and non-white as the subspecies, so that even bitterly recognizing it and critical of it, the postcolonial subject is still submitted to and unintentionally vindicate its logic. Today while benevolent white liberalism is busy barring racism from the domain of the social by offering calculative compensation and soliciting love and empathy for racial reparation, racism can now, unimaginably, be uttered by the ethnic themselves without prohibition (since prohibition is now righteously applied to the white domination). As Chow has noted,[20] this discreet and contradictory power of liberalism and imperialism can work as a way to permanently maintain racial violence throughout the social body in the name of preserving and safeguarding the ethnic life. Within this benevolent mechanism of racism, gratitude can now function as an alibi for the execution of the bad, the evil, while upholding the rights to life, happiness, freedom and equality. This management between the good and the bad, between the good Swedish who knows how to treat women well and the bad migrant, the inauthentic Swedish who is disrespectful of women's rights and gender equality, which eventually legitimizes the exclusionary feeling of gratitude, can also be read through Thu's narrative, given below.

Thu, a university-educated woman, migrated to Sweden twelve years ago as a housewife married to a man she describes as 'half-Swedish, half-Turkish', who is fifteen years older than her. She first met him when he was on a business trip to Hanoi. He stayed in a comfortable four-star hotel near the Old Quarter where she was working as a hotel receptionist. Desperately seeking a new life after her first break-up with a Vietnamese man, Thu quickly accepted the proposal from the half-Swedish half-Turkish man, who promised her a better life in a better country. Yet, things did not turn out the way she expected. Thu did not find her partner 'Swedish enough'. At home, he wanted to eat only Middle Eastern dishes and asked her to cook lamb stewed and soaked with melted herb butter, which for her was 'too greasy', and he listened to Middle Eastern music that was 'too uncanny' for her and didn't fit her mood. Her partner would be very pleased if she spent between four and six hours preparing a Middle Eastern-style dinner. He would be very glad if she spent several hours a day searching for some special Middle Eastern mints in a special Middle Eastern market in Stockholm. She did all that he required. But she was not happy and was not willing enough. She believed that she had travelled to Sweden to learn about the Swedish way of life, not the Middle Eastern life. She believed that she wanted to speak fluent Swedish and not a Middle Eastern dialect that for her was 'too weird'. She believed that she wanted to have a Swedish life, not a Turkish–Swedish life. She became angry and felt that everything he did was not just for her. She wanted to have freedom and equality. She believed Sweden to be a land of gender equality, and therefore it was not fair on her to have to stay at home serving a man who for her was not 'Swedish enough'. After several hesitations, she overcame her fear of a second broken marriage, packed and left him. She left him with the same luggage she had brought when she arrived. She did not demand any money or property, but freedom. 'I didn't want anything from him. I simply couldn't stand him anymore,' she said. Then she found a job, cooking Swedish dishes in a local school for mainly white Swedish kids. And finally, she found what she called her 'true love' with Johan, a white middle-aged working-class Swedish man, born in a suburb of Stockholm, whom she now believes is 'authentically Swedish', 'good', 'responsible' and 'caring'.

In this phantasmatic narration of difference between the good Swedish man and the bad other lies the myth of gender equality, propagated by Western civilization, where gender has become an apparatus of imperialist expulsion of the other, and at the same time of an emancipatory governmentality. Sweden has always been proud of itself as a leading country when it came to gender equality, as certified by the latest 2019 World Bank report for instance.[21] Yet, despite feminist demystification of the Swedish myth of gender equality,[22] this myth is still productive and alluring in producing the desiring migrant subject towards the white Swedish life. In Thu's narrative, it is not difficult to see that, as both a product of racializing power and an agent of that power, the ethnic subject has resorted to the governmental discourse of differences, for example, differences between a Swedish life and a half-Swedish life, differences between Swedish empowerment and a half-Swedish violation of rights, differences between the caring Swedish man and the uncaring Turkish–Swedish man, as a foundation for her abandonment of the inferior race. Only on the condition of this abandonment would her rights to life, happiness, freedom and equality be achieved. Because difference between the two races has become so ephemeral and indistinguishable, racism must be deployed as a reactionary strategic response to the lack of difference, and a race war must perpetually be stimulated in order to create and execute a scapegoat of difference.[23] Undeniably, in Thu's narrative, the binary scheme between the good responsible Swedish and the bad unempathetic Middle Eastern is invented and validated by her lived experience precisely due to this lack of difference. Without this fabricated difference, Thu, unaware of and vulnerable to the white world, would not have had any legitimate reason to thank the white world for her thriving, although it is a thriving in oblivion of herself and of the world that has already alienated her.

This Janus-faced nature of benevolent liberalism and imperialism in which the spectral difference is both celebrated and eliminated is precisely where the discourse of Swedishness is being produced and reproduced in the making of the non-Swedish subject. In Thu's narrative, this coercive discourse is no longer simply produced and reproduced by the superior race, but rather has already been embodied in the other, certified and gratified by the other through the other's gratitude in order to reinforce the fictitious Swedishness and simultaneously maintain the phantasmatic subordinated otherness. Read against Thu's celebratory narrative, the gift of love and its compulsion to thank is thus a conditional gratitude because it is predicated upon the self-coercion and self-complicity with the violence of the liberal imperialist empire. It is not only that the gift of a love is not delivered equally to everyone – as liberalism has promised – but it is also that this gift cannot be distributed by just anyone – as it can be distributed only by a certain group and a certain culture. Yet, unintentionally, on the condition of erasure of the other others, Thu's narrative appears to both preserve and annul an image of a loving and caring Sweden, since if that love ever existed, it would not have expelled its other others, even expelling them in the name of love. Furthermore, a pure gift of love would require an absolute forgetting of the gift.[24] When this gift of love has compelled Thu to thank, to pay back Johan by 'making a happy family together', as she states in her diary, then this gift has turned out to be an insolvent debt in a calculative trading discourse, a debt that Thu always has to remember – rather than forgetting and burning it in the memory – so that when I asked her to write her diary, she immediately started with a remembrance of the gift of love.

Reciprocal gratitude

As power enabled by benevolent liberalism and imperialism, gratitude functions as a self-contradictory mechanism. On the one hand, it is exclusionary, but on the other, it wants to be inclusive. It is the inclusiveness of gratitude's compulsion, conditioned by mutual benefits and mutual interests and desires, that brings gratitude into circulation, sets it to work and consolidates its power. In the liberal narrative, when reciprocity and coercion have been in mutual complicity, the feeling of gratitude is never one dimensional. If Johan is a gift to Thu, Thu is also a gift to Johan. For Thu, love is about sharing and giving. For Johan, love is about listening closely to each other, trusting each other and understanding each other deeply. Johan repeatedly confirms: 'Thu is a gift to me.' And he admits: 'I want to start something new, I want to restart my life, and she's here, sharing and giving out. She has made me a new life. I'm indebted to her.' Thu does not only offer love; she also takes out her savings and gives them to Johan as a way of showing her support for him to set up his own business. Johan has never been married, has no children, has been working as a social worker and is now unemployed. The gift of love and money from Thu is therefore more than he could have imagined. Mutual benefits, mutual interests and mutual desires thus erase anthropological differences. As Johan confesses: 'Sometimes I don't understand her because of linguistic barriers. But we've built trust and respect because we both share, we both give.'

Yet can one really give oneself to the other? Can Thu really be giving herself to Johan, although it appears that something like a mutual transaction, a mutual translation has occurred between the two? Displacing and sublating its binary position between the giver and the receiver, the liberal and imperialist empire is sustained by a fantasy of eternal reciprocal gratitude. Here, in this mutated structure of reciprocal gratitude, it is not difficult to see that not only has the yellow woman already benefited from the gift of love but the white man is also consolidated, resulting in a happy collaborative guarantee amidst the population policing of the anthropological liberal state.

The global circulation of gratitude: When the other is saving other others

Today, despite rapid economic growth, the postcolonial Vietnamese suffer from a double complex: on the one hand, the Vietnamese prefer to see themselves as the suffering others,[25] while, on the other, the Vietnamese are self-complacent with an inevitable national pride.[26] Yet, it might not be difficult to recognize that under mixed feelings of aggression against and admiration for the West, the Vietnamese see themselves as superior to some non-Western others in the global order, but at the same time, in its competitive rivalry with Western benevolent humanitarianism in the global order there is a strong desire and interest to help these other others, who are seen by the Vietnamese as the least developed.[27]

Hanh's narrative must be read within this inevitable nationalization and globalization of salvaging, when the national has gone global and the global has circulated in a gratitude circulation of mutual alliance and complicity. Hanh accompanies her Swedish husband during his diplomatic work to an African country, where she voluntarily works as a one-woman charity to help the locals. While her children go to expensive American schools with other international children from diplomatic and business expat families, she spends a great deal of time cooking food, baking cakes and inviting the poorest locals to her residence for meals and drinks because she wants to do something good for them. When her chef starts shopping for imported canned tomatoes instead of buying local produce because he thinks the taste of local tomatoes is too poor, Hanh objects and continues buying to support the locals and even buys more than she needs. Now, sitting on a sofa in her Stockholm apartment, in ellipses and stutterings as she tries to convey her difficult feelings, Hanh shares her thoughts with me:

> I feel very bad that I have so many things but people there don't have anything. I've never felt comfortable at all living there … not comfortable to see all that misery, poverty, corruption, gloominess in the country … There is no future there … no future … It makes me feel so sad, very sad … realizing that there are no bright signs for the country or for the lives of the people there … Even though apartheid has already been lifted from the continent, there, the country's economy is devastated, and the societal divisions are widening … The local residents treat me fairly and normally because they think I'm honourable … I have a yellow skin, I don't have a white skin, but they see me as honourable … I remember when I go to luxurious shops in the USA, I'm met with cold eyes … But there, I'm too honourable, too honourable.

'My children don't lack anything; I don't lack anything', Hanh repeats. 'I feel heartbroken when my life is filled with such comfort, but people there don't have anything … I'm not comfortable at all, not at all … with my situation … not at all, when I have so many things but they have nothing', Hanh repeats as though in a great fever. Hanh tells me that she does not regret accompanying her husband to that African country although the trip has disrupted her struggle to develop her own career in Sweden. 'Living there helps me broaden my worldview, despite the fact that my career has been interrupted … But I've earned some incredible richness for my soul, and that's the unique gift the local people there have given me', she concludes.

In a Freudian understanding, civilization is built on guilt as a sublimation to and a concealment of the desire to kill.[28] Yet, in Hanh's story, guilt is not exclusively ascribed to whiteness. Hanh's uncomfortable feelings and her administration of helping the other African could be read within guilt, *too*. However, in Hanh's narrative, it is not difficult to see that this act of helping is reducible to an act of consuming. Clearly, what Hanh can do to help the locals is limited to buying, eating and cooking. Since shopping and cooking are often seen as the most feminized acts, Hanh's narrative could be read as a feminization of aid, whereby this feminization is precisely an attempt by the liberal empire to de-masculinize, de-Westernize, decolonize the violence of the empire by a softer, more feminized, more decolonized and more humane face. In this de-masculinized, de-Westernized and decolonized act of helping, the private sphere of cooking, shopping and consuming has been transformed into a transnational public space of sharing, loving and devouring together.

From Hanh's gratitude for having a comfortable Western life to the local Africans' gratitude for Hanh's act of giving, from her Swedish husband's gratitude for having a non-Swedish wife with a good heart to Hanh's gratitude for receiving a unique gift of experiencing and enriching the soul while living in Africa, from a global transference of guilt passing through whites to non-whites, from the global administration of social missions passing through the former colonizer to the former colonized, through the white man to the non-white woman, and through the imperialist masculine face of salvaging the other to a friendly woman's face of helping, gratitude has encircled an eternal global distribution of compensation, satisfaction and moral complacency. As the new face of the global mission of the empire, the other woman, with all her capacities and possibilities, has devoted herself to a crucial task of rescue when beneath this rescue there remains a cruel destruction of the other others. Yet, this devotion or destruction to help the other others is both compulsory and voluntary, both enforcing and pleasing, since it is now proclaimed by the Vietnamese woman as 'a Vietnamese tradition to help' and is no longer exclusively Eurocentric.

When Hanh tells me that she is seen as 'honourable' in Africa, one can easily read this as an identification with, assimilation into or internalization of whiteness. Yet, what if this 'honourable' feeling is not an identification but an aggressive emulation and elimination of the white model?[29] When the marginalized have come to occupy a central position in the liberal discourse of history and revolution, this displacement and reversal of the old binary opposition between the empire and its objects of disciplinarity is facilitated by the global instrumentalization and accommodation of a new virtue, a new interest and a new passion for what the other of the West can do to the other others, rather than simply a sole coercion from the European benevolence.

On the other hand, reading Hanh's reference to the Vietnamese tradition of helping and her grateful indebtedness for having a comfortable Swedish life, it is not difficult to see that the multicultural migratory subject has accommodated the grand patriotic national narrative. Since national feeling of gratitude requires paying back, the multicultural migratory patriot consents to pay back by continuing to promote the image of Swedish loving and Vietnamese helping, and representing at both the national and the global scales a collaborative manufacturing of this consensus image. Hanh's self-sacrifice in giving up her own career for the mission in Africa could also be read as an act of paying back, and this endeavour continues to justify the existence of the liberal and imperialist empire, where the grateful diasporic subject acts as a moral safeguarding and as a successful targeted object of regulation. Thus continues the endless longevity of the global administrative society.

Throughout this chapter, I have critically deconstructed the privileged epistemic and moral standpoint of the subjugated subject in order to bring out a more nuanced understanding of postcolonial subjectivity and the dynamic condition of power in late modernity. I have demonstrated that gratitude as a power of self-coercion has become a productive condition of enablement and violation of the postcolonial subject. Without a prior position of the subjugated and the subjugator, this intricate subjugation of the self within the dynamic circulation of the structure of gratitude has not been easy to dismantle since it is relentlessly tied to the existence of the postcolonial subject and, therefore, to avow the subject, we must, paradoxically, efface the subject.

Notes

1 Lauren Berlant and Michael Warner, 'Sex in Public', *Critical Inquiry* 24, no. 2 (1998): 547–66; Lauren Berlant, 'The Subject of True Feeling: Pain, Privacy, and Politics', *Cultural Pluralism, Identity Politics, and the Law*, ed. Austin Sarat and Thomas R. Kearns (Ann Arbor: University of Michigan Press, 1999).
2 Lauren Berlant, *The Female Complaint: The Unfinished Business of Sentimentality in American Culture* (Durham: Duke University Press, 2008), 10.
3 Michel Foucault, 'Two Lectures', *Power/Knowledge: Selected Interviews and Other Writings, 1972–1977*, trans. Colin Gordon, Leo Marshall, John Mepham and Kate Soper (New York: Pantheon, 1980).

4 Michel Foucault, 'The Subject and Power', *Critical Inquiry* 8, no. 4 (1982): 781.
5 Mimi Thi Nguyen, *The Gift of Freedom: War, Debt, and Other Refugee Passages* (Durham: Duke University Press, 2012).
6 Gayatri Chakravorty Spivak, 'Righting Wrongs', *South Atlantic Quarterly* 103, no. 2/3 (2004): 523–81.
7 Nguyen Tran Phuong, *Becoming Refugee American: The Politics of Rescue in Little Saigon* (Urbana: University of Illinois Press, 2017); Nguyen Thanh Viet, *Nothing Ever Dies. Vietnam and the Memory of War* (Cambridge: Harvard University Press, 2016).
8 I conducted twenty-one in-depth interviews with Vietnamese migrant women living with their Swedish partners in Umeå, Stockholm, Örebro and Uppsala between October 2015 and February 2017 as a part of my PhD work. The interview processes have been complied with institutional ethics. All the names of the interviewees in this chapter have been changed.
9 Joan W. Scott, 'The Evidence of Experience', *Critical Inquiry* 17, no. 4 (1991): 773–97.
10 Melanie Klein, *Envy and Gratitude and Other Works 1946–1963* (London: Vintage, 1997).
11 Judith Butler, *Undoing Gender* (London: Routledge, 2004), 23.
12 Klein, *Envy and Gratitude*, 193.
13 Gayatri Chakravorty Spivak, *The Spivak Reader: Selected Works of Gayatri Chakravorty Spivak,* ed. Donna Landry and Gerald MacLean (London: Routledge, 1996), 28.
14 Jacques Derrida, *Given Time: Counterfeit Money*, trans. Peggy Kamuf (Chicago: University of Chicago Press, 1992), 12.
15 Gayatri Chakravorty Spivak, *A Critique of Postcolonial Reason: Toward a History of the Vanishing Present* (Cambridge: Harvard University Press, 1999), 36.
16 Ibid., 284.
17 Foucault, 'Subject and Power', 782–4.
18 Michel Foucault, *Security, Territory, Population. Lectures at the College de France, 1977–1978*, trans. Graham Burchell (New York: Picador, 2007), 72–3.
19 Klein, *Envy and Gratitude*, 179, 193.
20 Rey Chow, *The Protestant Ethnic and the Spirit of Capitalism* (New York: Columbia University Press, 2002).
21 Lucy Lamble, 'Only Six Countries in the World Give Women and Men Equal Legal Work Rights', *Guardian*, 1 March 2019.
22 Lena Martinsson, Gabriele Griffin and Katarina Giritli Nygren, *Challenging the Myth of Gender Equality in Sweden* (Bristol: Policy Press, 2016).
23 Michel Foucault, *Society Must Be Defended*, trans. David Macey (London: Penguin, 2004); Rene Girard, *Violence and the Sacred*, trans. Patrick Grego (Baltimore: Johns Hopkins University Press, 1989).

24 Jacques Derrida, *The Gift of Death*, trans. David Wills (Chicago: University of Chicago Press, 1995), 40–1.
25 *The Tale of Kieu*, a national epic by Nguyen Du (1765–1820), depicting the life of a prostitute – who has sacrificed herself, has been raped and tortured, and is living in exile – serves as an official narrative of the Vietnamese fate, despite the country's patriarchy. Nguyen Phu Trong, the Vietnamese president and general secretary of the Communist Party, taking office in 2018, cites *The Tale of Kieu*, identifying himself as Kieu, the most marginalized woman. P. Thao, 'Tổng Bí thư-Chủ tịch nước: 'Nhậm chức, tâm trạng có phần lo lắng hơn', *Dan Tri*, 23 October 2018.
26 Dang Hung Vo, 'Vietnam Opened to the World, and Has Gained Its Trust', *VnExpress*, 26 February 2019.
27 A newly released documentary entitled *Vietnam: Connecting East Africa* (aired on the Discovery Channel Southeast Asia in December 2018 and uploaded on YouTube in January 2019) has manufactured an image of a generous and trustworthy Vietnam pursuing the global capitalist mission of bringing technological revolutions to transform the lives of people in Tanzania.
28 Sigmund Freud, *Civilization and Its Discontents*, trans. James Strachey (New York: Norton, 1962).
29 Sianne Ngai, *Ugly Feelings* (Cambridge: Harvard University Press, 2005).

Bibliography

Berlant, Lauren, and Michael Warner. 'Sex in Public'. *Critical Inquiry* 24, no. 2 (1998): 547–66.

Berlant, Lauren. 'The Subject of True Feeling: Pain, Privacy, and Politics'. In *Cultural Pluralism, Identity Politics, and the Law*, edited by Austin Sarat and Thomas R. Kearns, 49–84. Ann Arbor: University of Michigan Press, 1999.

Berlant, Lauren. *The Female Complaint: The Unfinished Business of Sentimentality in American Culture*. Durham: Duke University Press, 2008.

Butler, Judith. *Undoing Gender*. London: Routledge, 2004.

Chow, Rey. *The Protestant Ethnic and the Spirit of Capitalism*. New York: Columbia University Press, 2002.

Dang, Hung Vo. 'Vietnam Opened to the World, and Has Gained Its Trust'. *VnExpress*, 26 February 2019. https://e.vnexpress.net/news/trump-kim-summit-vietnam/vietnam-opened-to-the-world-and-has-gained-its-trust-3886616.html.

Derrida, Jacques. *Given Time: Counterfeit Money*. Translated by Peggy Kamuf. Chicago: University of Chicago Press, 1992.

Derrida, Jacques. *The Gift of Death*. Translated by David Wills. Chicago: University of Chicago Press, 1995.

Foucault, Michel. 'The Subject and Power'. *Critical Inquiry* 8, no. 4 (1982): 777–95.
Foucault, Michel. 'Two Lectures'. In *Power/Knowledge: Selected Interviews and Other Writings, 1972–1977*, translated by Colin Gordon, Leo Marshall, John Mepham and Kate Soper, 78–108. New York: Pantheon, 1980.
Foucault, Michel. *Security, Territory, Population. Lectures at the College de France, 1977–1978*. Translated by Graham Burchell. New York: Picador, 2007.
Foucault, Michel. *Society Must Be Defended*. Translated by David Macey. London: Penguin, 2004.
Freud, Sigmund. *Civilization and Its Discontents*. Translated by James Strachey. New York: Norton, 1962.
Girard, Rene. *Violence and the Sacred*. Translated by Patrick Grego. Baltimore: Johns Hopkins University Press, 1989.
Klein, Melanie. *Envy and Gratitude and Other Works 1946–1963*. London: Vintage, 1997.
Lamble, Lucy. 'Only Six Countries in the World Give Women and Men Equal Legal Work Rights'. *Guardian*, 1 March 2019. https://www.theguardian.com/global-development/2019/mar/01/only-six-countries-in-the-world-give-women-and-men-equal-legal-rights.
Martinsson, Lena, Gabriele Griffin and Katarina Giritli Nygren, eds. *Challenging the Myth of Gender Equality in Sweden*. Bristol: Policy Press, 2016.
Ngai, Sianne. *Ugly Feelings*. Cambridge: Harvard University Press, 2005.
Nguyen, Mimi Thi. *The Gift of Freedom: War, Debt, and Other Refugee Passages*. Durham: Duke University Press, 2012.
Nguyen, Phuong Tran. *Becoming Refugee American: The Politics of Rescue in Little Saigon*. Urbana: University of Illinois Press, 2017.
Nguyen, Viet Thanh. *Nothing Ever Dies. Vietnam and the Memory of War*. Cambridge: Harvard University Press, 2016.
Scott, Joan W. 'The Evidence of Experience'. *Critical Inquiry* 17, no. 4 (1991): 773–97.
Spivak, Gayatri Chakravorty. *A Critique of Postcolonial Reason: Toward a History of the Vanishing Present*. Cambridge: Harvard University Press, 1999.
Spivak, Gayatri Chakravorty. 'Righting Wrongs'. *South Atlantic Quarterly* 103, nos. 2/3 (2004): 523–81.
Spivak, Gayatri Chakravorty. *The Spivak Reader. Selected Works of Gayatri Chakravorty Spivak*. Edited by Donna Landry and Gerald MacLean. New York: Routledge, 1996.
Thao, P. 'Tổng Bí thư-Chủ tịch nước: 'Nhậm chức, tâm trạng có phần lo lắng hơn'. *Dan Tri*, 23 October 2018. https://dantri.com.vn/chinh-tri/tong-bi-thu-chu-tich-nuoc-nham-chuc-tam-trang-co-phan-lo-lang-hon-20181023154801288.htm.

3

The *Beatitudes of Love*: Revisiting Stanley Spencer's ways of seeing[1]

Racheal Harris

Introduction

An emerging feature of recent art-history scholarship, academic and general, has been a concern with the fraught and volatile entanglements between artists and their significant others. This is particularly true of partnerships in which one lover functioned as either 'muse' or artistic contemporary to the other, or both. To serve this interest, collections including those from Chadwick & Courtivron,[2] Schuster,[3] and Stewart[4] have sought to bring together case studies of popular creative partnerships in something of a retrospective survey of the triumphant and tumultuous nature of love. Beyond print publications, the Barbican's 2018–19 exhibition 'Modern Couples' is another example of developing curiosities around this theme. While audiences may be intrigued by volatile, erotic entanglements and their associated melodrama, the overwhelming pattern of these outputs trend towards a formulaic discussion of relationships, and thus a limited focus on the same couples. Pairings such as Jackson Pollock and Lee Krasner, Frieda Kahlo and Diego Rivera, or John Lennon and Yoko Ono account for turbulent partnerships, strained by infidelity, illness and addiction, while the more tragic (though no less scandalous) pairings of Oscar Wilde and Lord Alfred Douglas or Virginia Woolf and Vita Sackville-West are similarly a common fixture. Though a case study of these relationships certainly has a value in any discourse on romance, in adopting such a limited field of vision, we fail to register a more textured experience of love and loving. With that in mind, this chapter seeks to adopt a different view in its discussion of love.

British artists Stanley Spencer CBE RA (1891–1959) and Hilda Carline (1889–1950) are the focus of my discussion of the complex and convoluted nature of love. I approach an analysis of their relationship through the lens of Stanley's artwork and the correspondences shared between them. Despite the litany of biographies and historical studies which examine almost exclusively Stanley's life and art, little has been written with a specific view towards the role of romantic love in his troubled partnership with Hilda. Such a chronic oversight is unfair to both, as artists and as lovers, but also to audiences. For, though their relationship was fraught with turbulence, it provides a compelling picture of love and its capacity to test and temper the fortitude of the lover. Specifically, the Stanley and Hilda union offers an insight into imperfect but enduring love and, in doing so, allows those of us with an interest in love more broadly a different interpretation or definition for what love *might* look like, how it can be both ugly and devastating, and yet still profound. Owing to Stanley's affection for the homely, domestic and familiar (all themes which pervaded his artworks), I have adopted the use of first names in my discussion of him, Hilda, and their union. This feels too, I believe, more in line with the thematic interests of this collection.

The definition of love I will use here is drawn from that offered by Hatfield and Sprecher[5] and revisited in the 2019 monograph *The Psychology of Love and Hate in Intimate Relationship*,[6] which frames love as follows:

> A state of intense longing for union with another. A complex functional whole including appraisals or appreciations, subjective feelings, expressions, patterned physiological processes, action tendencies, and instrumental behaviors. Reciprocated love (union with the other) is associated with fulfillment and ecstasy; unrequited love (separation) is associated with emptiness, anxiety, or despair.

This definition not only fits the experience of love that is expressed by Stanley in his artistic work and writing as it pertains to Hilda, but captures a universal truth of life – that love is not always about happy endings. Still, even when the experience of loving and being loved causes us pain, we would seldom choose to be without it. Admitting that it is part of a darker aspect of human nature to not only seek out, but take pleasure in, loving relationships which frustrate and confound as often as they comfort or console, is necessary to any examination of why love is so vital to the human experience.

Owing to geographical constraints related to the pandemic and the inability to access archival material, John Rothenstein's[7] and Adrian Glew's[8] publications of Stanley's collected letters have been used as primary source materials for discussion in this chapter, along with Nigel Rapport's[9] study of romantic love within the context of the *Beatitudes of Love* series. This series of works itself will act as the focal point for discussion throughout the chapter, though additional works by Stanley will be drawn upon. Kenneth Pople's biography,[10] along with Kitty Hauser's[11] analysis on the enduring impact of Stanley's work, provides much of the context for the artist's approach, while the limited titles that have attempted to examine Hilda as an artist in her own right,[12] and as the wife of Stanley,[13] have been consulted for context relative to her ideas about her relationship and further insight into how she continued to love Stanley even after the dissolution of their marriage. Sadly, both of these assess her largely as an extension of Stanley as opposed to an autonomous entity and accomplished artist, a fact most painfully illustrated in the title of the Wilcox volume. Since Hilda has undergone such scant discussion in comparison to her husband, Stanley's perspective is given more prominently throughout the chapter. This should not be interpreted as an attempt to depict him in a sympathetic light, nor to downplay Hilda's suffering throughout their relationship; it is merely a reflection of the source material available, which favours a patriarchal focus in its insistence of defining Hilda through the lens of her husband. Further exploration of the relationship between the pair, one which affords more time and attention to Hilda and her point of view, is the subject of a future project, which sits outside the scope of a single chapter.

The *Beatitudes of Love*

Completed between 1937 and 1938, the *Beatitudes of Love* series forms a part of what has been dubbed the second act of Stanley Spencer's career[14] and the apex of his artistic vision.[15] This phase and its output, unlike the work of Stanley's youth, capture his coming of age and (albeit belated) sexual maturity. There are seven surviving paintings within the sequence, with each given a name corresponding to a significant moment in the meeting and courting ritual of a pair of lovers. These include: *Romantic Meeting, Desire, Knowing, Worship, Contemplation, Consciousness* and *Toasting*. The images are mostly set among the milieu of daily life, with their characters engaging in the most common of circumstances, such as in the street or at a local dance. Frequently, there are also minor characters within the images and, as in the case of *Contemplation* and *Worship*, the expressions of these additional players highlight the intimacy and strength of emotion between the lovers, who are always primary characters within the works. For instance, in *Contemplation*, female and male are cast on the left and right side of the canvas, with several figures surrounding them. The image has the appearance of a social gathering, with people dressed formally, engaged in discussion and standing close to each other. Despite the closeness of bodies, the lovers stand in rapt attention, gazing across the space, their two selves joined by hands, which grip tightly to each other. The viewer is drawn into their wordless exchange and comes to feel, much like the additional figures in the background, that they are eavesdropping on an intensely private moment.

Toasting (also known as *Sociableness*) could be read as the odd one out within the sequence as, unlike the remaining works, it depicts its two lovers naked and ensconced firmly within a cosy, domestic setting. Based on Stanley's later diary entries, it is likely that there were additional nude works similar to *Toasting*, though these were either lost or destroyed by the artist in the face of public backlash about the provocative content of the images.[16]

Andrew Causey has described the *Beatitudes of Love* as a representation of intense mental suffering, arguing that Stanley is the key figure in each scene, even when the characters do not appear to bear a physical resemblance to him. He goes on to suggest that the women in the images appear intentionally disengaged or unsure of themselves, and that this too should be seen as indicative of the friction Stanley was encountering in his romantic life at the time.[17] Recently divorced from his first wife, Hilda, and largely estranged from new wife, Patricia Preece, rather than the blissful union he had imagined (which at one point included having both Hilda and Patricia simultaneously as wives) at this point in his life, Stanley was coming to understand that the reality of his situation was never going to compare to the fantasy he had concocted.[18] Looking at the series in this light, the figures are demonstrative of pent up desire, which seeks to be fulfilled on an emotional and metaphysical level.

In contrast to Causey's argument, Pople suggests that rather than being reflective of partnership, the series is instead indicative of the differing elements of Stanley's self, and that even the female figures are essentially representations of the oppositional elements of his own emotions, representing feminine and masculine.[19] As such, though Stanley's marital woes were an inspiration, his wives should not be seen strictly as the basis for the female characters within the paintings. While certain images certainly have a striking resemblance to Hilda and, to a lesser degree, Patricia, the renderings are about how Stanley understood himself *through* them as opposed to his desire or longing *for* them. For a male artist of Stanley's era, depicting oneself in such a quasi-hermaphroditic sense was uncommon and, perhaps, also presents an insight into why these works were often misunderstood by audiences. In his writings, he is clear however that his ideas about love were never completely understood by anyone other than himself,[20] neither were his enduring desires for perfect union with his partner. For him, such a union was not purely romantic or physical but deeply spiritual, taking on both feminine and masculine qualities, merging two parts into a singular, unified whole. Indeed, the reconciliation of all creation is a concept underpinning his entire oeuvre. The *Beatitudes of Love* sought to visually encapsulate these spiritual and philosophical ideals, and Stanley describes the works as such:

> I saw – and this interested me most – that the religious quality I had been looking for … in my sex pictures showed itself for the first time.[21]

Pople and Causey each offer detailed interpretations of the series, and yet to adopt either argument alone falls short in appreciating Stanley's deeply emotional nature and enduring attempts to draw nearer to his beloved. Stanley was a staunch advocate of his own beliefs, often unyielding when it came to altering them. While this lack served him in the role of artistic vision, it invariably complicated his ability to grow close to those he loved, particularly Hilda. When coupled with an overly nostalgic obsession with his childhood home and family unit, Stanley's idea of passionate love rendered him immature and unprepared for the amount of compromise that romantic relationships demand. In simply being her own self, Hilda was predisposed to fail in adhering to the shape Stanley imagined for her, and thus the couple were often at odds. Still, even when she fell short of his needs and (at times unrealistic) expectations,[22] it was she who came the closest to capturing the essence of the love that Stanley imagined was possible. It is his longing and desire to recapture their good moments together (no matter how fleeting) that we see expressed in the *Beatitudes of Love* sequence. That the images were primarily completed at a time when he was attempting to woo her back to him is telling and with this in mind, the series captures a deep longing to rebuild his union. Writing to Hilda many years after her death, he laments:

> I have never in my attempts to marry since [their divorce] been able to see and feel the marriage continuing endlessly into the future and through all the years ahead as I *was* able to feel about you and me … I *can* only feel that *one*ness I love,

with you. I could identify myself with you utterly so that I felt like a single being that was me and you.[23]

Despite being the object of Stanley's changing affections and, at times, callous treatment, it is evident that during her life, Hilda felt much the same way. Though it would take a tremendous toll on her mental health, she came to understand Stanley as being so interwoven with her own persona that the two could not be parted.[24] Even during their most bitter spats, she maintains a devotion to him, seeing him as someone with whom she is spiritually and emotionally linked. In a letter in which they were at odds over an impending court case for child support, she writes to him:

> I have known that I would rather, it were to injure *me* than you ... Either I love you or I don't, & if I love you I cannot hurt you. [25]

Reflecting on these sentiments, it is clear that Stanley's conception of love adheres strongly to a sense of self-identity and, in many ways, his self-esteem. For him this would prove to be quite difficult in the years after her death because, having lost that one person who anchored him to his ideas and experiences of love in its truest form, he was adrift, always searching for the stability which only she was able to provide. In later years, reflecting on his paintings and writing letters to her, even though she could not respond, would continue to be a comfort. With this in mind, a more compassionate view of his drives might be drawn from aligning his understanding of love to the model discussed by Robert C. Solomon:

> The primary motivation for love is not sex or companionship ... but a sense of self-worth ... when love fails, it is not usually because of flagging passion ... not because of disenchantment with one's lover but rather because one no longer likes or can no longer tolerate the person he or she has become ... It is in the first person plural – the 'we' – that not only our most private and personal but also our most important virtues are defined.[26]

Viewed in this light, we might better understand Stanley as looking towards Hilda in the hope she would fill something missing within himself. For many of us this is not dissimilar to our own desires, albeit a road that when we traverse it leads us almost invariably to disappointment. In an attempt to make up for his lack, Stanley turned, as he had so often before, to his artistic practice as an avenue of expression and thus, the *Beatitudes of Love* were born.[27]

Love as ugliness

Looking at the *Beatitudes of Love* aesthetically, the most distinguishing feature and certainly the one for which the series has attracted the most criticism, is the apparent ugliness of its subjects. A critic for *the Observer* described them 'exasperatingly pungent', while the *Daily Mail* was no less flattering in its accusation that the images, like the artist, seemed 'wishing to pillory moral frailties and physical defects'.[28] This last charge seems to have sat particularly poorly with Stanley, who offered this rebuttal:

> It would be better and truer to say 'Spencer likes degenerate, deformed-looking people … than to impute me with sniggering and laughing derisively …These people, every one of them, are beloved of my imagination'.[29]

It is important to note the use of the word 'degenerate' in this historical context, where it would have referred explicitly to an immoral or corrupt individual.

No matter the intent behind his works, it would be difficult if not impossible to argue that any of the figures in the works constitute a traditional notion of beauty; yet, through various elements each does depict a very strong notion of longing and desire, one which we could only equate with romantic love, sexual longing and Stanley's desire for the fusion of these feelings in the act of love making. It is in this facet that the beauty and the genius of the works is most evident, for in making his figures so odd and misformed, what Stanley is ultimately declaring is that love is not an emotion which is put aside purely for the young or the beautiful to experience; it is instead inseparable from faith or worship and in central to the attainment of joy. He reflects:

> Religion (or love I don't mind) brings happiness & happiness brings gratitude & gratitude brings aspirations: the wish to express it in the best possible way … And this brings passion & passion brings & reaches to creative power. This is the way of Vision. It ends with me seeing this special, & to me crucial, meaningfulness in ordinary appearance.[30]

A similar expression is felt in a later diary entry, in which he discusses the series and his enduring fondness for each of the images and what they strive to capture:

> I do myself love the 'disagreeably abnormal' persons in these paintings in the same way I love myself at home … I love them from within outwards and

whatever that outward appearance may be it is an exquisite reminder of what is loved within.[31]

Therefore, even as we consider the images in the aesthetic ugliness of their subjects, we are reminded that the individual is not loved because of their beauty but, because love is akin to a sacred, religious experience, despite their lack of it. Similarly, the act of loving itself can be ugly, clumsy and less than perfect at times. It is because of these factors that love is just as present, just as passionate, among normal (or even slightly abnormal) members of society as it is apparent among the idolized.

To highlight this concept, *Consciousness* (1938) casts its lovers as tall, thin, and unkempt figures, posed in a way that highlights their angular proportions. Based on their attire, it is hard to place either figure in a specific period, thus giving the impression of the timelessness of the exchange taking place between them. The male is unshaven, his clothes mismatched in a way that suggests a lack of means or the social skills required for engaging in formal occasions. His shirt is unbuttoned and he wears no necktie. Seemingly captured in mid-speech, the set of his mouth is pleading, as the female figure gazes back at him with a type of fondness, but also the hint of anxiety. In contrast to her suitor, the woman is more suitably attired, in a sequined top and formal skirt, but again her stance highlights the angularity and ugliness of her build. She is unshapely, her shoulders drooping, buck teeth jutting out from large lips and set off by heavy, wire framed spectacles. Her left arm turns towards her body at an odd angle, while her right-hand grips at the knee, in a way that suggests a lopsided, almost hunching stance. Taken together, the pair are comically unpleasant. When we think of a romantic interlude as it is expressed in other forms of visual media, neither figure would spring to mind.

In a similar way, *Romantic Meeting* (1938) depicts angular figures, although in this instance their stance mirrors each other, creating a sense of harmony as opposed to the awkward nervousness of the pair in *Consciousness*. The male figure in this painting (which is also known as *The Dustman* because of the appearance of a dustpan and broom in the background) is again attired in slightly mismatched clothing. Though clean shaven and less unkempt, he again wears no tie. His posture is stiff, with a slightly open mouthed expression and raised eyebrows elongating his face. He is stood with feet close together and has his hands placed in what appears to be very shallow pockets, obscuring them from view. This highlights the odd positioning and the immense size of the hands of his female love interest. Positioned in the front of the body, one signals between the breasts, which are lopsided and difficult to discern beneath her plum coloured, high neck frock, while the other is placed directly in front of the lower body, as though shielding her genitalia. There is an element to the composition of the woman that recalls Eve in the Garden of Eden, when she first recognizes herself as naked. Although the folds of her dress and her dark-coloured stockings cover any hint of bare skin, the gesturing of the hand between the thighs remains suggestive, and recalls a Western art-historical tradition dating back to Giorgione's *Sleeping Venus* (1510). The pair gaze at each other with rapt attention, their eyes are locked in an expression of anticipation and innocence, as if in a moment of shocked realization they have come to recognize what sexual desire feels like. If we consider both figures to be indicative of duelling aspects of Stanley's own self, the feminine figure is representative of his awakening sexual desire at that point while the male figure (who strongly resembles Stanley) speaks to the overwhelming challenge of trying to navigate these intensifying feelings. There is a clear sense of not only arousal, but also trepidation.

It is further interesting to note that unlike the other works in the series, both the above examples feature younger couples who, despite an obvious attraction, do not touch each other. Instead, communication is done with expression and stance. This speaks to love as it is experienced with that first sense of innocence before physicality enters into the exchange. Physical touch is of course central to the experience of romantic love and being loved and thus, I turn now to a consideration of how these tactile expressions are represented.

Love as touch and sight

Of the five senses, touch is central to the experience of love, as it is through the touching of a partner that we indicate and experience intimacy. As a highly visual species, sight is similarly a sense which is overwhelmingly interwoven with attraction, as well as to emotional and sensual bonding and communication with our beloved. When words fail us, a look or touch can convey all that is necessary. What is interesting about the figures shown in *Contemplation* is not only the way in which the fingers meet, in the top quarter of the trunk and level with the heart, but the way in which they parallel and strengthen the gaze of the lovers. In an interlocking grasp, the clasped hands form a conduit between the bodies, acting as a channel whereby the heart of each lover might touch the other. There is an obsessiveness about this type of connection, mirrored in their gaze, which suggests that love is not a temporary or shallow encounter. Rather, it requires the utmost devotion and dedication of one lover for the other.

This image is set amid a room of people, several of whom look upon the exchange between the couple, but are unseen by them. The rapture expressed between the two figures reflects the romantic desires present in Stanley's own life, specifically his need to be seen above all others. In the case of his relationship with Hilda, an enduring complaint was that he was unable to remain as close to her as he desired to be, particularly after the birth of their children. This was not limited to what he felt was a decline in the act of physical love making between them but encompassed a falling away of spiritual and mental closeness. The simpatico they shared on many of their religious beliefs and morals was something which had initially bought them together, though Hilda, as she matured, seemed to draw away from these elements of the relationship, leaving Stanley bereft.[32] Part of this problem might be attributed to a lack of verbal communication between the pair, an unwillingness to compromise or to place themselves into the role of the other. Of course, the entry of Patricia into their lives turned the fissure between them into a rupture, leading eventually to their separation. Though she never swayed in her love for Stanley, even during the most bitter aspects of their divorce, Hilda's devout religious beliefs would not be reconciled with his infidelity, even when it became apparent that his relationship with Patricia was over and he wanted to be reunited. The pair had discussed remarriage shortly prior to Hilda's death, and yet it seems that her stipulation for the reunion was that there would be no recommencement of a sexual union between the pair. This was a factor Stanley could not accept, writing to her:

> I am worried about your stipulation re condition of marrying you …
>
> The *fact* you tell me namely that there never never will be any sex relationship.
>
> The reason, allways [*sic*] difficult to give, you don't give … & my reply has to be I most ardently & spiritually wish & want to marry you but I cannot accept the condition.[33]

Touch and physicality were, unsurprisingly, a central factor for the expression of love as Stanley understood it, and yet they had been an ongoing hurdle in his relationship with Hilda. During his second turbulent marriage, he was similarly frustrated by the fact that Patricia kept him at a physical and emotional distance and this too, played out in his art. Rather than conveying the emotional or physical intimacy present in the *Beatitudes of Love*, his other compositions from this period, which include his most controversial nude pieces (including the notorious double nude portrait of he and Patricia) are indicative of the tensions between the spouses. In these, Patricia is always looking beyond Stanley, never meeting his gaze,[34] creating an element to these works which conveys a strong feeling of disconnection. The composition of the paintings recalls the argument of John Berger, specifically that it is a rarity for a nude to remove the artist from the dialogue of the image.[35] Although Patricia is the focal point and, in being so, becomes an object for the viewer, Stanley has captured her expression in such a way as to indicate that she does not register his presence and that despite their obvious intimacy as man and wife, she is emotionally and romantically absent from him. Even when he is in the images (such as is the case with *Self-Portrait with Patricia Preece* or *Double Nude Portrait: The Artist with His Second Wife*), there is an unmistakable sense of romantic disconnect. The *Double Nude* (1937) in particular captures this in the downcast look of Stanley, which is coupled with Patricia's far-off stare; though it is perhaps his flaccid penis, which sits, unavoidably, in the centre of the image that is the strongest indicator of his sense of romantic and sexual rejection within this period of his life. As Hauser has commented, Stanley could engage Patricia through looking, but their relationship was devoid of touch, especially that of the romantic and sexual kind.[36] It is widely believed that Patricia's affections were focused purely on Dorothy Hepworth, her constant companion both before and during her marriage to Stanley.[37] Their lesbian affair was something which even Hilda was able to see, though it caused her no less pain in recognizing it. In her personal correspondence with Stanley's art dealer Dudley Tooth, she refers to Hepworth as 'the girlfriend',[38] all the while scorning Patricia for her duplicity and general poor treatment of Stanley, and Stanley for his idiocy. For his part, Stanley seemed wilfully ignorant of his second wife's intimacy with Hepworth.[39] Though he often times expressed the desire to be wed to both Hilda and Patricia, there was never a desire to be involved in a similar three-way relationship with Patricia and Dorothy, though he did cohabit with the pair during his courtship of Patricia. This suggests that Stanley's thrall was not motivated by the sex act, nor simply by the desire for dominance over multiple women. Rather, there were intrinsic qualities, possessed by only Hilda and Patricia, which agitated his already complicated 'sex feelings', ultimately leading to the unrest experienced during his later life.

While the works which take Stanley and Patricia as a focal point are stunning examples of realism, they do not convey the emotional pull and certainly none of the intimacy present in the *Beatitudes* series, which despite a lack of visual realism is the more emotionally raw of Stanley's outputs at the time. While female figures depicted in the works fail to bear a striking resemblance to either Hilda or Patricia, each recalls other of Stanley's works which feature Hilda as his muse. Primary among these is the size at which females are often depicted. *Desire* (1938) adopts this theme, with the female figure appearing considerably larger than her male counterpart, so that she envelopes him with her voluminous curves and breasts. The pair recall figures from an earlier series on domesticity, modelled on the early years of Stanley's marriage to Hilda and in which she frequently covers his form with her body. As John Berger writes, the female form has generally been used in art as something consumed by both artist and viewer.[40] In this instance, however, it is the female body which consumes, literally and metaphorically, the form of her partner. Both *At the Chest of Drawers* (1936) and *On the Landing* (1936) are similar in their execution of the female form, which threatens to eclipse the male in various moments from the domestic mundane.

As in *Contemplation,* in *Desire* and in *Consciousness* Stanley's couples illustrate the importance of touch in the placement of their hands and use this as an extension of their gaze, highlighting the tactile experience of intimacy alongside the fusing of two halves into a single whole. For Stanley, lovers took on a unified persona, a 'you and me self' as he frequently described it. This was something secret, shared only between them, and which found its earthly expression in the act of love making, but also had a distinctly emotional and spiritual element. As such, it is unsurprising that devotional iconography is carried over through the elongation of the hands and fingers in each of the pieces. Even in *Worship* (1938), which is the only image not to feature a man and woman touching (and is said to be based explicitly on Patricia), the hands of the dancers, as well as the audience are their most prominent features. In his earliest images, such as *Apple Gatherers* (1912) and other standalone pieces from the figure drawing period like *Neighbours* (1936), hands are also a focal point of the images. Similarly, *Resurrection of the Soldiers* (1928–9) uses the clasping, joining and shaking of hands to bring together service men who, though in opposition during life, are reconciled upon resurrection through the power of a handshake. Not only do hands pass objects, but they fuse together the subjects of Stanley's work in an embrace which reads as platonic affection as easily as romantic love.

The interlinking of hands in an expression of communal touching, present throughout the *Beatitudes of Love* sequence, further recalls Stanley's resurrection images, notably *The Resurrection, Cookham* (1924–7), *The Resurrection of the Soldiers* (1928–9) and *Parents Resurrecting* (1933), which similarly feature masses of people in various types of intimate embrace. In this subgenre of image, the communal loving is again indicative of spiritual as well as physical love.[41] Looking upon them in the current time, particularly in the wake of the pandemic, it is difficult not to feel a pull of nostalgia, as they remind us of the intricacy and importance of touch to our experience of loving. Negotiating the ever-changing landscape of 'socially distanced living', it is difficult not to yearn for the familiarity of a loving touch.

Love as familiarity

> Being naked in their own sitting room … helps them in the realisation that the species called civilised conventional beings is different from the species husband and wife.[42]

Toasting is the only image in the series which brings love through to its consummated conclusion, which shows a woman and man poised naked before a fireplace. The female is shown in profile, standing on tip toes and warming herself over the fire, her orange hair splayed out across the mantle. She has voluptuous breasts, which hang heavily, while a soft stomach and pubic hair partly obscures the face of her lover, which is tilted to suggest that he may like to rest his cheek against her bare stomach. He is bent down in a crouching pose and leans towards the fire's grate to toast a piece of meat over the open flame. The nudity and exposure of both figures does not suggest any kind of vulgarity, but rather an intimacy which exists between lovers in the privacy of the world which they share. It is a visual representation of the 'you and me self' but also speaks to man and woman as separate entities, suspended in the act of reciprocal worship. There is none of the cool distance, evident in his nude work, between this couple.

In this instance, there seems little doubt that Stanley used both himself and Hilda as the inspiration for the piece. The quotation above is taken from one of his dairies, when he is recounting the role which memories of his early marriage to Hilda played in the construction of the image and is similar to a range of sentiments expressed in his letters to Hilda directly. In these he often refers to her by her pet name, Ducky, and recounts the bliss of their private rituals carried out within their domestic life. In a particularly poignant example, he recalls their honeymoon:

> we both knew each other's longings ... We blazed at each other, me being so me & you staggering me with your utmost Hilda. Confronting me with such positive you.[43]

Perhaps one of the most painful aspects of Stanley's writings *is* his sense of nostalgia and longing for the time which he and Hilda shared at the start of their marriage, and the echo of this, present within his work, is what continues to make it so arresting. Towards the end of his own life, and having recently returned from a trip abroad, he writes to Hilda:

> What I like about our marriage ... is that we are to each other all & any place near & far.[44]

Note that he refers to the marriage in the present tense, as though in his mind, it continues on in her absence, in a spiritual union. It was this desire to revisit their shared self, the closeness of the unique bond which he was unable to replicate with any other woman, which drove Stanley's obsession with Hilda after her death, and saw her cast as the primary figure of many of his later works, including unfinished pieces he was constructing at the time of his own passing. In these later examples, however, Hilda often transcends from the role of wife to that of quasi-spiritual deity.[45] In his final (unfinished) work *The Apotheosis of Hilda* (1959), she appears amid a crowd of villagers, her figure twice their size as she seems to rise above them, while they look on in splendour.[46] The meaning of 'apotheosis' is the elevation of someone into divine status and should be read here as another indication of Stanley's veneration of his wife.

What Stanley tells his audience in the domestic scenes present in the *Beatitudes* series and *Toasting* specifically is that, rather than being an unfamiliar, and necessarily youthful experience, the deepest sense and expression of love comes from a love which has developed over time – one which takes place within the home, between established, devoted lovers. In his estimation, it is in the growing together of two souls that love becomes ultimately recognized. An essential part of this is the aging of the physical forms which house these souls, and with this ageing imperfection is an unavoidable side effect. In a world which constantly suggests that outward perfection is a prerequisite for attracting love, Stanley's works demonstrate a more realistic truth: that it is through an accumulation of time, and the acceptance of its tangible and intangible imperfections, that one comes to fully embrace love in its most authentic guise.

Reflecting on an image called *Age* (since lost or destroyed), Stanley writes explicitly about the comfort and beauty of the ageing body and the enduring attraction that it conjures between older lovers, writing 'each new fold of her skin appearing as her age increased was a new joy to him … She stood and he surveyed her … he does so from every angle.'[47] A prolific scholar on Stanley Spencer and his obsession with love, Rapport ultimately sums up the enduring appeal of Stanley's art being in that fact that he 'is happy to depict the perfection of a relationship where love is the recognition of the true identity of another: something neither heralded by convention nor obstructed by circumstance.'[48]

Conclusion

If there are such things as 'mistakes' in love, then Stanley Spencer surely made them all. Like many of us, however, he was simply trying to make sense of a conflict existing in the space between lovers. He was naïve and, in many respects, ignorant to the fact that love cannot always be an act of worship and adoration from the other party, but sometimes requires these actions of us. We can argue that Stanley's romantic life was steeped in disappointment and heartbreak, but it is also a story of love, experienced in the real world. All too often this lived experience, unlike its fictionalized and sentimental counterpart, offers lovers the harsh truth of irreconcilable difference, and only too often the best of intentions result in the failure of a relationship. But does this mean that the love on which they were built was not worth experiencing, that it should be forfeited in favour of something which is more clean, more pleasing, more satisfactory in its resolution? If we believe this is so, we are cheating ourselves by examining only half of the picture. If we are to know and understand love, in all its complexity, then triumph needs to be measured in proportion to tragedy; the aesthetically pleasing, in contrast to the mundane and ugly. Stanley Spencer's work, like his life, achieves a telling of this story. His figures, while peculiar in appearance, are indicative of love and its realities, which are, for most of us, quite far removed from love and romance as it appears in popular culture. Even for audiences with no understanding of the particulars of Stanley Spencer's vision or the oddities of his life, the sense of comfort which comes from the familiar, from a mature and intimate love, is one that transcends time. Thought often ugly, it is perfect in its imperfections.

Notes

1. *Dedication*: Racheal's chapter is dedicated to T … *with love*.
2. Whitney Chadwick and Isabelle de Courtivron, *Significant Others: Creativity and Intimate Partnership* (London: Thames and Hudson, 2018).
3. Clayton Schuster, *Bad Blood: Rivalry and Art History* (Atglen, PA: Schiffer Publishing, 2019).
4. Louise Stewart, *Love Stories* (London: National Gallery Publications, 2020).
5. Elaine Hatfield and Susan Spreecher, 'Measuring Passionate Love in Intimate Relations', *Journal of Adolescence* 9, no. 4 (1986): 383.
6. Elaine Hatfield, Cyrille Feybesse, Victoria Narine and Richard L. Rapson, "'Passionate Love: Inspired by Angels or Demons,"' In *The Psychology of Love and Hate in Intimate Relationships*, ed. K. Aumer (London: Springer, 2019), 65.
7. John Rothenstein, *Stanley Spencer the Man: Correspondence and Reminiscences* (London: Paul Elk, 1979).
8. Adrian Glew, *Stanley Spencer: Letters and Writings* (London: Tate Publishing, 2001).
9. Nigel Rapport, *Distortion and Love: An Anthropological Reading of the Art and Life of Stanley Spencer* (Oxfordshire: Routledge, 2018).
10. Kenneth Pople, *Stanley Spencer: A Biography* (London: Collins, 1991).
11. Kitty Hauser, *Stanley Spencer* (London: Tate Publishing, 2001).
12. Thomas Wilcox, *The Art of Hilda Carline: Mrs Stanley Spencer* (London: Lund Humphries, 1999).
13. Richard Carline, *Stanley and Hilda Spencer* (London: Anthony d'Offay Gallery, 1978).
14. Jane Alison, *Stanley Spencer: The Apotheosis of Love* (London: Barbican Art Gallery, 1991), 13.
15. Pople, *Stanley Spencer*, 353.
16. Rapport, *Distortion and Love*, 175.
17. Andrew Causey, *Stanley Spencer: Art as a Mirror of Himself* (Surrey: Lund Humphries, 2014), 11.
18. Tom Bromwell, 'Stanley Spencer', in *Critical Dictionary of Apocalyptic and Millenarian Movements*, ed. James Crossley and Alastair Lockhart, www.cdamm.org/articles/stanley-spencer 2021.
19. Pople, *Stanley Spencer*, 390–1.
20. Rothenstein, *Stanley Spencer*, 67–8; Causey, *Stanley Spencer*, 12.
21. Richard Collis, *Stanley Spencer: A Biography* (London: Harvell, 1962), 142.
22. Carline, *Stanley and Hilda Spencer*, 4.
23. Rothenstein, *Stanley Spencer*, 72, italics in original.
24. Wilcox, *Art of Hilda Carline*, 38.
25. Rothenstein, *Stanley Spencer*, 65, italics in original.

26 Robert C. Solomon, *About Love: Reinventing Romance for Our Times* (Indianapolis: Hackett Publishing, 2006), 239.
27 Pople, *Stanley Spencer*, 385.
28 Rapport, *Distortion and Love*, 166.
29 Hannah Neale, *Stanley Spencer: Love, Desire, Faith* (Cumbria: Abbot Hall Art Gallery, 2002), 50.
30 Glew, *Stanley Spencer*, 253.
31 Rapport, *Distortion and Love*, 177.
32 Carline, *Stanley and Hilda Spencer*, 5–6.
33 Rothenstein, *Stanley Spencer*, 70, italics in original.
34 Mary Kisler and Justin Paton, *Everyday Miracles in the Art of Stanley Spencer* (Dunedin: Dunedin Art Gallery, 2003), 28.
35 John Berger, *Ways of Seeing* (London: Penguin, 2008), 56–7.
36 Hauser, *Stanley Spencer*, 52.
37 People, *Stanley Spencer*, 353–60; Bromwell 'Stanley Spencer'.
38 Rothenstein, *Stanley Spencer*, 84.
39 Wilcox, *Art of Hilda Carline*, 60.
40 Berger, *Ways of Seeing*, 52.
41 Alison, *Stanley Spencer*, 30–1; Richard Heathcote and Anna Jug, *Stanley Spencer: A Twentieth-Century British Master* (Mile End, South Australia: Wakefield Press, 2016), 18.
42 Neale, *Stanley Spencer*, 48.
43 Rapport, *Distortion and Love*, 172.
44 Glew, *Stanley Spencer*, 241.
45 Wilcox, *Art of Hilda Carline*, 47.
46 Hauser, *Stanley Spencer*, 60.
47 Rapport, *Distortion and Love*, 175–6.
48 Nigel Rapport, *Cosmopolitan Love and Individuality: Ethical Engagement beyond Culture* (London: Rowman & Littlefield, 2019), 63.

Bibliography

Alison, Jane. *Stanley Spencer: The Apotheosis of Love*. London: Barbican Art Gallery, 1991.
Berger, John. *Ways of Seeing*. London: Penguin, 2008.
Bromwell, Tom. 'Stanley Spencer'. In *Critical Dictionary of Apocalyptic and Millenarian Movements*, edited by James Crossley and Alastair Lockhart. www.cdamm.org/articles/stanley-spencer 2021.

Carline, Richard. *Stanley and Hilda Spencer*. London: Anthony d'Offay Gallery, 1978.
Causey, Andrew. *Stanley Spencer: Art as a Mirror of Himself*. Surrey: Lund Humphries, 2014.
Chadwick, Whitney, and Isabelle de Courtivron. *Significant Others: Creativity and Intimate Partnership*. London: Thames and Hudson, 2018.
Collis, Richard. *Stanley Spencer: A Biography*. London: Harvell, 1962.
Glew, Adrian. *Stanley Spencer: Letters and Writings*. London: Tate Publishing, 2001.
Hatfield, Elaine, and Susan Spreecher. 'Measuring Passionate Love in Intimate Relations'. *Journal of Adolescence* 9, no. 4 (1986): 383–410.
Hatfield, Elaine, Cyrille Feybesse, Victoria Narine and Richard L. Rapson. 'Passionate Love: Inspired by Angels or Demons'. In *The Psychology of Love and Hate in Intimate Relationships*, edited by K.Aumer, 65–84. London: Springer, 2019.
Hauser, Kitty. *Stanley Spencer*. London: Tate Publishing, 2001.
Heathcote, Richard, and Anna Jug. *Stanley Spencer: A Twentieth-Century British Master*. Mile End, South Australia: Wakefield Press, 2016.
Kisler, Mary, and Justin Paton. *Everyday Miracles in the Art of Stanley Spencer*. Dunedin: Dunedin Art Gallery, 2003.
Neale, Hannah. *Stanley Spencer: Love, Desire, Faith*. Cumbria: Abbot Hall Art Gallery, 2002.
Pople, Kenneth. *Stanley Spencer: A Biography*. London: Collins, 1991.
Rapport, Nigel. *Cosmopolitan Love and Individuality: Ethical Engagement beyond Culture*. London: Rowman & Littlefield, 2019.
Rapport, Nigel. *Distortion and Love: An Anthropological Reading of the Art and Life of Stanley Spencer*. Oxfordshire: Routledge, 2018.
Rothenstein, John. *Stanley Spencer the Man: Correspondence and Reminiscences*. London: Paul Elk, 1979.
Schuster, Clayton. *Bad Blood: Rivalry and Art History*. Atglen, PA: Schiffer Publishing, 2019.
Solomon, Robert C. *About Love: Reinventing Romance for Our Times*. Indianapolis: Hackett Publishing, 2006.
Stewart, Louise. *Love Stories*, London: National Gallery Publications, 2020.
Wilcox, Thomas, ed. *The Art of Hilda Carline: Mrs Stanley Spencer*, London: Lund Humphries, 1999.

Part 2

Love and communal pedagogies of care

4

Symbiosis masquerades as love in the (post-) apartheid world of Marlene van Niekerk's *Agaat*

Shekufeh Owlia

Introduction

Apartheid, defined as 'the segregation of non-whites from whites', was established in South Africa with the rise to power of the National Party in 1948.[1] Discriminatory laws, such as the Prohibition of Mixed Marriages Act (1949); the Population Registration Act (1950), which classified people according to their race; the Group Areas Act (1950), which called for residential segregation; the Reservation of Separate Amenities Act (1953), which enforced segregation 'at beaches, on buses, and in hospitals, schools, and parks', further contributed to the entrenchment of racist views in the country.[2] After years of initially non-violent protests and later militant actions, the African National Congress (ANC) and Pan Africanist Congress (PAC) succeeded in dismantling the apartheid state by late 1991. Democratic elections held in 1994 resulted in victory for the ANC and Nelson Mandela becoming president of the Republic after nearly three decades of incarceration. Following his election, he appointed a Truth and Reconciliation Commission (TRC) with the aim of uncovering grave human rights violations of the apartheid era that initiated a process of national healing. This process included public hearings which started in 1996 and heralded a new era where forgiveness and love would be the basis for a new social order.[3]

Marlene van Niekerk's *Agaat* (2004), a post-apartheid novel steeped in the violence of the age, is narrated principally by Milla de Wet, a solitary seventy-year-old Boer farmer who is suffering from Amyotrophic Lateral Sclerosis (ALS).[4] The now paralysed and mute Milla, whose brutal husband Jak, also of Dutch descent, has passed away and whose only child Jakkie has emigrated to Canada, is cared for by her nurse Agaat Lourier. Milla, who suffered regular abuse by her husband in her youth, had brought Agaat, a girl of 'colour' with a stunted arm who was raped as a child on her mother's farm, to live with her family on Grootmoedersdrift.[5] The novel's climax is reached when the childless Milla who initially raises Agaat as her own daughter eventually becomes pregnant and begins to treat her mercilessly, casting her in the role of servant. *Agaat* has attracted a flow of articles from a range of critical positions, particularly postcolonial theory through the prism of Homi Bhabha. There have also been studies focusing on the author's subversion of the conventions of the *plaasroman* (farm novel), a genre that conventionally silences the voice of women. What makes *Agaat* stand out among farm novels of the period is the agency accorded to women, particularly the female subaltern, and the deep psychological insights it offers into the lives of its principal characters. The novel has surprisingly stimulated very few studies examining it through the lens of psychoanalysis, and recent work on Erich Fromm's psychoanalysis in the South African context is confined to two journal articles written by Maryam Beyad and Hossein Keramatfar.[6] To address this gap, this chapter provides a close reading of the novel, arguing that Fromm's concept of symbiosis can be construed as a mode of social organization through which the relationships of the main characters to one another can be understood. Van Niekerk explicitly mentions in an interview that her obsession in writing the novel was to show the 'workings of power in intimate relationships' and how love and abuse often coexist.[7] The following analysis also examines this statement in relation to love across racial lines in (post-)apartheid South Africa and its likely perversion into sadomasochism.

Any discussion of Frommian symbiosis and sadomasochism needs to begin with the premise that human beings avoid solitude which is conducive to insanity by any necessary means. According to Fromm, the need for relatedness is stronger in human beings than lust and the wish to survive.[8] Based on respect and equality, love is the true mode of relatedness that does not undermine the subjectivity and freedom of the parties involved. Those who cannot bear independence resort to another mode of relatedness that Fromm labels symbiosis.[9] He posits that human beings 'can relate to others symbiotically – i.e., by becoming part of them or by making them part of himself'.[10] Through symbiotic relationships, humans 'strive … either to control others (sadism), or to be controlled by them (masochism)'.[11] In other words, what distinguishes pseudo-love in both its masochist and sadist variants from genuine love is the fact that the individual adopts 'a negatively individuated dependency', which stems from his inability to stand alone.[12]

This chapter opens by looking into the reasons behind Milla's abduction of Agaat, arguing that it constitutes an instance of sadism that masquerades as love and shows how Milla's sadism is exacerbated after she gives birth to Jakkie. I will then discuss how Agaat as servant relates to Milla in apartheid South Africa as a dominant masochist, yet attempts every now and then to reverse the dynamic by exerting a measure of indirect control over her son's life. As for Agaat's subordinate sadism, it is predominantly directed towards the farm labourers who are more helpless than herself, and it also finds expression in acts of arson. I suggest that Milla's unravelling of the truth about Agaat's past in a fashion reminiscent of the TRC proceedings is no prelude to love between the two women, because Agaat cannot forgive Milla for the sadistic treatment she has received at her hands in the apartheid past. By way of conclusion, this chapter proposes that Agaat, who cannot overcome her loveless upbringing, is likely to further resort to forging symbiotic bonds with the farm labourers to overcome her solitude after Milla's death in the post-apartheid future.

Milla's abduction of Agaat and her rising sadism

The novel is principally narrated by Milla using a variety of narrative methods, including first-person monologues, passages of stream of consciousness and diary excerpts. Crucially, there are passages where the protagonist addresses herself in the second person, especially when reflecting on past events. Using these narrative techniques early on in the text, Milla describes her deteriorating relationship with her husband who batters her, her childlessness and her loneliness on the farm during the first seven years of her marriage, which make her admit that solitude was beginning to seriously affect her.[13]

Wishing as she does to experience motherhood, Milla decides to abduct the daughter of her former nanny Maria on the Day of the Covenant, a day that marks the anniversary of the sadistic defeat of some 12,000 Zulu combatants at the hands of Afrikaner nationalists in the 'Battle of Blood River' back in 1838.[14] The significance of the date is not coincidental and implies that her plans for the child have sadistic overtones from the very start. She grabs the girl, throws her on the floor, sprawls over her and screams:

> You're not getting away! … You're mine now … I'll thrash your backside blood-red for you if you don't behave yourself now … If you carry on being naughty

and running away I'll tell the kleinbaas and he'll take off his belt and flog you till your backside comes out in red welts and then we'll tie a rope around your neck and tie you to a pole like a baboon, the whole day long until you're tame. (572)

Milla then doses her with valerian and sleeping pills that keep her sedated for days so she may forget about her past life. This passage depicts child abuse which is 'one of the most widespread manifestations of nonsexual sadism' and can be analysed through Fromm's notions of physical and mental sadism which constitute the main thrust of this chapter.[15] While the former expression denotes physical suffering, the latter denotes a form of psychic cruelty aiming to demean the individual by hurting his feelings through verbal abuse.[16]

If one is to believe that 'if you call things by their names, you have power over them' (450), then Milla who baptizes her foundling 'Agaat' has ultimate control over her. It is important to stress at this point that power does not necessarily imply a tendency for sadism; it denotes both potency which has positive connotations and domination which carries negative ones. Power in the second sense is 'the perversion of potency' and is widespread in apartheid South Africa, a society that does little to foster any sense of solidarity across racial lines, and thus forces individuals to occupy positions of sadistic control and masochistic subordination.[17] Milla tries to 'escape that painful and practically deathlike aloneness through the forging of symbiotic bonds with' Agaat to whom she cannot relate on an equal basis and truly love under apartheid laws.[18] She strives to make the weak and vulnerable child 'a part of [her]self', and thus 'transcend [her] individual existence by domination'.[19]

While Milla is childless, her relationship to Agaat verges on a benevolent vein of sadism whereby exercising control over other people's lives does not intend to hurt them but actually works for their own benefit.[20] Milla asserts that all she wanted 'was to make a human being of her, to give her something to live for, a house, opportunities, love' (492). She teaches Agaat how to use the potty, speak, play music, embroider and farm, giving her 'everything except … the right to be free and independent' in the parent–child bond.[21] In *The Art of Loving*, Fromm posits that genuine love 'implies the absence of exploitation' whereby one 'want[s] the loved person to grow and unfold' in their own right and 'not for the purpose of *serving*' them.[22] Early on in the narrative, Milla betrays her true intention behind Agaat's 'adoption':

Sometimes I feel as if the child is a dark little storage cubicle into which I stuff everything that occurs to me and just hope for the best and that one day when

I open the door, she'll walk out of there, fine and straight, all her limbs sound and strong, grateful and ready to *serve*, a solid person who will make all my tears and misery worthwhile. (493, italics added)

Fromm asserts that people tend to rationalize sadistic desires more frequently than masochistic tendencies, and one of the most frequently recurring rationalizations is the following, 'I have done so much for you, and now I am entitled to take from you what I want.'[23] He stresses moreover that it is possible for a person to be animated by sadistic impulses and yet 'consciously believe that he is motivated only by his sense of duty'.[24] Both attitudes seem to ring true in Milla's case, who takes Agaat into her care, believing that she is acting based on the biblical commandment to 'love thy neighbour as thyself' (409). Interestingly, Fromm interprets the true meaning of the phrase 'love thy neighbour as thyself' as 'Be fair when you exchange. Give what you expect to get. Don't cheat!'[25] Milla looks upon Agaat precisely in those terms of exchange, extending effort to care for the little girl in the hope that it will pay back in the future. Overwhelmed by the daily farming chores she performs on Grootmoedersdrift without any support from her husband, Milla wishes to raise a conscientious servant who would act as her right hand on the farm and nanny to her future children. Little can she guess that Agaat will one day save her life and that of her son, during Jakkie's difficult birth.

Jak sees through Milla's rationalizations for her benevolent sadism, accusing her of thinking only of herself and using other people for her own purposes (404). His accusation suggests that Milla is sadistically domineering to Agaat and wishes to utilize her to further her own goals in life. Elsewhere, Jak cries, 'Now you've broken her in. Clay in your hands. A blank page. Now you can impress anything upon her' (408), bringing forward clear resonances of Fromm's definition of sadistic love as 'the desire to swallow its object to make him a will-less instrument in one's own hands'.[26] From the very beginning of her education, Milla sets herself the task of 'taming' Agaat, and yet by the end of the first year they live together, she admits that she is far from being tamed (493). Such moments in *Agaat* bring into question Milla's conscious belief that she is acting out of love and compassion towards the helpless Agaat whom she has taken under her care. Still, raised in the sadomasochistically charged environment of South Africa under apartheid rule, the protagonist cannot relate lovingly to the 'coloured' Agaat whom she ruthlessly kidnaps. When Milla becomes pregnant herself and gives birth to Jakkie, she relegates Agaat to the role of servant and

Milla's initially benevolent sadism gives way to a malevolent streak, in which domination over another individual aims directly at 'crippling', 'choking' and 'thwarting' them.[27] The intensity of Milla's sadism is well illustrated in the passage depicting Jakkie's christening. Agaat who, despite her wish to attend, is prevented from being present at the ceremony due to the segregation laws starts misbehaving. Milla first threatens to 'skin her alive' then adds 'tanned & brayed you must be that's punishment number one' and warns of other punishments she has in store for her (190). As though the threat of this punishment were not enough, she makes her 'plough an acre with a handplough & a mule' (192). The harshness of this treatment makes Jak wonder what is to happen if Agaat 'drop[s] dead with exhaustion' (192) and tells Milla that he has had enough of her 'concentration-camp movie' (193). This passage is another instance of the physical and mental sadism that motivates Milla's desire 'to make others suffer or to see them suffer', to use Fromm's formulation. In his view, 'this suffering can be physical, but more often it is mental' and aims to 'humiliate, embarrass others', which is the case of Agaat who is forced to manoeuvre the plough with her only remaining hand in the presence of the other labourers.[28] Their relationship contains a racial dimension too. As a white woman belonging to the social elite of South African society, Milla's sadism is directed towards Agaat, a 'coloured' servant, who is more powerless than herself. Milla acknowledges that she feels guilty, but the guiltier she feels, the angrier she gets, each time employing harsher techniques to coerce Agaat into submission.

Decades later, the dying Milla unravels the real reason behind her 'adoption' of Agaat: '*I was alone, I felt useless, I wanted to do something for my fellow humans*' (373, italics in original). In the process of individuation, one is overcome by a sense of impotence, feeling thoroughly passive in an overwhelming world. Thus, the need to 'be able to effect', to show the capacity of an active human being emerges. Much like relatedness, the need for effectiveness can be answered by 'the potency to effect love or to effect fear and suffering'.[29] Milla consciously thinks that she is driven by the need to 'effect' love, but Agaat questions the sincerity of her intentions, '*Do something for your fellow humans? Or do something with your fellow humans or to your fellow humans? Fellow human or in- or superhuman? Or half human? Less human than yourself?*' (373, italics in original). She seems to be implying that Milla's answer is of the second order. It is only in the final pages of the novel that Milla admits that she 'appropriated' Agaat for her own purposes without consulting the girl or her parents, and 'locked' her up upon her arrival on the farm to prevent her from fleeing, wondering: 'What made me abduct you over the pass? What made me steal you from beyond the rugged mountains?' (462). She now realizes how ill-conceived the project of kidnapping Agaat may have been and the answer to all her rhetorical questions is that she sought a symbiotic relationship to the discarded Agaat who fell prey to her sadistic schemes.

Agaat's subordinate sadism enacted

Living in apartheid South Africa subjects Agaat to experiences that are sadistic in nature from early childhood. She was raped as a child by her kinsmen, abducted and briefly 'loved' by Milla in a sadistic fashion, only to be thereafter cast aside and relegated to the servants' quarters; an experience that makes her *'heart … very very sore. But not for long and then it grew as hard as a stone and black as soot and cold as a burnt-out coal'* (589, italics in original). In Fromm's theory, violent treatment one suffers in early childhood can be conducive to manifestations of sadism later in adulthood.[30] In a key passage, Milla is depicted as punishing the small Agaat for her transgressions by pretending to call the police, telling them how mischievous she is and asking them to 'lock her up in a cell with bars behind a great iron door without food and without pee-pot' (492).

Fromm describes two kinds of authority situations relevant to this discussion: the first is best exemplified in the teacher–student relationship and the second in the master–slave relationship.[31] As long as Milla is childless, her relationship to Agaat verges on the first kind, which implies 'elements of love, admiration, or gratitude'.[32] Agaat's love for Milla reaches a point where she even tells her 'Même you're my only mother' (541).[33] After Jakkie's birth, however, Agaat becomes a servant and her condition closely approximates the second kind of authority, where 'resentment or hostility will arise against the exploiter, subordination to whom is against one's interests', which makes her behavioural patterns towards her foster mother develop, as we shall see, in a sadistic direction.[34] According to Chancer, each person primarily relates to those living in his surroundings through either sadism or masochism, which is one's dominant mode of relatedness to the world, yet also has the potential to enact one's subordinate sadism or masochism on other people under particular circumstances.[35]

Agaat, who relates to Milla as dominant masochist, exerts a measure of indirect control over her mistress's life by appropriating Jakkie. In a climactic moment in the novel, Agaat saves Milla's life while the latter was giving birth to Jakkie and claims him for herself saying '*You-are-mine*' (590, italics in original). This scene is disturbingly reminiscent of the words Milla utters as she prepares to abduct Agaat earlier in the novel: 'You're mine now' (572). What's more, Agaat repeats the phrase '*I am a slave but You-are-mine*' (590, italics in original) as part of the bedtime story she tells Jakkie every night while cuddling him in bed. This is the revenge Agaat enacts on Milla for kidnapping her as a child and later making her a servant after having a child of her own. Quick to realize the profundity of Agaat's influence on his son, Jak reluctantly admits, 'she has Jakkie more than you [Milla] or I have him or had him or ever will have' (267). Milla broods over this question for many years to come and even on her deathbed where, unable to speak, spells out 'S·T·O·L·E H·I·M F·R·O·M M·E, exclamation mark. T·O·O·K H·I·M O·U·T O·F M·E F·U·L·L O·F B·L·O·O·D + S·L·I·M·E + W·R·A·P·P·E·D H·I·M + T·O·O·K H·I·M + N·E·V·E·R R·E·T·U·R·N·E·D H·I·M' (419). Such passages may be read in light of Chancer's assertion that the anger the masochist feels can 'be subverted back toward the sadist through exercise of *indirect controls*'.[36] Paradoxical though it may seem, it is not Milla but Agaat, the slave, who 'controls' Jakkie's life.

In addition, Agaat, who relates to the de Wet family as a dominant masochist, enacts her subordinate sadism towards the farm labourers who are even more helpless than herself, eventually earning her the nickname 'tyrant' (520). On one occasion, she humiliates the labourers' children over their poor hygiene:

> she grabbed the children by the hair and pulled their heads back and clamped their noses until they opened their mouths. With every spoonful she scolded. This is what you get for shitting in the bushes like wild things! Open your porridge-hole! This is what you get for wiping your arses with your hands! … Will you pee on my shoes, you little hotnot! Stand that way, shut your trap and swallow or I'll wind up your little prick for you like flypaper … If I catch one of you dropping your pants in the veld then I'll string barbed wire through his arse! (245–6)

On hearing the scolding, Milla wonders, 'where did the words come from?' (247), astonished by their cruelty. Agaat, caught as she is in the sadomasochistic dynamics of South Africa under apartheid, forcibly uses abusive language to displace the frustration that she cannot 'directly express … at authorities onto those less powerful'.[37] Since it is hardly possible for her to 'express dissatisfaction … at the person or party who is actually generating such responses', that is Milla and the racist apartheid state that routinely undermine her very basic rights, she enacts her subordinate potential for sadism in this fashion.[38]

Another means of control exercised by Agaat over the farm is her power to extinguish fires she is suspected, in true arsonist fashion, of having started in the first place. This point is explicitly developed by Jak when he wonders, 'How come, Gaat, that you're always the first on the scene?' (244) whenever a disaster occurs. This issue torments Milla until the very end of her days when she spells out 'D·I·D Y·O·U S·T·A·R·T T·H·E F·I·R·E' (368); yet Agaat who completes her sentence for her slyly refrains from providing an answer. She is animated by 'the sadistic wish' for once in her lifetime 'to reverse the situation by controlling others instead of being controlled'.[39] This is best exemplified by Agaat's appearance on the scene to extinguish the fire at Jakkie's farewell party: 'The one to whom all looked, the one who turned round, lifted her good hand for silence, and started issuing orders left and right: You and you and you do this that and the other!' (526). Unlike his parents who are at a loss to understand the real motive behind the sadistic atrocities Agaat commits, Jakkie cleverly remarks, 'It's you who made her like that, Ma, you and Pa. She's more screwed up than Frankenstein's monster' (520). As Van der Vlies rightly points out, Agaat is actually 'a monster of Milla's own making'; so fed is she with violence and sadomasochistic social psychology that she 'stand[s] to Milla as the monster does to Dr Frankenstein'.[40]

Jakkie urges Agaat to leave Grootmoedersdrift forever as he himself is planning to do but she wonders why, 'I have food, I have clothes, I have a house … and everything' (468). Another advantage of living on the farm according to Agaat is that she and the de Wets keep each other company, which is 'also better than nothing' (470). Jakkie is percipient enough to recognize that such relationships are sadomasochistic based as they are on the unfreedom of the individual. He tells his mother that Agaat ought to climb aboard the aeroplane for a short flight above the farm on his farewell party to experience: 'how it feels to be as *free* as a bird. Because that's what she's scared of. That's what you're all scared of. You're more scared of *freedom* than you are of the communists' (520; italics added).

After Jakkie's departure to Canada and Jak's untimely death, Milla believes that her life with Agaat is replete with love and harmony. But her increasing dependency on Agaat, including as a nurse, after she becomes paralysed make the young woman 'more rancorous, more furious' (136), 'a tyrant who in a battle of wills controls her as she herself had been appropriated as a child'.[41] Milla significantly wonders what has made Agaat so bitter: 'When did it change? When

I could no longer speak … when I became completely helpless and had to come and lie here? Was it that that released the poison? That I was more dependent on her than I'd ever been? I've always been that, from the beginning' (136). She acknowledges her lifelong dependence on Agaat, which points to the symbiotic nature of their relationship. In her will, Milla passes her farm and homestead on leasehold to Agaat provided that she nurses and keeps her company to the very end of her days. It is possible to read this act from an interpersonal psychoanalytic point of view and argue, following Fromm, that 'only in the love of those who do not serve a purpose' does genuine 'love begin … to unfold'.[42] In other words, Milla's 'love' for Agaat could be seen as sadistic based as it is on the premise that she needs her care while going through the terminal stage of ALS. Milla's prophesy that bringing Agaat into her life would repay all her pains someday seems to have come true now that her nurse works herself 'to the brink of exhaustion' (183), trying to meet her dying patient's every need now that she is all alone on her farm with no one else to keep her company.

After losing the ability to speak, Milla wonders if she and Agaat could 'devise an adequate language with rugged musical words in which [they] could argue and find each other' and wonders what 'the joy of finding each other without having been lost to each other' would have been (474). This is an important first step for Milla towards the realization of true love. A characteristic moment in the novel is the scene in which Agaat brings the dying Milla the maps of Grootmoedersdrift that she had begged to see one last time. At this particular moment, the servant's voice and, more importantly, feelings are restored to her. Agaat whose voice has been silenced up to this point in the narrative is given the chance to unravel 'the cruelty of the omissions and exclusions she has had to suffer' during the forty-year time span of her life with Milla on the farm.[43] Agaat forcefully 'presses with her finger … on all the places' (348) on the map that she was prevented from entering because of apartheid laws that forced segregation. She angrily chants Milla's past mistreatment of her: how she was once locked up in a room without a potty, how she was relocated in a 'skivvy-room' (348) after Jakkie's birth and, most importantly, how she never had the opportunity to voice her emotions after becoming a servant 'Heartburied! Nevertold! Unlamented!' (348). As Carvalho and Van Vuuren correctly point out, what is memorable in Agaat's song is that it captures 'her emotional response to this event' which has not been shared until then.[44]

Glancing at the calendar one day, Milla realizes that there are only two days left until 16 December, 'the Day of the Covenant, the Day of Reconciliation' and asks Agaat to pray to God to 'forgive us our trespasses' (422). Curiously, Agaat's response to this request for prayer is to expose her stunted arm and cry, 'Lord God in heaven ... Hear me! Foot-rot! ... Pip! Roup! Glanders! ... Contagious abortion! ... Who do I have other than you? Don't go away from me! ... Have mercy on me! ... Amen' (423–4). The language she employs is replete with the names of infectious diseases, which suggests that even though her wounds of the apartheid past have not yet healed, Milla is the only person she has left on earth and begs for God's mercy in fear that she will be taken from her.

In her final days, Milla even wonders what made her abduct Agaat in the first place and why she 'only now love[s her] with this inexpressible regret' (462). Unlike Milla who attempts on her deathbed to be reconciled with Agaat by conceding that she kidnapped her as a child, Agaat remains adamant in her hatred and suffering. The novel's suspicion regarding the possibility of love in the post-apartheid era once the truth about bygone atrocities is unveiled in a fashion reminiscent of the TRC proceedings is reflected in Agaat's inability to forgive Milla for the sadistic control she exerted over her life and to love her now that she is terminally ill and willing to repent.

A further question one can ask is whether Agaat, who has a penchant for subordinate sadism, will be able to actively love the farm labourers in the post-apartheid era now that Milla can no longer speak and will pass away in the near future. One should bear in mind that she is a solitary figure whose favourite riddle even as a child was 'Why do you always sit *alone*? Because I'm the one in *alone*' (498; italics added). Even Milla seems to be preoccupied with this question on her deathbed as she considers whether Agaat will be able to overcome her increased loneliness after her death (461). In an interview, Van Niekerk reassures us that 'as "boss-girl" [Agaat] has learnt all the worst lessons of coercion and oppression and corrupting of the poor from her former masters'.[45] Chancer significantly argues that subordinate sadism is a relative concept 'dependant on time'.[46] Thus Agaat, whose subordinate sadism was developed during apartheid in relation to the farm labourers, treats them as a dominant sadist in the new post-apartheid era. This is reflected in the scene where Agaat announces to Dawid that only three of the six families can stay living on the farm after Milla's death and that she plans to fix the women if they keep on breeding (281–2). Thus, it seems likely that she may attempt to overcome her solitude by forging further symbiotic bonds with the farm labourers, cementing her sadistic control over them with the tools she has inherited from her previous masters. Historical records are replete with instances of former masochists turning into sadists under new circumstances; Agaat under the new post-apartheid dispensation is hardly an exception to the rule.

Conclusion

Marlene van Nierkerk's *Agaat* represents South African society in the apartheid past as well as in the current post-apartheid era as consisting of 'atoms' that are 'estranged from each other but held together by selfish interests and by the necessity to make use of each other'.[47] At a loss to explain why Milla's relationship to Agaat is colder than ever, his marriage is in tatters and his evasive son's relationship to his parents has deteriorated to the point where he is preparing to leave the country without telling them where he plans to go, the perplexed Jak summons a poetic voice to characterize their experience of love on the farm 'Love is the empty glass. And then? Bitter? Dark? That holds the hollow heart? Is that how it goes?' (465) he asks Milla and Agaat. In this key passage, Jak displays a vague understanding of love turned hostile in South Africa. The aim of this chapter was precisely to delve into the psychological roots of pseudo-love that has replaced genuine love in the apartheid era, arguing that the highly hierarchal structure of society tended to propel individuals towards sadomasochism. Milla's abduction of Agaat is an instance of sadism that masquerades as love for her real intention behind bringing the child to live with her was to experience motherhood and to raise a maid who would act as her right hand on Grootmoedersdrift. Milla, who primarily related to Agaat as benevolent sadist before Jakkie's birth, later relates to her as malevolent sadist, channelling her own sadism towards her.

Agaat, however, is situated masochistically vis-à-vis her mistress, and yet, in turn, she sadistically domineers the farm labourers, exerts indirect control over her mistress's life by claiming her son for herself and commits arson. Van Niekerk undermines the possibility of love after the end of apartheid even after Milla tells her foster daughter the truth about her abduction in the past. Precluding egalitarian relationships based on love, the apartheid regime was the epitome of a society based on destructive interpersonal relationships that bred violence, the vestiges of which linger in the post-apartheid setting of the novel, where Agaat is depicted as an heir to apartheid sadism.

Fromm's famous dictum that the only plausible answer to the individual's need for relatedness resides in the 'practice of the art of loving' resonates with particular force in South African context where genuine love could be a motivator of non-violent relation to the world.[48] His insistence that love does not consist in loving only one person while turning one's back on the rest of humanity is what prevents an accurate practice of love across racial lines in the country.[49] If taken seriously, this admonition could be a prelude to love in the post-apartheid present. What's more, reading post-apartheid novels through the prism of Frommian (pseudo)love can help continue work initiated by the TRC since the wounds of the past are far from being healed.

Acknowledgements

This chapter benefited greatly from comments by Prof. Neil ten Kortenaar, Chair of the Department of English at the University of Toronto on an early draft.

Notes

1 Robert Cottrell, *South Africa: A State of Apartheid* (Philadelphia: Chelsea House Publishers, 2005), 92.
2 Ibid., 87.
3 Richard Wilson, *The Politics of Truth and Reconciliation in South Africa: Legitimizing the Post-Apartheid State* (Cambridge: Cambridge University Press, 2001), 13–15.
4 *The Way of the Women* is the title Michiel Heyns gives to his 2006 award-winning translation of Marlene van Niekerk's *Agaat* (2004). His translation was the recipient of many awards such as the South African *Sunday Times* Fiction Prize and the South African English Academy's Sol Plaatje Prize for Translation (see Andrew van der Vlies, "'MÊME DYING STOP CONFIRM ARRIVAL STOP": Provincial Literatures in Global Time – The Case of Marlene van Niekerk's *Agaat*', in *Institutions of World Literature: Writing, Translation, Markets*, ed. Stefan Helgesson and Pieter Vermeulen [New York: Routledge, 2016], 191–208, 193). All quotes in this chapter are from Heyns's translation of *Agaat* into English.
5 In terms of apartheid's racial categorization grid, South African society is composed of four races: whites, Africans, coloured and Indians. Van Niekerk uses the term 'coloured' throughout the novel to refer to Agaat and so will this chapter.
6 For a Jungian reading of *Agaat*, see Rossmann's 'Complexio Oppositorum: The Integration of Good and Evil in Marlene van Niekerk's *Agaat*'. Also see, Keramatfar and Beyad's 'Subjection and Survival in J. M. Coetzee's *Disgrace*' and 'The Worm in the Apple: Wretched Bonds in J. M. Coetzee's *Disgrace*' for a sustained analysis of symbiotic bonds in J. M. Coetzee's novel *Disgrace*.

7 Leon de Kock, 'Intimate Enemies: A Discussion with Marlene van Niekerk and Michael Heyns about *Agaat* and Its Translation into English', *Journal of Literary Studies* 25, no. 3 (2009): 141.
8 Erich Fromm, *Beyond the Chains of Illusion: My Encounter with Marx and Freud* (1962; New York: Continuum, 2009), 94.
9 David Ingleby, 'Introduction', in Erich Fromm, *The Sane Society* (1955; London: Routledge, 1991), xxviii.
10 Erich Fromm, *The Anatomy of Human Destructiveness* (New York: Holt, Rinehart and Winston, 1973), 233.
11 Ibid.
12 Kieran Durkin, *The Radical Humanism of Erich Fromm* (New York: Palgrave Macmillan, 2014), 87.
13 Marlene van Niekerk, *The Way of the Women*, trans. Michael Heyns (London: Abacus, 2008), 79. All subsequent references will be made in text.
14 Wilson, *Politics of Truth*, 115–16.
15 Fromm, *Anatomy of Human Destructiveness*, 284.
16 Ibid.
17 Erich Fromm, *The Escape from Freedom* (New York: Avon Books, 1969), 184.
18 Lynn S. Chancer, 'Fromm, Sadomasochism, and Contemporary American Crime', in *Erich Fromm and Critical Criminology: Beyond the Punitive Society*, ed. Kevin Anderson and Richard Quinney (Urbana: University of Illinois Press, 2000), 34.
19 Fromm, *Sane Society*, 29.
20 Fromm, *Anatomy of Human Destructiveness*, 320.
21 Fromm, *Escape from Freedom*, 168.
22 Erich Fromm, *The Art of Loving* (1956; New York: Open Road Media, 2013), 52, italics added.
23 Fromm, *Escape from Freedom*, 166.
24 Ibid., 185.
25 Fromm, *Sane Society*, 169.
26 Erich Fromm, 'Selfishness and Self-Love', *Psychiatry* 2, no. 4 (1939): 518.
27 Fromm, *Anatomy of Human Destructiveness*, 289.
28 Fromm, *Escape from Freedom*, 165.
29 Fromm, *Anatomy of Human Destructiveness*, 235 and 237.
30 Ibid., 298.
31 Fromm, *Escape from Freedom*, 186–7.
32 Ibid., 187.
33 Même is a vernacular expression for mother (Van Niekerk, *Way of the Women*, 593).
34 Fromm, *Escape from Freedom*, 187.

35 Chancer, 'Fromm, Sadomasochism, and Contemporary American Crime', 36–7.
36 Lynn S. Chancer, *Sadomasochism in Everyday Life: The Dynamics of Power and Powerlessness* (New Brunswick: Rutgers University Press, 1992), 192, italics added.
37 Chancer, 'Fromm, Sadomasochism, and Contemporary American Crime', 37.
38 Chancer, *Sadomasochism in Everyday Life*, 91.
39 Fromm, *Anatomy of Human Destructiveness*, 200.
40 Andrew van der Vlies, *Present Imperfect: Contemporary South African Writing* (Oxford: Oxford University Press, 2017), 86.
41 J. U. Jacobs, '"As I Lay Dying:" Facing the Past in the South African Novel after 1990', *Current Writing: Text and Reception in Southern Africa* 24, no. 1 (2012): 85.
42 Fromm, *Art of Loving*, 80.
43 Gail Fincham, '"Reterritorialising" the Land: *Agaat* and Cartography', *Tydskrif vir Letterkunde* 51, no. 2 (2014): 137.
44 Alyssa Carvalho and Helize van Vuuren, 'Examining the Servant's Subversive Verbal and Non-Verbal Expression in Marlene van Niekerk's *Agaat*', *Journal of Literary Studies* 23, no. 3 (2009): 45.
45 Marlene van Niekerk, 'So It Is a Risk, This Business of Writing', Interview with Hans Pienaar, *LitNet*, 2 June 2005, quoted in Van der Vlies, *Present Imperfect*, 87.
46 Chancer, *Sadomasochism in Everyday Life*, 91.
47 Fromm, *Sane Society*, 135.
48 Fromm, *Art of Loving*, 181.
49 Ibid., 95.

Bibliography

Beyad, Maryam and Hossein Keramatfar. 'Subjection and Survival in J. M. Coetzee's *Disgrace*'. *Journal of Black Studies* 49, no. 2 (2018): 152–70.

Carvalho, Alyssa, and Helize van Vuuren. 'Examining the Servant's Subversive Verbal and Non-Verbal Expression in Marlene van Niekerk's *Agaat*'. *Journal of Literary Studies* 25, no. 3 (2009): 39–56.

Chancer, Lynn S. 'Fromm, Sadomasochism, and Contemporary American Crime'. In *Erich Fromm and Critical Criminology: Beyond the Punitive Society*, edited by Kevin Anderson and Richard Quinney, 31–42. Urbana: University of Illinois Press, 2000.

Chancer, Lynn S. *Sadomasochism in Everyday Life: The Dynamics of Power and Powerlessness*. New Brunswick: Rutgers University Press, 1992.

Cottrell, Robert C. *South Africa: A State of Apartheid*. Philadelphia: Chelsea House Publishers, 2005.

Durkin, Kieran. *The Radical Humanism of Erich Fromm*. New York: Palgrave Macmillan, 2014.

Fincham, Gail. '"Reterritorialising" the Land: Agaat and Cartography'. *Tydskrif vir Letterkunde* 51, no. 2 (2014): 130–43.

Fromm, Erich. *The Anatomy of Human Destructiveness*. New York: Holt, Rinehart and Winston, 1973.

Fromm, Erich. *The Art of Loving*. 1956. Reprint. New York: Open Road Media, 2013.

Fromm, Erich. *Beyond the Chains of Illusion: My Encounter with Marx and Freud*. 1962. Reprinted with a foreword by Rainer Funk. New York: Continuum, 2009.

Fromm, Erich. *The Escape from Freedom*. New York: Avon Books, 1969.

Fromm, Erich. *The Sane Society*. 1955. Reprinted with an introduction by David Ingleby. London: Routledge, 1991.

Fromm, Erich. 'Selfishness and Self-Love', *Psychiatry* 2, no. 4 (1939): 507–23.

Ingleby, David. 'Introduction'. In Erich Fromm, *The Sane Society*, xvi–lv. London: Routledge, 1991.

Jacobs, Johan U. '"As I Lay Dying": Facing the Past in the South African Novel after 1990'. *Current Writing: Text and Reception in Southern Africa* 24, no. 1 (2012): 72–87.

Keramatfar, Hossein, and Maryam Beyad. 'The Worm in the Apple: Wretched Bonds in J. M. Coetzee's *Disgrace*'. *African Identities* 16, no. 3 (2018): 318–32.

Kock, Leon de. 'Intimate Enemies: A Discussion with Marlene van Niekerk and Michiel Heyns about *Agaat* and Its Translation into English'. *Journal of Literary Studies* 25, no. 3 (2009): 136–51.

Rossmann, Jean. 'Complexio Oppositorum: The Integration of Good and Evil in Marlene van Niekerk's *Agaat*', in *Live Evil: Of Magic and Men*, edited by Sophia Vivienne Kottmayer, 95–102. Oxford: Inter-Disciplinary Press, 2011.

Van der Vlies, Andrew van der. '"MÊME DYING STOP CONFIRM ARRIVAL STOP": Provincial Literatures in Global Time – The Case of Marlene van Niekerk's *Agaat*'. In *Institutions of World Literature: Writing, Translation, Markets*, edited by Stefan Helgesson and Pieter Vermeulen, 191–208. New York: Routledge, 2016.

Van der Vlies, Andrew. *Present Imperfect: Contemporary South African Writing*. Oxford: Oxford University Press, 2017.

Van Niekerk, Marlene. 'So It Is a Risk, This Business of Writing'. Interview with Hans Pienaar, *LitNet*, 2 June 2005.

Van Niekerk, Marlene. *The Way of the Women*. Translated by Michiel Heyns. London: Abacus, 2008.

Wilson, Richard A. *The Politics of Truth and Reconciliation in South Africa: Legitimizing the Post-Apartheid State*. Cambridge: Cambridge University Press, 2001.

5

Parenting as a political pedagogy: Love as methodology, parenting as praxis

Shelley Maddox

Introduction

Relationships between parents and children are often understood to be natural, to exist outside of the political realm, but feminist theorists have long called attention to the family as a unique site of early socialization wherein children are taught to perform their gender in accordance with patriarchal norms.[1] For example, Andrea O'Reilly calls such familial naturalization a patriarchal tactic of ideological depoliticization.[2] And in the black feminist tradition, Patricia Hill Collins and bell hooks delineate the depths of these connections, pointing out the extent to which the home is a reflection of the surrounding culture and a key source of patriarchal indoctrination. As children's experiences teach them to operate within various hierarchies in the family, they enter the larger social world prepared to accept a variety of other manifestations of hierarchical human associations. Unable to discern the paradoxical model of what Collins calls 'hierarchy within unity', the child's consciousness is intentionally produced to accept hierarchy as natural insofar as dominator ways of being is a patriarchal requirement that is associated 'with seemingly "natural" processes of the family'.[3] The family, hooks tells us, is the site where we first experience 'coercive domination and learn to accept it', yet these intimate relationships are also defined by 'relations of care and connection', blurring our ability to recognize their partiality and perversion while also making it difficult for us to see beyond and imagine otherwise.[4] It is within the intimate relations of the family that we are most likely to implicitly endorse and perpetuate patriarchal social relations through our everyday interactions. If the family is a key site for the production of social subjects in alignment with dominator ways of being, it must also be a key site in the disruption of and intentional resistance against such seemingly natural reification.

I come to this work as a mother. Tasked with the daily care and co-creation of the world with two growing humans in the intimate closeness of the home, I am aware of the disproportionate amount of power bestowed upon me by society in this relation, and I feel an immense responsibility to teach my children a way of being that will enable them to experience the fullest potential of their humanity. However, when I reflect upon my parenting practices, I see contradictions between my practices and the ideal ethic of love. Facing the reality that I engage my children from an ethic of domination is painful, as it conjures the many experiences that have shaped my own understanding of love and defined it in ways that are deeply entangled with domination. This project is, then, an attempt to consciously incorporate my values into my everyday actions, and it is to do so with a recognition of the special role of the parent–child relationship as the space in which we first learn about power, domination and love. Despite the inevitable difficulties of overcoming these understandings, this way of being, I have a responsibility to my children to move against the practices of domination that define the status quo.

If a shift in educational methods can help to bring about a radical societal transformation in Paulo Freire's *Pedagogy of the Oppressed*, it becomes possible to envision a comparable transformation brought about by a shift in parenting methods within families. When we collectively acknowledge parenting as a site of informal education, apply a critical consciousness to our interactions with our children and intentionally develop parenting practices based on an ideal ethic of love, I believe we can facilitate a transformative project of restructuring social hierarchies in pursuit of liberation for all. Parenting as a political pedagogy posits parenting as an educative site with political implications, imploring us to harness the political power of the family in order to intentionally shape our children's first lessons in power, domination and love. In what follows, I will explore hooks's suggestion that we turn our attention to the patriarchal family as a specific situation of oppression followed by a look at Freire's presentation of love as the possible alternative consciousness towards which we can strive. Combining these two perspectives, I will argue that it is possible to approach the family from a place of love in order to transform parental domination into mutual humanization.

The patriarchal family as a situation of oppression

In a six-page zine essay entitled 'Understanding Patriarchy', bell hooks aptly characterizes relations of domination within the patriarchal family. Using her own narrative, she weaves her personal experiences of being dominated as a child with her analysis as she calls attention to the themes that she believes broadly characterize relations within the patriarchal family and represent its central role in the perpetuation of relations of domination. This includes the socialization of children into gendered behaviour roles, corresponding gendered expectations guiding appropriate emotional expressions, explicit physical violence, blind obedience and a culture of silence regarding the realities of our family situations. According to hooks, it is within the patriarchal family that children are socialized into a paradigm of human relations based on a dominator model of interaction and, as a result, are unable to enter into personal relationships in ways that allow for experiences of true intimacy and genuine wholeness. In addition to children's socialization into psychological patriarchy as a means of maintaining multiple systems of domination, hooks attends to the ways that patriarchy harms all people, including men and boys, and the ways that women, as well as men, engage in patriarchal behaviour and otherwise support the perpetuation of patriarchal rule, in order to highlight a feminist politics that seeks to liberate people of all genders.

Defined by hooks as 'a political-social system that insists that males are inherently dominating, superior to everything and everyone deemed weak, especially females, and endowed with the right to dominate and rule over the weak and to maintain that dominance through various forms of psychological terrorism and violence', patriarchy is the primary system of domination that structures our daily experiences and shapes our consciousness to be complicit in relations of domination and subordination.[5] Patriarchy is of principal concern for hooks because its presence in children's lives marks it as the first system of domination that humans encounter, making it chronologically prior to, and therefore foundational, to all other systems of domination. A multitude of early and consistent experiences with physical and psychological violence within the patriarchal family prepares us for a lifetime of acclimation to expected gendered expressions and provides us with the knowledge that to fail to comply will be accompanied by a barrage of potential risks to our safety. hooks elaborates:

> But the most common forms of patriarchal violence are those that take place in the home between patriarchal parents and children. The point of such violence is

usually to reinforce a dominator model, in which the authority figure is deemed ruler over those without power and given the right to maintain that rule through practices of subjugation, subordination, and submission.[6]

The desire to dominate, the lust for power over others, parallels the dominator model at the heart of all systems of domination and is taught to children as natural within specific familial situations. Given the general idea that parental domination of children, including physical abuse, is a widespread phenomenon that crosses many racial, gendered and class boundaries, hooks's argument is meant to reinforce the notion that, as she tells us, 'there is nothing unique or even exceptional about this experience. Listen to the voices of wounded grown children raised in patriarchal homes and you will hear different versions with the same underlying theme, the use of violence to reinforce our indoctrination and acceptance of patriarchy.'[7]

By choosing to focus on the patriarchal family, hooks is naming it as an origin point of oppression within which we all experience our formative understandings of relationships as existing within a paradigm of domination. For hooks, patriarchy shapes the family to be a place where children acquire the understanding that hierarchy is necessary, that all relations consist of a person dominating and a person being dominated. Because these understandings permeate children's lives, they come to accept this notion as an axiom and become comfortable applying it to a variety of other personal and professional relationships, perpetuating the patriarchal cycle of violence that is, for many, implicit in family life.

hooks's call to understand patriarchy is addressed to everyone. She wants us to understand that we have all been schooled in the rules of patriarchy. It is embedded in our very consciousness, and it shapes our everyday lives in ways that limit our ability to relate to others from a place of true intimacy. hooks wants wholeness for all people through a feminist politics that acknowledges the complexity of the dominator consciousness and the potential of all humans to engage with one another outside of the paradigm of the dominator model. She wants us to believe that another way of being is possible and that it is everyone's responsibility to bring this alternative into being.

Love/dialogue as method in *Pedagogy of the Oppressed*

In the preface to *Pedagogy of the Oppressed*, Freire writes, 'From these pages I hope at least the following will endure: my trust in the people, and my faith in men and women, and in the creation of a world in which it will be easier to love.'[8] This introductory quote expresses three specific components of Freire's project. First, he seeks to relate to all humans as subjects, as persons in whom he trusts and has faith. This requires a shift in the ways that we relate to others, moving from subject–object to subject–subject relations. Second, he lists three components of his pedagogical method of dialogue: trust, faith and love. His emphasis on these components highlights the need to understand the important role of dialogue in his pedagogy, as well as to understand his project as a process that is always capable of being altered, always in the process of becoming. Third, he tells us his aim (which is also a component of his method), a world in which it will be easier to love. For Freire, love is the means and the end, the process and the goal. Love is an essential component of his method, a requirement in the liberatory transformation of human relationships, a part of this never-ending process, and it is also the ideal ethic towards which we should strive.

In Freire's liberatory, problem-posing pedagogy, it is through dialogue that we name the world, and it is through naming the world that we recognize our humanity.[9] Inherent in this practice is a particular orientation towards interactions with others and with the world that emphasizes subject–subject relations, encourages critical engagement with reality and makes the space for collective engagement through open communication that enables the realization of critical consciousness and praxis in the collective co-construction of reality. This orientation towards the world is realized when we dialogue with others from a place of love, humility, faith, trust, hope and solidarity. Freire tells us, 'Dialogue cannot exist, however, in the absence of a profound love for the world and for people.'[10] Without love, we cannot achieve dialogue. Love is, therefore, both chronologically prior to our engagement with dialogue, and it remains present throughout our dialogical encounters. In fact, Freire ties love to dialogue in ways that overcome the dualities of action/reflection, means/ends and naïve understandings of temporality, stating that 'love is at the same time the foundation of dialogue and dialogue itself'.[11] In order to engage in dialogue, as action, we must have established an orientation towards humanity that is grounded in love, through reflection. In the act of dialogue, which is at the same time an act of love itself, the duality between the means, love/dialogue, and our desired ends, a world in constant process towards humanization, dissolves. As such, love/dialogue is to become the foundation for parenting as a political pedagogy.

Freire tells us that the submerged consciousness of fear that keeps us trapped in relations of domination can be replaced with an alternative – love. 'Because love is an act of courage, not of fear, love is commitment to others. No matter where the oppressed are found, the act of love is commitment to their cause – the cause of liberation. And this commitment, because it is loving, is dialogical.'[12] It is love that encourages people to enact a revolutionary praxis in pursuit of humanization. It is love that leads the radical to desire another way of being that can enable the realization of our collective freedom. Love, as such, is courageous; it cannot be fearful. As commitment to others, love guides the way in this project of collective humanization. Freire adds:

> I am more and more convinced that true revolutionaries must perceive the revolution, because of its creative and liberating nature, as an act of love … What, indeed, is the deeper motive which moves individuals to become revolutionaries, but the dehumanization of people? The distortion imposed on the word 'love' by the capitalist world cannot prevent the revolution from being essentially loving in character, nor can it prevent the revolutionaries from affirming their love of life.[13]

Love is the orientation towards the world that results from an acknowledgement of our collective immersion in situations of oppression. Through a recognition of the dehumanizing nature of our situations, we find the ability to overcome our fear and engage our incompletion because we desire a world that enables its opposite, that of love.

Love, as dialogue, is the means and the end. Love is a component of the dialogical method, it is the purpose of this method, and it is the method itself. If situations of oppression are to be overcome through a pedagogy of the oppressed, Freire provides an alternative theme around which to build a liberated society, and this theme is love. The achievement of this new reality is never-ending, always in process, encompassed by the means as much as the intentional move towards its goal.

Love as methodology, parenting as praxis

For Freire, love and dialogue represent the praxis of a liberatory pedagogy, within which the means and the ends, the practices and the values, perpetually influence and reinforce one another. As a requirement in the liberatory transformation of human relationships, love, conveyed through our methods of communicating with others, is an act of commitment to the liberation of all. When we work together to develop love as an ethic that can guide our actions, we develop love as a practice that allows for true intimacy within our personal relationships.[14] To consciously infuse our personal interactions with an ethic of love is to prioritize the potential for humanization that exists when we engage love as the practice of freedom.[15] Situations of love become possible when we purposefully interact with others and the world through circular practices of love guided by an ideal ethic of love. To do so is to courageously choose love and overcome a consciousness of fear.

Following hooks's critique and applying Freire's framework to the family, when parents engage in intentionally loving parenting practices based on an ideal ethic of love in the pursuit of transforming patriarchal families from situations of domination to situations of love, parenting becomes a praxis. To parent as praxis, as the expression of a desire to consciously attend to power, requires that we check our own internalization of the dominator consciousness and work to establish an alignment between practices and values.[16] It requires that we meet our children as subjects and engage with them in love/dialogue. When we allow parenting to be guided by a loving ethic, we parent *for* the establishment and continuous development of loving practices of communication and *against* subjugation, subordination, submission, blind obedience and forced submission to authority. The dominator-dominated relationship that characterizes the parent–child relationship in patriarchal families can then become that of lover–beloved in families as situations of love.

Pedagogy is a term used to denote a method or style of teaching in educational settings and has highly variable interpretative potential.[17] When pedagogy is approached critically, it entails an intentional attendance to power dynamics for the purpose of enabling critical consciousness and praxis through the recognition of contradictions.[18] To understand the parent–child relation as educative and to embrace it intentionally is to develop a means of interaction that can be collapsible with our ends, a praxis.[19] A pedagogy is, then, a specific manifestation of praxis that refers to intentional practices within education. To engage parenting intentionally is to accept the asymmetrical power relation granted to the parent as an educative site rich with potential contradictions, and through coming to see, name and grapple with these contradictions, parents can intentionally engage in means of interaction that work to co-create a world with their children in which it will be easier to love. Parenting as a political pedagogy, a specific manifestation of praxis, entails engaging in a continuous, dialectical cycle of action and reflection about parenting practices and values between parents and children for the purpose of maximizing the potential for the family to manifest as a situation of love. Parenting as a political pedagogy is an educative process occurring between relational individuals whose relationship is characterized by asymmetrical power relations and through which all parties consciously attend to the power that exists between them.

To say that parenting is a political pedagogy is to call attention to its role in teaching children about love and domination. It is to be conscious of the ways in which we grapple with the power that is bestowed upon us as parents, to refuse the dominator model of interaction and to use parental authority for the purpose of liberation. To acknowledge the parent–child relationship as a relation partly constitutive of each individual's foundational understandings of power, domination and love is to acknowledge the parent–child relationship as the first power struggle in each individual's life and, therefore, as the first potential site for the implementation of a political pedagogy. As praxis, the means and the ends are one.[20] Enabling those in our care to come to critical consciousness through subject–subject relations and love/dialogue is a purposeful mediation of power intended to disrupt the child's socialization into an acceptance of the dominator consciousness. Parental actions must reflect their words, and their words must reflect their actions if they are to engage in a praxis that teaches children about power and domination through a political pedagogy intent upon mutual humanization.

Parenting for critical consciousness

To overcome the patriarchal family as a situation of domination, we must work to dismantle the practices that maintain our dehumanization, instead working towards the process of establishing situations of love. When we come to see how patriarchy, as a system of domination, defines and constrains the material conditions within the patriarchal family that shape our foundational understandings of love and domination, we begin to see how it promotes a culture of fear and suppresses relations based on love in the very place we are supposed to learn it. Because part of a parent's job is to socialize their child into the world, an intentional approach to parenting requires that they also reveal the power dynamics and potential for domination that exists within the patriarchal family and the parent–child relationship. Because they want to be accountable, the parent must expose their children to the patriarchal underpinnings of the social order and of the expected family organization. The potential abuse of their own power must be actively mediated through open, honest dialogue with their children from a place of love. The pedagogy of the oppressed is a method of engaging with others in a variety of educative settings that attempts to alter the situation of oppression and enable a more fully human experience for all. Parenting as a political pedagogy, in turn, is an attempt to engage the parent–child relationship as a specific educative site in order to create a new everyday reality that transforms the patriarchal family from a situation of oppression to a situation of love.

Because of the centrality of our interactions with others in the creation of an alternative way of being, Freire insists that we attend to the dynamics of our personal relationships. Whereas the teacher–student relationship represents a vital contradiction between values and practices in education, the parent–child relationship within families must also be transformed from subject–object relations to subject–subject relations in order to overcome its contradiction and enable true dialogue.[21] To begin the work of diminishing the hierarchical distinctions that structure oppressive situations, we must meet the other from a place of vulnerability. When parents engage with children in ways that promote their humanization, they recognize the potential inherent in human incompletion, help children understand the material conditions of their historical realities, nurture practices of critical thinking, love them from a place of humility and faith in humankind as well as work in solidarity with them for the purpose of elevating consciousness. To think of parenting as praxis is to parent from a place of intentionality, undermining the action/reflection dichotomy through the emphasis on aligning parenting practices with the highest possible human value, love. To alter the authority present in the parent–child relationship in such a way that establishes subject–subject relations and allows for the collective co-creation of action influenced by reflection in perpetuity, we realize social transformation in the process towards humanization represented by the parent–child relationship.

In Freire's *Pedagogy of the Oppressed*, he presents the problem-posing concept of education as the means through which to achieve praxis and critical consciousness.[22] When we are hopeful for the future, we believe that transformation is possible and seek methods that will help us to systematically change our daily, lived realities. As an educative attempt to bring about a new reality that alters the situation of domination within patriarchal families, parenting through the problem-posing concept of education would entail a collective discussion regarding the material conditions of reality. This critical interrogation of reality reveals the specific daily manifestations of patriarchy within particular family situations, allowing for the recognition of contradictions through the questioning and criticizing of authoritative, and presumably natural, means of organizing and conducting life within families.[23] Prompting discussions by grappling with problems that are directly applicable to parents and children's daily lived realities, they can work together to overcome contradictions between practices and values, co-creating a world that allows for a fuller expression of everyone's humanity. Parenting for critical consciousness becomes not only possible, but necessary.

To name patriarchy is to call attention to its existence as a system of domination that structures our material reality. Through praxis and critical consciousness, breaking the silence surrounding patriarchy enables us to see the contradiction that it poses to the realization of our humanity, the ways that it underlies a dysfunctional understanding of love and human relations, keeping us mired in our own dehumanization and encouraging parents and children to rebel against it in pursuit of freedom, in pursuit of its transformation.[24] The act of naming is a process enabled by our very humanity and, as such, engaging in this process represents the praxis of striving towards humanization that allows for the collective realization of critical consciousness. Once we name patriarchy as the system of domination structuring our family lives and relations with others and with the world, as hooks suggests, we can work towards the co-creation of a situation of love, allowing love as an ethical ideal to guide our praxis towards humanization. This act of naming occurs within subject–subject relations through dialogical encounters.

Transforming parental domination

The move to subject–subject relations between parents and children is necessary if parents and children are to engage in dialogue. Moving to lover–beloved (subject–subject) includes a collective questioning and revising of the role of parental authority, in which power is diminished in pursuit of a synthesis between values and practices. Within the parent–child relationship, however, given the varying degrees of cognitive and physical capacities of children throughout the duration of their childhoods and the necessity that parents work to nourish and ensure the safety of these growing beings, it does not entail a complete dissolution of authority. The authority that remains within the parent–child relationship, then, 'must be *on the side of* freedom, not *against* it', according to Freire.[25] Parental authority must not be implemented in the service of creating submissive behavioural orientations that are shaped to be in alignment with the dominator consciousness. Instead, we must come to a new understanding of the 'good' child as active, engaged, aware and capable – a child who embodies a willingness to question authority, to engage in dialogue in ways that clarify and alter previous understandings and to think imaginatively and creatively. To parent from this perspective is to encourage children to question, to critique, to challenge ways of being that are understood to be natural and necessary, to go up against the authoritative status quo, to be disobedient, to defy the informal rule of silence.

Within an everyday context, the move to subject–subject relations between parents and children focuses on a shift to methods of communication as the foundation of a loving practice. Within this dynamic, it is necessary that parents accept children's understandings and expressions of their feelings as legitimate and create the space for children of all genders to express a full range of human emotions. This requires that parents help children to acquire a vocabulary with which to understand and name their feelings and that they take responsibility for the actions they engage in when they feel heightened emotions. Parents can be conscious of the extent to which their actions serve as the primary model for their children's socialization into expected gendered performances by attending to the ways their own actions either disrupt or reinforce gendered expectations of behavioural and emotional expressions. In addition, parents must value children's contributions to the family, helping them to understand themselves as agentic and autonomous, ultimately strengthening their potential to acquire a critical consciousness through praxis. Meeting children as subjects includes encouraging them to grapple critically with their material realities and making space for them to engage in conversations about their perspectives and their preferred ideals towards which to strive. The parent–child relationship as lover–beloved values children's experiential realities in their construction of their own understandings of the world. At its heart, parenting through subject–subject relations is an intimate co-construction – based on honesty and mutual trust – of new ways of being with one another in the pursuit of humanization.

In addition to these characteristics of parent–child relations as subject–subject relations, engaging children as subjects also requires that parents consciously refrain from suppressing children's voices or engaging in other acts of anti-dialogue, domination, coercion or manipulation.[26] The practice of actively working against the dominating tendencies we absorb from our patriarchal families can be understood as refusing to parent through anti-dialogical means. For Freire, this means that we are conscious of the ways that we communicate, refusing to treat others as objects existing for our domination, possession or control. Our parenting practices cannot consist of attempts at conquest over and above our children. Parents cannot manipulate, coerce or otherwise abuse the power assigned to them in this relation. They must work to transform the dominator tendencies learnt from their families, establishing instead dialogical practices with children in pursuit of transforming these very tendencies. Parents have the obligation to work towards the co-construction of situations of love within the family through our means of interacting with one another in our day to day lives by placing our highest values on our mutual humanization through love/dialogue that is premised on humility, faith, trust, hope, critical thinking and solidarity.

Love/dialogue is the method of problem-posing education that Freire believes fosters an engagement with others that is enabled by subject–subject relations. As a means of communication that allows for the transformation of the hierarchical *dominator–dominated* parent–child relationship to become a more horizontal *lover–beloved* parent–child relationship, dialogue allows for a purposeful grappling with power in the process of enabling another to become more fully human. The ways in which we communicate with children can set them up for a lifetime of liberatory practice. If the process of humanization is encapsulated in our collective striving to experience a full range of human emotion in genuine relations with others, learning to engage in dialogue is the foundation of a lifetime of living in process with others as subjects in a continuous transformation of reality. By centring love/dialogue as method, as the paradigm through which we engage with others and with the world, as means and end, in the here and now, we centre the continuous process of engaging critical consciousness and praxis, allowing our lives to be living expressions of our desire for freedom.

As an aim, love is an orientation towards humanity, an ethic, a value, a goal, an ideal. As a means, love is a practice. It is the way that we engage with others in the pursuit of understanding our world. This is why love is central to dialogue. If love is dialogue itself, then at its core, love is the way that we communicate with others, requiring us to be fully present with others as subjects in solidarity. To love our children means to engage with them in practices of communication that encompass humility, faith, trust, hope, critical thinking and solidarity – all of Freire's components of dialogue.[27] Because love is presented as an essential component of the method of dialogue, the purpose of the method and the method itself, love is necessarily chronologically prior to our engagement with our children in dialogue and present throughout our dialogical encounters, dissolving any duality between the means, love/dialogue and our desired ends, a world in constant process towards the realization of our fullest humanity. Love enables dialogue, which further enables love and vice versa in perpetuity.

Mutual humanization

Because dialogue requires humility, faith, trust, hope, love and critical thinking in solidarity with others and with the world, parents must recognize that they are not all-knowing; the parent is in fact fallible, capable of making mistakes and learning from them. Facing the limits of our understanding, acting with humility, requires an acceptance of our vulnerability, our incompletion as humans. It is to take seriously the critiques and conceptions of reality as they are held by others, including our children, as we are all always learning and growing and changing and loving. To engage in love/dialogue, I must have an orientation towards the world that is hopeful for the future and has faith in the abilities of others to work collectively towards our mutual humanization. If I trust my children, I must believe in their abilities to think for themselves and to help unveil the world of oppression that defines our reality. The understandings accessible to all are expanded when critical thought is engaged in communion with others, helping to reveal a fuller account of the material reality that shapes all our lives. As beings who have not yet fully internalized their indoctrination into the status quo through their socialization into patriarchal ways of being, children have access to a particularly critical perspective of human interaction that adults have long grown accustomed to. Without solidarity with our children, we cannot learn mutual trust, engage in dialogue about reality, think critically about how to achieve a world that better enables the humanization of all, overcome the fear that has previously defined our consciousness or come to realize the family as a situation of love. To engage parenting as a political pedagogy is to foster a praxis that is a continual process of love/dialogue and action/reflection.

If dialogue is love, when we communicate, we are also teaching/learning about love and domination. Within the family, moments that teach us about love and domination are inherently entangled with one another. How we communicate within the family sets the tone for the ways that we will communicate/love for the rest of our lives. Choosing to communicate intentionally within the family is a way to teach kids about love and the possibility that we can purposefully mediate relations of asymmetrical power between humans and check the potential for domination; it is a political pedagogy. As a mother, I engage my children from a place of love because my love for my children holds the highest possible value in my life, because I want them to know a form of love that is openly communicative about the power dynamic between us and experienced in abundance. I accept my role as their teacher of love and domination, and I humbly accept the lessons I learn in return.

Love is the purpose of life, the ideal ethic towards which we should strive because it represents the fullest expression of the freedom of humanity, which is to experience ourselves as whole, as capable of genuine emotional expression and true intimacy. It is the means and the end, the method and the goal. As a practice, it is to communicate with one another intentionally, to meet the other as subject from a place of vulnerability, trust, humility, hope, faith and solidarity, to actively work against the dominating tendencies that we absorb from our families and our societies. It is to live as if our very existence *is* love, to continuously engage in reflection about our loving practices with those we love in an attempt to perfect it, to realize its ideal. As an ethical ideal, love guides our moral decision-making in everyday situations through these practices.

Situations of love are possible when we purposefully engage others and the world through practices of love as guided by love as an ethical ideal. Parenting as praxis with the use of love/dialogue as methodology is one way to achieve a fuller experience of humanity for all. When we understand life as always in process and seek to understand the material reality that constitutes the limits of our everyday situations, we come to critical consciousness and engage in praxis, realizing our own liberation through our everyday interactions. The achievement of this new reality is never-ending, always in process, encompassed by the means as much as the intentional move towards its goal.

Conclusion

In conclusion, I contend that breaking the silence about our everyday experiences with patriarchal families is a necessary practice, however painful. Coming to see our intimate relationships as structured by patriarchy is the first step towards revealing the potential that lies in our incompletion as humans. When we believe that another way is possible, we can begin the work of overcoming the dominator model of human relationships and bringing into being a new reality systematically structured by love.

Parenting carries with it revolutionary potential in this process. When parents choose to act in accordance with a belief in the abundance of love and give it to their children without fear, together they co-create a world in which an abundance of love becomes the norm, the expectation and the foundation of everyday material reality. Through an understanding of the dominator consciousness, I can pay close attention to those moments in which I want to control my children, when I want to force them to accept my version of reality, when I cannot hear their voices for my own submersion in fear. Resisting the ways that I was parented and the ways that society tells me I should parent, I can choose to meet my children as subjects in dialogue and in love.

Given my own socialization into love and domination within a patriarchal family, I can only begin to use my imagination to envision a world in which life is always experienced in its fullness. I can choose love over and over again as the ideal ethic through which to guide my life, knowing that I will stumble and make mistakes. I can only hope that my children will be there to call me in, to lovingly challenge me to live my life as a tribute to love. Our actions make the world what it is, and through these actions, we can choose every day to live our ideals. Because I am hopeful, I believe it is never too late to initiate parenting as a political pedagogy with our children, and our children can take their understandings of life lived as love into the world in ways that make it easier for everyone to love.

Parents hold an awesome power to create the world for their children, and this chapter asks parents to engage parenting as a political pedagogy in order to collectively co-create a world that fosters a more loving way of being for all of us.

Notes

1 Definitions of 'family' are historically, culturally and geographically specific and as such have changed over time to accommodate particular social realities. The only thing that has remained constant in definitions of the family is a general lack of consensus. Legal definitions often exist at odds with actual social practices and lived realities. The use of 'family' in this chapter should be understood to extend

beyond the normative to fit whatever household organization makes sense for you, and I encourage you to think and live family beyond its association with imperialist white supremacist capitalist patriarchy.

2. Andrea O'Reilly, *Matricentric Feminism: Theory, Activism, and Practice* (Bradford, ON: Demeter Press, 2016), 14.
3. Patricia Hill Collins, 'It's All in the Family: Intersections of Gender, Race, and Nation', *Hypatia* 13, no. 3 (1998): 64.
4. bell hooks, *Talking Back: Thinking Feminist Thinking Black* (Boston: South End Press, 1989), 21.
5. bell hooks, 'Understanding Patriarchy', Louisville's Radical Lending Library, No Borders Collective, 2013, http://imaginenoborders.org/, 1.
6. Ibid., 2–3.
7. Ibid., 2.
8. Paulo Freire, *Pedagogy of the Oppressed* (New York: Continuum, 2003), 40.
9. Ibid., 88.
10. Ibid., 89.
11. Ibid.
12. Ibid.
13. Ibid., footnote 4.
14. For hooks, intimacy equates to genuine human wholeness, comparable to Freire's process of freedom, or humanization.
15. Because of the centrality of the idea of becoming more fully human in Freire's project, the pedagogy of the oppressed can also be called a quest for humanization, understood as an attempt to realize the origins of human oppression and engage in a systematic attempt to overcome them. Freire equates this project of humanization with the pursuit of freedom.
16. Freire, *Pedagogy of the Oppressed*, 79.
17. Carmen Luke, 'Introduction', in *Feminisms and Pedagogies of Everyday Life*, ed. Carmen Luke (Albany: State University of New York Press, 1996), 1.
18. Freire, *Pedagogy of the Oppressed*, 48.
19. Ibid., 79.
20. Ibid.
21. Ibid., 75.
22. Ibid., 83.
23. Ibid., 81.
24. hooks, 'Understanding Patriarchy', 3.
25. Freire, *Pedagogy of the Oppressed*, 80, italics in original.
26. Ibid., 141.
27. Ibid., 91.

Bibliography

Collins, Patricia Hill. 'It's All in the Family: Intersections of Gender, Race, and Nation'. *Hypatia* 13, no. 3 (1998): 62–82.

Freire, Paulo. *Pedagogy of the Oppressed*. New York: Continuum, 2000.

hooks, bell. *Talking Back: Thinking Feminist Thinking Black*. Boston: South End Press, 1989.

hooks, bell. 'Understanding Patriarchy'. Louisville's Radical Lending Library, No Borders Collective, 2013. http://imaginenoborders.org/.

Luke, Carmen. 'Introduction'. In *Feminisms and Pedagogies of Everyday Life*, edited by Carmen Luke, 1–27. Albany: State University of New York Press, 1996.

O'Reilly, Andrea. *Matricentric Feminism: Theory, Activism, and Practice*. Bradford, ON: Demeter Press, 2016.

6

Caring with, voice and under-represented expressions of love in and through *The Undefinable* by She Goat: An artist-researcher's perspective

Eugénie Pastor, with Shamira Turner

Introduction

I am a researcher and an artist, and since 2014, I have been one half of the performance company She Goat. In December 2019, we premiered our second theatre piece *The Undefinable*[1] at Camden People's Theatre, London, UK, which aimed to explore and give a place, sonically and theatrically, to under-represented or misunderstood forms of love and relationship arrangements. The piece, and its process, were born out of mine and my collaborator Shamira Turner's personal lives as well as of a desire to create a space, for the duration of each performance, where ambivalence, nuance and slippery feelings could coexist and where audiences could reflect on the under-represented relationships in their lives. One of the stimuli behind the making of the piece was a desire to continue to find ways for Shamira and I to be together at times where we were feeling increased pressure on our relationships, with each other and with others, and a latent expectation that we should categorize and hierarchize them.

The piece takes the form of a dream-like radio show, with a focus on voice, speech and original music. This radio format, put into a theatre context, was one way we had found in the creative process to incorporate audio-description in our performative language from the early stages of the show's development. This choice enabled us to make the piece inherently accessible to visually impaired audiences, rather than this aspect of the work being added retroactively. We experimented with audio-description in consultation with Maria Oshodi, artistic director of Extant, 'the UK's leading professional performing arts company of visually impaired artists and theatre practitioners'[2] and the piece was awarded the Extant Enhance mark.[3] This dimension was essential to Shamira and I, as we felt that, at the time at least, the offer of work accessible to visually impaired audiences from small-scale experimental companies was sparse. Integrating audio-description also afforded a performative language that echoed the intentions of the work in that it permitted ambiguity, especially in the way our relationship is defined – 'queerplatonic' being one possible term for it – and in the way we speak about forms of love and loving that do not have a name, or whose name restricts our understanding of them. On another level, and an acknowledged motivation behind the making of the piece, creating and performing the show together was also a way to explore our love for each other and give it a place on the stage and in a wider societal conversation. We did so through one of the trademarks of our work: the use of singing, especially close harmonies that contribute to blurring the sonic delineation between our two voices. Combined with our use of audio-description, voice is used in *The Undefinable* as a tool that carves out, sonically and thematically, a space for under-represented expressions of love to be felt, crystallizing our exploration of the love that binds us.

In the next few pages, I will draw on my embodied, lived experience of the making and the performing of *The Undefinable* to argue that this physical and vocal co-presence constitutes an act of care towards each other and our audience. It opens up a space for us to be together, with feelings and ways of describing them that, for once, do not need to be labelled or defined. I am inspired here to use a term introduced by Bojana Kunst that offers a framework within which to hold what is at stake in *The Undefinable*. Kunst calls for a 'dimension of care' which she terms 'the practice of *caring with*'.[4] *Caring with* is defined as 'the attendance to others', which Kunst argues is 'scarce' and is hard to sustain due to the 'accelerated professionalization of the artistic work and the instability of the institutional surroundings in which' it is developed and shared.[5] In this respect, how we worked together was a way of *caring with*: a means of challenging the making and sharing of work that is inherently violent towards artists and audiences in their commodification of time spent together, and to enact this *caring with* through our moving, touching, speaking, singing bodies and through the additional layer of audio-description.

As will become clear in the next few pages, the interconnectedness of our relationship is at the heart of She Goat as a company, and of *The Undefinable* as a piece of work. Before I go further however, I would like to pause on the fact that while talking about this interconnectedness, I am authoring this piece alone. The question of unpaid labour is one we constantly come up against, as the necessity of working for free or for low pay is endemic in the sector we work in. Alongside She Goat, Shamira works as a successful actor and as a highly skilled arts producer, while I work part-time as a senior lecturer at a university. This research is part my job and is to an extent supported by the salary I get from the university, which Shamira, as a freelancer, doesn't get. However, it felt important and consistent with our collaboration to offer Shamira a space to voice her views. When I shared a draft with her, Shamira said this: 'I felt compelled to have an interactive experience while reading, as it felt like a conversation I was present in, so I followed this impulse and added comments for you to read me chipping in or responding.' We have decided to leave these asides and additions in the body of the text, included as text highlighted in bold, a way, as Shamira said, of

bringing multiplicity to this 'academic' context: output harmonizes with process.

In this regard, we are enacting a practice of *caring with* in ways which I hope will become clearer in the next few pages.

I will start by presenting *The Undefinable*, and how its creation is mirrored by the way She Goat was formed and operates today. This will lead me to speak briefly about my relationship with Shamira and to reflect on how it is an essential underpinning of both the company and this piece of work. I will then explore how the making and performing of *The Undefinable*, and the logistical and practical decisions that motivated it, feed into an act of gentle resistance to dominant ways of working together: an expression of our desire to *care with*. I then move on to exploring how audio-description first, then sung voice, allow a sharing of what these forms of love are like, or feel like, in a way that is embodied, rather than labelled. In doing so, I will use scholarship on voice and on music as vibrational practice. Finally, I will close with some thoughts on the form that *The Undefinable* took during the Covid-19 lockdowns, reimagined and expanded into a new audio-only version, which we released as a six-part podcast miniseries, and question whether this aural space can function in a way akin to the physical space of the performance, asking whether our recorded voices can provide a similarly safe exploratory space for audiences. I will suggest how the way the piece was made, centring around care for oneself and for each other, and who for, with accessibility at its heart through audio-description, which also

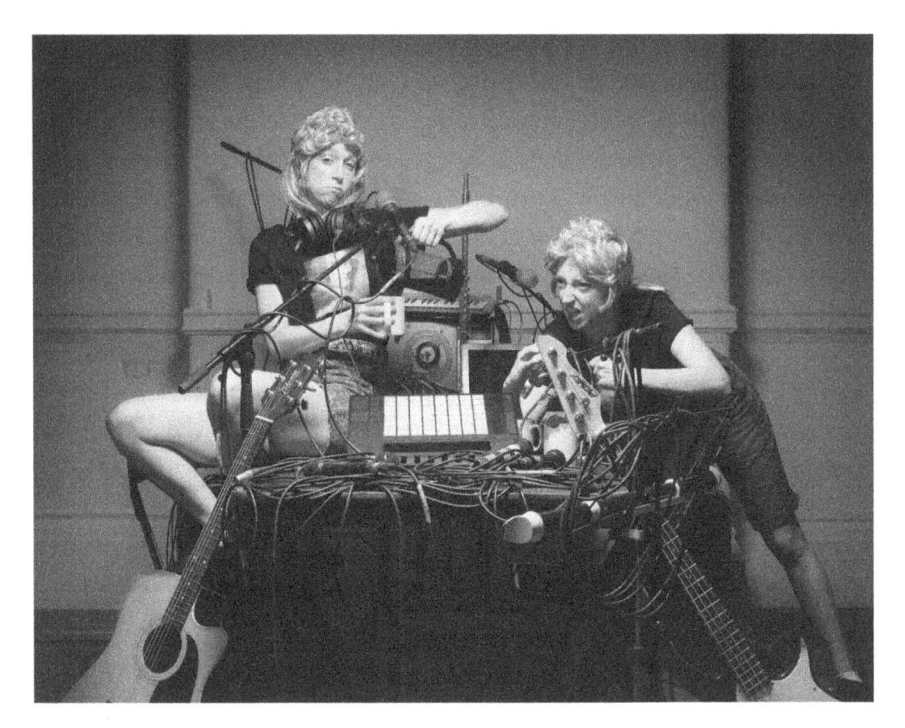

Figure 6.1 The Undefinable by She Goat. Picture by James Allan, 2018.

became an artistic language of love in itself, as well as through the fact that the radio format suggests the idea of reaching out to potentially solitary underdogs, contribute to creating ways of *caring with* in the theatre, forming temporary communities brought together in our exploration of all that love is and can be.

The Undefinable as a practice of 'caring with'[6]

1. The birth of She Goat

The Undefinable emerged out of a two-year development period as She Goat's second show. Our first piece, *DoppelDänger* (2015),[7] had come out of a desire to interrogate and playfully further confuse a pattern that had been recurring in our lives ever since the first days we met in the summer of 2009: the fact that many people, in eerily large numbers and on a bemusing number of occasions, would mistake us for one another. This would range from thinking we were siblings or even twins, to believing we were one and the same person, not two distinct beings. At times, when corrected, an interlocutor would then go on to ask if we were lovers. This confusion would happen to acquaintances, close friends, strangers, audience members, collaborators and the like; it would happen while we were on stage, in character, or off, as ourselves. After years of, in turn, finding the confusion amusing or exasperating, depending on what effect it seemed to have on our sense of self, belonging and adequacy, we decided to lean into the feeling and performatively explore what it could be.

> **These experiences created unique foundations for our relationship. Others compared or combined us, defined us in relation to each other. How would we respond? Have we reclaimed the narrative placed onto us … now owning, playing with and even encouraging this 'doppelgänger' mythology within our She Goat identity?**

Out of this came *DoppelDänger*, 'an exploration of dangerous doubling'[8] which also marked the start of She Goat as a company in its own right. *The Undefinable* then led us to interrogate our aesthetics and modes of working while developing a company identity beyond the visuals and themes of *DoppelDänger*. As our first piece had directly emerged from real-life experiences, so were the motivations behind *The Undefinable* born out of what we were experiencing in our lives at the time.

Shamira and I met in early 2009, as I started working with the company Little Bulb Theatre which she had co-founded a year earlier.[9] From our ongoing collaboration in several Little Bulb shows and out of the constant mistaking of one for the other and the strange uncanny solidarity this created came a strong and layered relationship. She Goat emerged from this relationship and continually invites us to rethink and shift the way we are with each other, which has involved an incredible amount of complex, shifting relational set-ups that have encompassed devising together, making and playing music, living together, being close friends and feeling like siblings at times.

2. The making of *The Undefinable*

This is how Shamira describes *The Undefinable*, in an interview She Goat conducted with Duška Radosavljević and Flora Pitrolo:

> we're in this interdependent relationship … sonically, and with the text we're constantly supporting each other, finishing each other's sentences, setting each other up for the next moment in terms of tech, helping with cueing each other

up, chipping in … [I]t is something quite specific to what we crave in a kind of onstage relationship and the kind of work we want to make … [I]t is a two-person experience.[10]

The fact that it 'is a two-person experience' is linked to the solidarity and complementarity we have developed with each other. The piece, the company and mine and Shamira's relationship intersect in ways that overflow neat or tidy delineations.[11] Making and performing the show together was then also a way for us to explore what our love for each other is/was/will be,

and 'would' or 'could' be, with a sense of responsibility towards the future/ fuelling of that love + what this love 'does'. Love as a verb,

and to give it a place on the stage and in a wider societal conversation. This was born out of a feeling of being erased, or talked over, in conversations about what our present and future should be as we were entering our thirties. We would often feel at odds with the ways people around us had decided to live but would find a refuge in the exchanges we would have with each other, where it was possible to have space and time to voice the feelings of alienation or incomprehension we were experiencing. This feeling of not 'fitting in' was compounded by our working lives as artists, experiencing financial precarity and unusual working schedules at a time when friends or family around us would be moving in a different direction. Deciding to go on with being an artist therefore also translated as continuing to have a different lifestyle to most of the people around us, working 'in flexible and instable ways'.[12] In this respect, our physical co-presence in the performance space (and as I will show later, our vocal co-presence) constitutes a way of *caring with* towards each other, opening up a space for us to be together.

Working with love, loving our work: Risks and precarity

1. *The Undefinable* as an attempt to *care with*

I would like to focus on one aspect of Kunst's definition of *caring with*, and argue that what we do with *The Undefinable* extends this practice into our ways of working and being. Reflecting on the lockdowns brought on by the Covid-19 pandemic at the end of April 2020, Kunst elaborates on what she terms the *right* care, which she argues was what we were then collectively performing: 'being *right*, being up to the measure'.[13] But as Kunst explains:

while we were performing the skills of the *right* care, we also radically abandoned another dimension of care, the practice of *caring with*. *Caring with* in the attendance to others, … this kind of caring radically collapsed already some time ago.[14]

Kunst argues that we can see this collapse 'in our exhausted environment, in our political and economic solutions, but also in our precarious micro-relations, where the time for *caring with* is scarce, because we work so relentlessly for our (calcul)able future'.[15] Kunst emphasizes how the *right* care creates some of the imbalances that make the work of artists so difficult: 'many current precarious professions and precarious institutional surroundings in arts originate from this shift in the notion and experience of care'. Kunst explains that this shift 'does not mean that the hierarchies, inequalities, and violent power relationships do not continue in this, more involved, caring and affective way of making art'. In this context, the possibilities of *caring with* seem forever further away from reach, especially since, as Kunst states, 'many of you work in flexible and instable ways, you belong to the precarious forms of life, … familiar with the hierarchies, exclusions, and power relations, continuing with all their forces inside the call for the imagination', when 'there should really be no obstacles to our imagination, the performance is a space of imagination of a better world and living, an unexpected, rich, and poetic practice of reciprocity and entanglement'.[16] The final call from Kunst, then, is for artists to imagine different ways of making performance, without the relentless productivity and professionalization of our work. What Shamira and I attempted to do when making *The Undefinable*, with gentle timelines to begin with, a commitment to prioritizing our well-being and our relationship over being productive, in our desire to be transparent and ethical with our collaborators, and to open up this space for audiences at the time of the performance, echoes with Kunst's invitation to experiment 'with, and searching for, other modes of working, … collaborating and building a practice together'.[17] This feels particularly poignant as the pressures placed on this act of collaboration, and of 'building a practice together', feel sometimes unsurmountable.

2. Generosity and collaboration

Elsewhere, in the book *Artist at Work*,

> **which I have on my bedside table because you bought it for me,**

Kunst quotes choreographer Eleanor Bauer, who explains that, 'in a neo-collective or post-collective model, the artists that remain in pro-community engagement must maintain a highly individual-oriented strength and productivity while remaining connected to the world and to each other'.[18] Bauer notes, however, as many artists working now in the UK might, that such a definition is 'ambitious considering what it requires in terms of time and energy, and generosity of course'.[19] Generosity is a useful term here: there is a desire to be generous with our audience in the way we approach our subject matter in *The Undefinable*, and in how much of ourselves and our relationship we give in the process; but being generous in performance has consequences off-stage too, in what it requires in terms of energy and commitment. As Bauer notes, while this generosity is a condition of working collaboratively in the socio-economic contexts within which artists operate today in the UK, and while, as Kunst explains, it is expected of the artist, it places us at risk of further exploitation as 'it is precisely [our] extra time and energy[20] that are demanded from [us]',[21] Underlying these demands is the expectation that artists will not mind gifting time and energy because they *love* their work. There seems to be a commonly accepted idea that a labour of love does not need to also be paid labour.

These points unfortunately resonate greatly. This paradox, and the Sisyphean effort required in order to pursue deep forms of collaborations, some of which do not neatly fit expectations or definitions of work, co-creation, relationships and love, are continually felt by Shamira and I, and the immense pressures that our collaborative approach within a system that constantly undermines such practices places on us take their toll. This also has the potential of hurting the very love that is at the heart of our collaborative effort. The constant pressure and demand that we be 'generous' within a system that continually makes such generosity precarious and commodifies it always runs the risk of destroying the fragile, living equilibrium we are constantly reimagining in the ways we work together, in the work we make and how we share it.

Another way in which this risk is real is through what Kunst calls the 'merger' of art and life, which 'underlies the capitalisation of human powers and their exploitation for the generation of profit'.[22] There is a risk of us capitalizing on our lives as a way of making every instant productive, of countering that terrible accusation of 'laziness' which Kunst identifies as being at the core of society's disdain towards artists and the internalized accusations we have learnt to pre-empt and work hard to counter – often at the expense of our well-being. The risk in this, Kunst suggests, is that the artist 'loses any critical power to hold up a mirror to the true layabouts at the core of the capitalist system',[23] presumably by partly playing its game. But finding ways out of the game while having to partake in it to ensure one's survival as an artist – Kunst points out, rightly, that in a capitalist society, an artist is only an artist when they produce art, not in and of themselves[24] – seems, from where I am writing, a fairly impossible task. The irony is not lost here: I am an artist and an academic trying to write in a way that *cares with* about a show that *cares with* while feeling how much of my 'generosity' this act demands – due to the fact that a lot of my work continues to be done at the expense of rest, or for free, always at risk of burning out. One of the gentle ways *The Undefinable* resists this is by harnessing our generosity – towards audiences, the work and its subject matter, each other – while finding pockets of resistance. While our relationship in *The Undefinable* blurs the boundary between art and life, some of it remains unsaid, un-shown, disguised, as we decided we would keep some secrets to ourselves but share others, discussing and deciding on these in the quiet of our rehearsal room at the times when it was just the two of us there, playfully weaving truths and half-truths within the script of the work we were making. What this process affords is a way of protecting ourselves and our relationship, as well as resisting the forces that make the making and performing of art an exhausting and all-encompassing activity.

> **The 'show' as a deadline and paid development time also importantly allows us to *have* our relationship. We create space, context, and commitment (even a schedule!) to work/be together.**

In this way, we perform a state of being that shifts and morphs, not in transit or in flux, not on its way somewhere or towards some definition, but instead, being what it *is*, for us and for the audience, in the time of the performance. In this way, we intend to 'confirm ... what Puig de la Bellacasa writes: that the burnout, anxiety, etc., do not have to be the only way to care',[25] instead following Kunst's suggestion that

> there is so much joy in experimenting with, and searching for, other modes of working, shifting and distributing the value of [our] work ..., collaborating and building a practice together ...; there is so much joy in writing and thinking in a more *caring with* way.[26]

Audio-description as a way of voicing the undefined

These ways of being and working with each other open up a space for less represented forms of love to be explored. As I will show in the next few pages, it is through words and sound, especially our voices, that this can happen. It is also fitting to explore what expressing one's voice, in this context, can mean, especially because of the way our work complicates autobiography as I have suggested above. I will start by concentrating on words, and how these are at the heart of the question of what is or not *un-definable*: what do words say, how, with what terms, and what evades them and remains unsaid?

When we remounted *DoppelDänger* to take it on tour in 2018, we worked on creating an audio-described introduction to the piece, as well as a pre-show touch tour, but with *The Undefinable*, we wanted audio-description to be a creative tool in its own right. Another key element was the music we played, unlikely cover songs and our own compositions, and finding a dramaturgical framework that would support both live music within a theatrical context[27] and audio-description. This led us to explore radio and its tropes. In this context, our use of audio-description became extensive and playful: the two hosts are addressing each other as well as their listeners (real or imagined), and so describe their surroundings as well as their actions as they perform them.

Audio-description becomes an act of care to the listener and each other. It feels unnatural at first but has become habitual in how we communicate as a duo off-stage now too. Our first time out 'in public' together in 2021 I noticed we were narrating our actions to each other. Have we always been this way? Or has the performative language we crafted infused our personal interactions?

The need to clearly delineate, in our description, the slippages between the different personae that we adopt on stage meant working with modulating and altering our voices, as well as the difference between speaking 'on mic' and speaking 'off mic'. These changes in timbre, modulations, intonations, amplification and to an extent, our perceived gender in the way we used voice, allowed subtle changes in our relationship on stage to be heard, whether they were shown or not. It was a way to voice the *undefinable* nature of this relationship, without needing to label it, but on an experiential, phenomenological level. It was also a way for us to explore an autobiographical dimension to the work, while layering and complicating it with personae. In this respect, it is not obvious for anyone outside of the relationship between Shamira and I as to which parts are autobiographical, and which are not – or not fully. Integrated within the sonic and verbal world of the show are secrets only we know – another way for us to be together in that moment. Like the secrets we opted not to tell, the ways we voice throughout *The Undefinable* is both a way of *caring with* and resisting the demands that we be generous with our lives when making art.

Another function of audio-description in *The Undefinable* is to open up layers of meaning through an interplay between the description and the way we modulate our voices, or the timings of songs or asides. Audio-description becomes what Maria Oshodi and Amelia Cavallo call an important 'storytelling tool for everyone, sighted or otherwise, as it offers imagery and depth to the performance'.[28] This echoes what Electa S. Behrens, in an article on devising a voice practice with drama students, argues 'can work almost like film' in that it allows shifts that instead of affecting the 'physical scenography' of the piece become 'the imaginative film in the mind's eye/ear'.[29] What audio-description affords in *The Undefinable* is the opening up of spaces where what remains unsaid or undefined can exist, specifically because it is expressed through the mediums of sound and voice. Audio-description requires from audience members that they listen, an activity which Lynne Kendrick, drawing on Jean-Luc Nancy's definition, allows 'an engagement in and with … substance and depth'.[30] Kendrick suggests that 'one of the tenets of this is that listening can liberate the subject from understanding the world as it is, instead moving towards new versions of what it might be',[31] taking us 'towards meaning which exists outside of our sphere of knowledge, in relation to other voices yet to be encountered, to sounds hitherto ignored and, arguably, beyond the world we consider to be the same'.[32] Audio-description as we voice it in *The Undefinable* invites the audience to listen to ways of being together, of loving each other and of working together, ways of *caring with*, that are otherwise unimagined. This is made all the more powerful that this layering happened in a state of physical co-presence, where the audience shared a physical space with us. In the following paragraphs, I explore what sharing a physical space in this way allowed our voices, through song, to create, in our attempt to explore experiences of love which do not necessarily have –

have, or want, or need–

a name yet.

Singing close harmonies: Whose voice is whose?

The Undefinable contains a lot of music, most of it performed live, with some tracks played from recordings.[33] The audio-description, the text and music are mostly mediated through our voices. A key dimension of our work is the use of close sung harmonies. When working on *DoppelDänger*, we wrote our music in this way to convey a sense of doubling or merging together, a means of echoing sonically the themes we were exploring in the piece. This paralleled the fact that our voices can feel harmonious across a similar range, and we share vocal techniques we adopted, hijacked or repurposed to explore gendered or a-gendered vocalizations. In an article on voice training, Konstantinos Thomaidis explores an idea in relation to hearing and monitoring one's own voice that sheds an illuminating perspective on what I feel is happening when Shamira and I are singing in this way – and I argue that this is another instance where the in-betweenness of certain states of love that we explore on stage can be felt. Thomaidis' analysis is concerned with the idea of presence, or rather, the fact that this striving for presence in the act of 'voicing' is complicated by the acts of 'voicing' and hearing: they are 'potentially … contradictory ways of thinking about presence'.[34] This is due to the 'micro-phenomenal experience of voicing' which 'sets into motion a shift in emphasis towards its embodied future and past' due to the feedback loop that happens between the muscular proprioceptive awareness required to vocalize and the act of hearing oneself once the voice has been uttered.[35] In Thomaidis' terms: 'voicing in front of an audience engages with an understanding of voice as an in-between, as equally pertaining to the moment of production and the moment of reception'.[36] Thomaidis, quoting laryngologists D. Garfield Davies and Anthony F. Jahn, writes: 'the voice produced by the singer is constantly being monitored in two ways: by audition and by proprioception'.[37] This means that 'the voicer listens to the pitch, volume and timbre of the auditory outcome through acoustic feedback from the space and, further, relies on physical, vibratory sensation engendered by voicing within the body'.[38] Thomaidis explains later that this 'proprioceptive self-experiencing' of one's own voice happens 'in the moment following phonation', in the question to oneself: *'did this feel right?'*, but also in the 'proprioceptive sensation of prephonatory onset',[39] in the way one activates one's muscles prior to emitting a sound.

This definition of self-listening by Thomaidis finds echoes in the way Shamira and I work: singing close harmonies requires a certain level of self-listening, as well as listening to the other, in order to check that it sounds (and feels) *right*.

> **We build harmonies through instinct, trial and error, rather than checking what the notes could or should be … to find idiosyncratic 'She Goaty' choices.**

As Thomaidis suggests, this is not an exact science once the voice has been uttered, and it is further complicated by the fact that should one of us feel like her harmony is not sounding *right*, she might start altering it in a way that leads the other to also alter hers. There is no third ear in the room when we are devising or rehearsing, and by the time we are performing, any changes to the composition or pitching will have to happen while also believing that what comes out of us is how it should sound. In this lies an act of trust and a loving act of care: trusting that we will have each other's vocal back. This act of self-listening and listening to the other simultaneously is further complicated by the closeness of the harmonies we are singing and the timbre we are singing them with: we both experience uncanny moments, which we have learnt to feel comfortable in, where we cannot for certain delineate whose voice is whose. The feedback loop between the muscular proprioception of knowing I am vocalizing is complicated by the fact that I am not sure who I am hearing back. This is made even stronger when our voices are amplified through speakers located away from where our voices feel, to us, like they are originating. This leads to an uncanny experience of self-othering, but also of sonically becoming the other person singing with me in the room, and of singing in 'one voice'.

> **I'm recalling this uncanny sensation and blurring happening in the spoken text too. Sometimes we end up swapping lines, discovering ourselves saying the other's lines in the relentless back and forth 'score' of the co-created script, before getting back onto the *right* track … We share custody of the sound and text.**

This experience of self–othering and other–othering, instead of being distressing, is actually comforting: it offers an audible representation of the solidarity, the love and the complicity that unite Shamira and I, in the moment of performance and beyond it as well, in a way that cannot be fully discerned by the audience – I am not sure they always know who is singing which part either, or that they are fully distinguishing the two voices from one another at times – and, importantly, in ways that cannot be dismissed or taken away: they are a way for us to *care with* each other in a violent neoliberal context that makes the conjoining of two artistic entities in deep and sustainable ways extremely difficult or impossible. There is something, in the moment where our voices merge, that belongs solely to Shamira and I; it is a way of being physically intimate with each other, in a way that could be described as 'queerplatonic'.[40]

Music as vibration

In her book *Sensing Sound*, Nina Sun Eidsheim proposes that 'not only aurality but also tactile, spatial, physical, material, and vibrational sensations are at the core of all music'.[41] Eidsheim suggests we can understand music as 'nonstatic, not limited to the aural sense and dimension', concluding that 'music is the practice of vibration'.[42] Eidsheim also specifies that music understood this way is 'relational',[43] coming 'into being through an unfolding and dynamic material set of relations'.[44] This claim feels particularly relevant here to exploring the ripples that sound in *The Undefinable* makes, in carving a space for Shamira's and my togetherness to be heard, and for slippery unnamed feelings to be voiced, especially so because sound is uttered and heard in a space of co-presence. Thinking of the performative event through this lens is meaningful: if as Eidsheim writes 'vibrations that enter my body are transmitted by and through the body at the very point in time that I sense it',[45] then there is something inherently unique to each performance. There is also the suggestion that, through our collective presence in the room, there is the emergence of a vibrational community: if sound is relational, then the sounds created on a specific night are unique to the collection of people through whom it vibrated. In this respect, there is a physical, vibrational dimension through which the intention of the show is realized and activated. Each iteration of the show carves out a unique space where we, as a collective of people in a room, can spend time with feelings, thoughts, ideas, vibrations that resist meanings and labels.

Eidsheim also suggests that because we understand music as strongly linked to 'the figure of sound', it 'pulls us towards certain ways of experiencing and naming sounds and limits our access to other ways'.[46] The consequence of this is that 'we are not entirely free to experience sound idiosyncratically or to experiment unrestrictedly with that experience beyond agreed-on names and meanings'.[47] This latter idea resonates with both the intention and the hoped-for outcome of *The Undefinable*: that by questioning the way we use our voices that are simultaneously our own,

(and with this: I notice that my 'own' voice isn't even a fixed point. It shifts and slides in pitch, timbre, (age?) and vocal quality responding to my internal and external world – sometimes revealing or betraying my feelings before my 'brain' seeks to interpret them. This is further complicated by putting myself on stage. My voice is 'employed' to work; it is sometimes overworked)

but also our character voices, our singing voices, our voices when we audio describe and our voices when they are a complement to each other, we allow such an experience of sound in the show to uncover a shared experience 'beyond agreed-on names and meanings'.[48] It allows a way of voicing the undefined.

Sharing a space through audio only

At the heart of *The Undefinable* is a desire to provide a space and a time for a group of people to let themselves feel ways of doing love differently that many of us will have experienced at times, without having a name for them. In doing so, it incorporated the bond Shamira and I share, and placed our desire to *care with* at the core of our process by looking for ways of being and making work together at a time where the very existence of that endeavour was antithetical to the pressures placed on us. In doing so, we have hoped to extend this act of *caring with* to the audiences sharing a time and a space with us, and we have been thinking in performance through ways of working and community-building in order to afford care, love and representation in contexts where these are hard to access. Using voice and audio-description enabled a phenomenological understanding of what alternative ways of doing love could be, by becoming the place where what Thomaidis has called 'logos-as-language' and vocalization as meaning-making[49] are joined. I have argued how this act of meaning-making through words, as well as through voice and the self-othering it invites, are further helped when we think of voice in *The Undefinable* as a way of creating a vibrational community through whom unnamed forms of love can be felt and explored. In so doing, the piece gives aural and physical space for the forms of love that elude definition. To conclude, I would like to think about how these aspects are differently complicated especially in an audio-only set up, as is the case for *The Undefinable* as a six-part audio art series. The appeal of the radio format was also to reach out to potentially solitary underdogs, creating communities of listeners across the airwaves and enabling anyone to tune in without having to reveal anything about themselves. We liked the idea of transposing this into theatres and creating similar communities of care there, centred around the idea of love. The audio-only version of the show has the potential of reaching far beyond the confines of a theatre building and including anyone for whom accessing a theatre space is complicated. This was also echoed in the partner project to *The Undefinable*, *The Curious Hearts Song Club*,[50] where communities of care were created around the sharing of songs and personal histories in carefully curated Zoom 'listening parties'.[51] Through these endeavours, She Goat hopes to continue to *care with*, in spite of all the ways this is made near impossible, to open up

liminal and interactive spaces

about 'the unknown future and forgotten past of doing love differently'.[52]

Notes

1   *The Undefinable*, performance by Eugénie Pastor and Shamira Turner (London: Camden People's Theatre, London, December 2019).
2   'Access', Extant, n.d., https://extant.org.uk/access/enhance/, accessed 9 April 2021.
3   On Extant's website, the Enhance process is explained as a 'bespoke consultation on the best creative ways to integrate appropriate aesthetic audio-description in [a] production'.
4   Bojana Kunst, 'Lockdown Theatre 2: Beyond the Time of the Right Care', *Schauspielhaus*, April 2021, https://neu.schauspielhaus.ch/en/journal/18226/lockdown-theatre-2-beyond-the-time-of-the-right-care-a-letter-to-the-performance-artist.
5   Ibid.
6   Ibid.
7   *DoppelDänger*, performance by Eugénie Pastor and Shamira Turner, multiple locations, UK, 2016–18.
8   'DoppelDänger', She Goat, https://www.shegoat.co.uk, accessed 9 April 2021.
9   With Alexander Scott, Clare Beresford and Dominic Conway, later joined by Miriam Gould and Tom Penn.
10 Eugénie Pastor and Shamira Turner, 'Everything in Harmony: An Interview with She Goat'. Interview by Flora Pitrolo and Duška Radosavljević, *Auralia.Space*, 22 April 2020, transcript, https://www.auralia.space/gallery5-shegoat/, accessed 8 April 2021.
11 It is evident that our work within Little Bulb, and the 'collective intimacy' I have argued elsewhere this produced for members of the company (Pastor, Time, Friendship and Collective Intimacy', 206), played a part in the shared intimacy between Shamira and I.
12 Kunst, 'Lockdown Theatre 2'.

13 Ibid., italics in original. Here, Kunst suggests that there was a need 'to give at least a feeling of relentless productivity (in work and in leisure)'.
14 Kunst, 'Lockdown Theatre 2', italics in original.
15 Ibid.
16 Ibid.
17 Ibid.
18 Bojana Kunst, *Artist at Work* (Winchester: Zero Books, 2015), 80.
19 Ibid.
20 Time and energy that, as Bauer notes, are not always paid for, thus perpetuating unsustainable patterns of work and art-making (Kunst, *Artist at work*, 80).
21 Kunst, *Artist at Work*, 79.
22 Ibid., 176.
23 Ibid., 187.
24 Ibid.
25 Kunst, 'Lockdown Theatre 2'.
26 Ibid., italics in original.
27 This is a recurring concern of our work and can be traced to pieces with Little Bulb, where live music in a show is always justified by a fictional framework that explains why the performers or the characters are playing music, that is: a gig (*Operation Greenfield*), a cabaret-opera (*Orpheus*), a TED talk that is a performance art experiment (*The Future*), for example.
28 Amelia Cavallo and Maria Oshodi, 'Staring at Blindness: Pitch Black Theatre and Disability-Led Performance', in *Theatre in the Dark: Shadow, Gloom and Blackout in Contemporary Theatre*, ed. Adam Alston and Martin Welton (London: Methuen Drama, 2017), 178.
29 Electa W. Behrens, 'Devisers in the Dark: Reconfiguring a Material Voice Practice', *Theatre, Dance and Performance Training* 10, no. 3 (2019): 401.
30 Lynne Kendrick, 'Aural Visions: Sonic Spectatorship in the Dark', in *Theatre in the Dark: Shadow, Gloom and Blackout in Contemporary Theatre*, ed. Adam Alston and Martin Welton (London: Methuen Drama, 2017), 122.
31 Kendrick, 'Aural Visions', 126.
32 Ibid., 126.
33 Launched from the stage by Shamira or I: almost all sounds are played from an Ableton PUSH, a black pizza box-shaped machine with squares that flash when they are played.
34 Konstantinos Thomaidis, 'The Always-Not-Yet/Always-Already of Voice Perception: Training Towards Vocal Presence', in *Time and Performer Training*, ed. Mark Evans, Konstantinos Thomaidis and Libby Worth (Oxon: Routledge, 2019), 153.
35 Ibid., 153.
36 Ibid., 154.

37 D. Garfield Davies and Anthony F. Jahn, *Care of the Professional Voice* (London: A&C Black, 2004), 10, in Thomaidis, 'The Always-Not-Yet', 156.
38 Thomaidis, 'The Always-Not-Yet', 156.
39 Ibid.
40 The term 'queerplatonic' was first brought to my attention by Shamira when we were making *The Undefinable*, in Summer 2019.

> **I first encountered it through the 'Multiamory Podcast' and that 'it seems the term was first coined in 2010'. I remember using Urban Dictionary to check on the definition. Urban Dictionary can be a strong indicator of emerging terminology being shaped by the people who seek terms that don't 'exist' yet: https://www.urbandictionary.com/define.php?term=queerplatonic.**

In the *Undefinable*, we borrow the Urban Dictionary's definition and refer to it as describing 'a relationship which is more intense and intimate than is considered common or normal for a 'friendship', but doesn't fit the traditional sexual-romantic couple model'.
41 Nina Sun Eidsheim, *Sensing Sound: Singing and Listening as a Vibrational Practice* (Durham: Duke University Press, 2015), 8.
42 Ibid., 155.
43 Ibid., 6.
44 Ibid., 10.
45 Ibid., 155.
46 Ibid., 7.
47 Ibid.
48 Ibid.
49 Konstantinos Thomaidis, 'The Revocalization of Logos? Thinking, Doing and Disseminating Voice', in *Voice Studies: Critical Approaches to Process, Performance and Experience*, ed. Ben MacPherson and Konstantinos Thomaidis (Abingdon: Routledge, 2015), 18.
50 "She Goat," She Goat, accessed April 9, 2021, https://www.shegoat.co.uk.
51 *The Curious Hearts Song Club*, participatory performance by Eugénie Pastor and Shamira Turner, online, 2020–1.
52 *The Undefinable*, She Goat, https://www.shegoat.co.uk, accessed 9 April 2021.

Bibliography

Alston, Adam, and Martin Welton, eds. *Theatre in the Dark: Shadow, Gloom and Blackout in Contemporary Theatre*. London: Methuen Drama, 2017.

Behrens, Electa W. 'Devisers in the Dark: Reconfiguring a Material Voice Practice'. *Theatre, Dance and Performance Training* 10, no. 3 (2019): 395–409.

Cavallo, Amelia, and Maria Oshodi. 'Staring at Blindness: Pitch Black Theatre and Disability-Led Performance'. In *Theatre in the Dark: Shadow, Gloom and Blackout in Contemporary Theatre*, edited by Adam Alston and Martin Welton, 169–91. London: Methuen Drama, 2017.

The Curious Hearts Song Club, by She Goat. Created and performed by Eugénie Pastor and Shamira Turner. https://www.shegoat.co.uk/curious-hearts-song-club, 2020–1

Davies, D. Garfield, and Anthony F. Jahn. *Care of the Professional Voice*. London: A&C Black, 2004.

DoppelDänger, by She Goat. Created and performed by Eugénie Pastor and Shamira Turner. Multiple locations, UK, 2016–18.

Eidsheim, Nina Sun. *Sensing Sound: Singing and Listening as a Vibrational Practice.* Durham: Duke University Press, 2015.

Extant. 'Access'. https://extant.org.uk/access/enhance/. Accessed 9 April 2021.

The Future, by Little Bulb Theatre. Performed by Clare Beresford, Dominic Conway, Eugénie Pastor and Shamira Turner. Directed by Alexander Scott. London: Battersea Arts Centre, 2019.

Kendrick, Lynne. 2017. 'Aural Visions: Sonic Spectatorship in the Dark'. In *Theatre in the Dark: Shadow, Gloom and Blackout in Contemporary Theatre*, edited by Adam Alston and Martin Welton, 113–30. London: Methuen Drama, 2017.

Kunst, Bojana. *Artist at Work*. Winchester: Zero Books, 2015.

Kunst, Bojana. 'Lockdown Theatre 2: Beyond the Time of the Right Care', Schauspielhaus, April 2020. https://neu.schauspielhaus.ch/en/journal/18226/lockdown-theatre-2-beyond-the-time-of-the-right-care-a-letter-to-the-performance-artist. Accessed 1 May 2010.

Operation Greenfield, by Little Bulb Theatre. Performed by Clare Beresford, Dominic Conway, Eugénie Pastor and Shamira Turner. Directed by Alexander Scott. Multiple locations, UK, 2010–12.

Orpheus, by Little Bulb Theatre. Performed by Clare Beresford, Dominic Conway, Miriam Gould, Eugénie Pastor, Charlie Penn, Tom Penn, Alexander Scott and Shamira Turner. Directed by Alexander Scott. Multiple locations, UK, 2013–18.

Pastor, Eugenie. 'Time, Friendship and Collective Intimacy: The Point of View of a Co-Devisor from Within Little Bulb Theatre'. In *Time and Performer Training*, edited by Mark Evans, Konstantinos Thomaidis and Libby Worth, 204–6. Oxon: Routledge, 2019.

Pastor, Eugénie, and Shamira Turner. 'Everything in Harmony: An Interview with She Goat'. Interview by Flora Pitrolo and Duška Radosavljević. *Auralia.Space,* 22 April 2020. Transcript. https://www.auralia.space/gallery5-shegoat/. Accessed 8 April 2021.

Pastor, Eugénie, and Shamira Turner. *The Undefinable*. Podcast audio, 2020. Spotify. https://open.spotify.com/show/4A551yLaBqNxAHNQ6eiqS8.

'She Goat'. https://www.shegoat.co.uk. Accessed 9 April 2021.

Thomaidis, Konstantinos. 'The Always-Not-Yet/Always-Already of Voice Perception: Training Towards Vocal Presence'. In *Time and Performer Training*, edited by Mark Evans, Konstantinos Thomaidis and Libby Worth, 151–65. Oxon: Routledge, 2019.

Thomaidis, Konstantinos. 'The Revocalization of Logos? Thinking, Doing and Disseminating Voice'. In *Voice Studies: Critical Approaches to Process, Performance and Experience*, edited by Ben MacPherson and Konstantinos Thomaidis, 10–21. Oxon: Routledge, 2015.

Tomlinson, Gary. 'Evolutionary Studies in the Humanities: The Case of Music'. *Critical Inquiry* 29, no. 4 (2013): 247–75.

The Undefinable, by She Goat. Created and performed by Eugénie Pastor and Shamira Turner. London: Camden People's Theatre, December 2019.

Urban Dictionary. 'Queerplatonic'. https://www.urbandictionary.com/define.php?term=queerplatonic. Accessed 4 November 2021.

Part 3

Love and neoliberal care

7

Not in the mood: Reading love in the contemporary university

Karen Schaller

Let us imagine a scholar.[1]

Introduction

Here is how someone imagines me: 'academic staff who are devoted to teaching and scholarship are able to focus their energies on the development of curricula that are genuinely innovative'.[2] This submission to the UK's first Teaching Excellence Framework (TEF) highlights 'carefully planned' developments in teaching and learning evidence excellence to gain purchase on the higher tuition fee the TEF secures.[3] Devotion is translated here as 'intensification of teaching' that has grown the affective capital of student satisfaction: 'increasing the student-facing academic staff resource (through increasing academic staff numbers) by 88%, over the period 2007/08 to 2013–14 has allowed us to deliver our commitment to building personalised learning relationships with students'.[4] While many contemporary accounts of the neoliberal university as a meritocracy assume a distinction between the affective and the countable, here we can see that affect *is* what counts. Yet although the value of personalization is accompanied by the depersonalization of 'academic staff resource', I can't agree with Stefan Collini's analysis of university business-speak as a discourse that 'depends on harnessing but devitalizing the language of the emotions'.[5] We need only to look at the loving, and the not so loving, affects mobilized by the remarkable valence of academics 'who are devoted'.

From the Latin 'to vow', the term 'devote' names the action of devoting, or applying, to a particular purpose.[6] The labour zoned by contracting someone *as* devoted is inseparable from the labour affects being evoked – enthusiastic, earnest, 'akin to religious', devoted denotes a service of attachment. Staff 'who are devoted' are contracted for, and defined by, a labour service whose value is in the quality, and qualities, of attachment they provide and perform. Affording the university a performance of appreciation, 'devoted' here enables contractual designation and restriction to teaching to be reimagined as institutional dedication to teaching students, to teaching-intensive staff and to the practice of teaching itself. Crucially, imagining staff as 'devoted' transfers 'devotion' from something the university actively determines to a natural academic attachment being merely described. The institutional grammar is notable: 'who are devoted' enables the university to disappear as the agent of that devoting, as if getting out of the way of academic vocation. Passive construction works here to institute academics' passion. The coincidence between the passive and passion is telling: sharing their Latin origin in 'pati', to 'suffer', the document materializes the contingencies between loving and suffering already inscribed in the passionate attachments of devotion. After all, as the *OED* reminds us, 'devote' includes in its orientations the giving of another over, or up, to destruction. Embodiments concealed by academics who are 'devoted': exhaustion, abscess, IBS, chronic infection, myalgic encephalomyelitis, insomnia, fistula, clinical depression, migraine, eclampsia, heart attack, fibromyalgia, addiction ... Bodies impassioned, inflamed by their devotions. It is a love scene, just not the one we hoped to imagine.

This chapter addresses a growing claim, among academics, that love and its range of affects can counter the neoliberal university. To do so, I look at critical scholarship on love and the twenty-first-century university and reframe contemporary arguments about the transformative potential of love as a prolonged ideological marriage to academic subjectivities we know to be injurious, but still desire. To rethink the critical attachments at work in how academics imagine love, I turn to a particular kind of love scene: how we imagine academics *in* love. I position Donna Tartt's *The Secret History* (1992) and A. S. Byatt's *Possession: A Romance* (1990) as late-twentieth-century novels preoccupied by academic passions and prescient in their alertness to how these might work for and with neoliberal academia, before developing the politics of love in twenty-first-century representations of academics in Zadie Smith's *On Beauty* (2005) and Luca Guadagnino's film *Call Me by Your Name* (2017). I finish by returning these questions to our critical imaginaries: must we relinquish love?

Love's labour: Academics on love in the contemporary university

Critical scholarship on affect and the neoliberal university addresses a range of feelings. But love and the attachments it comprises (passion, care, eros, devotion, agape, etc.) have a special status.[7] Growing accounts of academics' attachments identify how integral love is to the neoliberal university: as Mona Mannevuo observes, 'contemporary academic capitalism works through affects and languages of love, flexibility, and productivity'.[8] Sandro Busso and Paola Rivetti point out that love functions to legitimate increasing demands for flexibility and productivity, normalize precarity, perpetuate competitive individualization, replace job security, and depoliticize discourses about quality and excellence, while maintaining an image of the university as an institution concerned with knowledge rather than capital and ranking.[9] Their interviews with precarious academics show how love is 'an actual reason motivating actions and professional choices and … a rhetorical genre, a motif or "motive" that social actors deploy to build consistent and socially acceptable narratives about their jobs'.[10] In these accounts, love is how academics imagine and sustain themselves under neoliberalism – perhaps even how they become attached to it. Rosalind Gill summarizes the situation neatly: by reinvesting us in myths of the academic good life, love is 'ultimately making things worse'.[11]

But we are also seeing an upsurge of scholarship that positions love as missing from, and/or a force for resisting, the neoliberal university. Millicent Churcher and Debra Talbot, for example, describe the latter as a bureaucratic atmosphere whose primary mode of relating is a passion-free workplace.[12] Al-Mahmood et al. argue that an ethics of love for, and in, teaching has the power to resist agendas of competition, efficiencies, measurement and performance culture, creating a radical affective counter to the feeling that 'the soul of academic labour is being lost in performativity'.[13] Emma Bell and Amanda Sinclair call for us to reclaim eros: 'an antidote to the increasingly factory-like experience that many encounter … [eros] could re-inspire meaning, enjoyment and pleasure in university life'.[14] Rebecca Lund and Janne Tienari expand this call, arguing that the transformative power of a non-commodified eros derives from being independent of dominant institutions and uncapturable by, nor reducible to, managerialist discourse and gender norms. They contrast eros to other forms of love, specifically passion and care, determining these as 'lesser' versions that 'coexist' with neoliberalism and 'serve institutional interests that are not necessarily conducive to a longing for knowledge and growth'.[15]

We can see a tension between what academics know about how the neoliberal university engages their attachments, and how academics continue to imagine these as having transformative potential. The contemporary revival of critical interest in love is similarly strained. In their survey, Anna Jónasdóttir and Ann Ferguson argue that while critics increasingly position love as a positive political force, love studies is actually a 'heterogenous and conflicted field of knowledge' that claims love 'for both revolution and maintaining power'.[16] So what are we attached to when we are attached to love? And what do we risk professing when we make professions of love? We should notice a set of interlocking ideals that surface when we position love (or one of its forms) as a corrective to the neoliberal university. First, the ideal mode of an academic's relation to their work and identity is, ultimately, still imagined as a loving one (even when disavowing it or lamenting its loss from our professions). Second, these attachments are positioned as natural resources for transformation or resistance. Third, that resource is implied to derive from being naturally distinct from the realm of capitalism and neoliberalism. In Churcher and Talbot's analysis, for example, bureaucracy, metrification and corporatization delineate a machinic order whose defining practices are a 'rational calculation and instrumentalisation' combined with a tactical orientation to feeling through which 'strong affect' is constrained, policed, regulated and managed while permissible feelings are, merely, strategic displays of 'overt levels of enthusiasm and zeal in relation to work in order to gain a competitive edge'.[17] Here two further assumptions are worth noticing: neoliberal attachments aren't real feeling, and the reason is because they are instrumentalizable, performative and serve economic functions. These ideals index a logic of opposition between real, authentic, personal feeling, and that which is performed, pretended and capitalized on. This paradigm endorses a model of political transformation that imagines neoliberalism as de-animating or de-vitalizing the human subject, while positioning love as a vitalizing and animating resource that, reinserted into the neoliberal environment, can activate agency, resistance and, ultimately, an authentic, and authentically sovereign, subjectivity. But theorizing politicization in this way risks imagining academics' attachments as not political until the economic conditions of the late twentieth and early twenty-first centuries and posits the existence of a version of real, non-bureaucratized and anti-capitalist love whose positive valance belongs, naturally, to academic subjectivity. Lauren Berlant describes the idea of 'real' love as 'a political question about the way norms produce attachments to living through certain fantasies'.[18] The affective politics of these scenes from our critical imaginaries contract around an attachment to living, and loving, that institutes a natural difference between the work of love under capitalism, and the labours of love through which academics imagine themselves. In so doing, these arguments register critical desire for the restorative promise of a bifurcation between academia and capitalist economies of affect, a distinction supposedly disturbed by the neoliberal university's ability to turn our loving attachments into labour, commodity and capital. These scenes are also enmeshed with ideologies of feeling in which valance corroborates values: that enmeshment invites us to ask, vis-à-vis Berlant, what happens 'when feeling bad becomes evidence for a structural condition of injustice? ... when feeling good becomes evidence of justice's triumph?'[19] Zeena Feldman and Marisol Sandoval remark that the neoliberal academic self as we experience it in the twenty-first century has 'little in common with the ideals of passionate vocation so often invoked in the popular imaginary'.[20] I don't think this is quite true: our cultural imaginaries are highly attuned to how love works in academic lives, if we attend to what they teach us.

Love lessons: *The Secret History* and *Possession*

Recent scholarship on the neoliberal university tends to represent corporatization, managerialism and bureaucratization as uniquely twenty-first century. But Sheila Slaughter and Gary Rhoades's seminal work in the 1990s described the neoliberal university as an intensifying, rather than emerging, economic configuration.[21] *The Secret History* and *Possession* can be situated, then, as not divergent from but contemporaneous with this development in critical attention. Prescient in their preoccupation with academic feeling, these novels anticipate the eventual turn to affect in twenty-first-century arguments about the neoliberal university by registering cultural anxieties about the place, and disappearance, of passion from academic vocation.

In Tartt's *The Secret History,* Richard Papen transfers to a New England liberal arts college where an exclusive clique – materially and academically privileged beyond their peers – are handpicked by a professor for private tutelage in Classics.[22] From the beginning, the novel entangles academic passion with economic and cultural capital: their means are what affords the level of dedication to study demanded by Professor Morrow, and each other. This devotion is a source of fascination in the novel, but it is also a source of anxiety – the novel's structuring question is how the ancient passions studied are transformed from objects of academic interest into deadly academic orientations. Academic passion authorizes abuses of privilege and power that culminate in murder. Continually prodding at the relation between, and consequences of, their passions for what they study and for their own superiority, the novel construes these attachments as dangerously uncontained and out of control. Indeed, it is a lesson in desire for middle-class Richard, who is the only one in the group to go on to become an academic, albeit an unimpassioned and unhappy one, haunted both by his unrequited love for Camilla (one of the elite group) and for a version of academia on which he never gains purchase.

For critics of the novel, Tartt's vision of academia is purposefully antiquated and opposed to – or perhaps even reclusive from – both the late-twentieth century and the everyday. But *The Secret History* works as a grotesque fantasy, registering cultural anxieties about the line between passionate inquiry and dangerous obsession, as well as the value of knowledge derived from such interests. In this sense, the narrative preoccupations of *The Secret History* speak to a late-twentieth-century preoccupation with the pleasures and dangers of academic intimacies that we can also track across films such as Rob Cohen's *Skulls* (2000), based on conspiracy theories about Yale University's Skull and Bone's society; the sexual initiations at private prep schools in Roger Kumble's *Cruel Intentions* (1999); and the epistemerotic fantasy of and for a passionately intimate masculine pedagogy in Tom Schulman's *Dead Poet's Society* (1989). Anxious fantasies of a neoliberalized culture, these are all concerned with the consequences of academic passions left unregulated. In *The Secret History*, these are self-indulgent, diverging from public good, from value, and, importantly, from the very ethics with which the humanities claim a particular kind of concern – that is, the humane. Indexing a twinned cultural fascination with, and distrust of, the kinds of claims academics make about universities as being primarily concerned with making knowledge for the public good, the novel amplifies the neoliberal university's managerial rhetoric which, with its emphasis on multi-tiered monitoring, accounting and operationalization, imagines academics as in need of regulation, managing and self-responsibilization. But the novel also, in the form of Richard's own unhappy academic career, wonders at the value of such a vocation if it is pursued without passion. By pointing us to a cultural narrative in which passion signs the academic subjects' sovereignty, the novel registers how the neoliberal university recruits cultural anxieties about the threat of that sovereignty into justification for marketization. Yet it also signals, in Richard's nostalgia for the academic passions of that elite group, a longing for a subjectivity known to be enmeshed with structures of violence. Like his love for Camilla (who is part of the elite group), Richard's desire for the academia he'd imagined is unrequited: his mourning marks the persistence of an attachment to a scene of desire that has not – yet – offered him a return.

A. S. Byatt's *Possession: A Romance* also worries about the disappearance of passion, but romance promises the conditions for requitement.[23] Roland Michell appears as a figure of the academic who has, thus far, been unable to adjust to the new demands of professionalized academia. Still employed on part-time and fixed term contracts, Roland has yet to convert his academic passion (the work of Victorian poet Randolph Henry Ash) into an academic career. His scene is the conflict between a romantic and out-of-date idea of passionate academic vocation, and the demands for competitive individualism and careerism in the academic marketplace. It is a neoliberalism embodied in the cliché of dispassionate Maud Bailey, a women's studies scholar who specializes in minor Victorian poet Christabel LaMotte and runs a Women's Resource Centre at Lincoln University. Their coming into possession of a packet of letters that Roland has stolen on impulse (later revealed to be Maud's inheritance) unites both the poets they research, and themselves, in romance, and offers proof of a romantic entanglement that ends up transforming their futures. For Roland, the possession of these love letters literalizes the promise of an academic career: despite the controversy of how they came into his possession – perhaps even because of the affective orientations his theft signals – he is offered several full-time research positions.

Like a love letter to passion's future within the academic marketplace, *Possession*'s narrative arcs towards renewed investment in, and attachment to, academia. The ending amplifies this desire: by leaving the question of Roland's choice open (we don't find out which position he takes), the novel finishes with a sense of unlimited choice. Roland is now a free agent. Rather than a marriage of opposites, of academic passion and neoliberalism, the novel's education-in-becoming-academic evinces an intimate relation between Roland's passion and his neoliberal career potential. Note that the means by which he succeeds is a passion whose orientation to artefacts, to academia and to others, is possessive. Not only does he steal the letters, but the race against other academics is one in intellectual property, of who will be the first to put their name to this capital.

Rekindled, Roland's academic passion is revealed to be not only enmeshed with, but also a passion for, the competitive individualism promoted by the neoliberalism that was, initially, a source of threat. Crucially, what converts his passion into purchase is the possession of Maud's property – and her erotic attachment. It is the kind of conversion Richard, in *The Secret History*, was never able to secure. Here intimacy offers Roland ownership-by-proxy, smoothing over questions of piracy or illegitimacy, or indeed, the ethics of appropriation. That Maud's property passes, through her feelings for Roland, to him, is a naturalizing logic with an economic structure remarkably proximate to the historical period to which they are both so attached. And what of Maud? Her flourishing takes the form of consummation, of being sexually possessed by Roland. It is as if as an academic she has no further becoming to do. Whether the doubling of love plots, here, reinscribes or critiques these essentializing gender norms is debatable. But what we should notice is that *Possession* imagines academic subjectivity as no less subject to the heteropatriarchal project by which men are allocated women's capital for their own flourishing in the public sphere, and women dedicate theirs to the cruel optimism of heterosexual attachment. Love works here to legitimate annexation, naturalizing – and depoliticizing – the economic conditions of Roland's academic becoming. *Possession* speaks to the anxiety that neoliberalism threatens academic subjectivity by reassuring those who can possess another's capital of their sustained potential for flourishing. Passion earns for Roland the capital of an orientation to, and way of being in, academia that appears to uncouple economic and epistemic desires while, simultaneously, benefitting from their marriage. Summoning questions about the future of an academia that is increasingly professionalized and market driven, *Possession* romances with passion's restorative promise – for some. At the heart of this love plot are the heteropatriarchal institutions underwriting that repair.

The Secret History and *Possession* tendered, at the beginning of the 1990s, an intimacy between academics' affective orientations to academia and the means by which the neoliberal university functions. Attentive to the different forms that intimacy takes, the novels predict love's capacity to resource the neoliberal university, reminding us that academia and neoliberalism can marry because they are already attached through heteropatriarchal economies of affect. Critical work on affect and academia published in the decades since demonstrates just how prescient these novels are in representing academics' attachments as a scene for debates about the neoliberal university. But these novels should also alert us, in their use of romance, to how a politics of desire compels our attachment to subjectivities and feelings we know to be injurious. While those late-twentieth-century scenes of academia might now seem hopelessly out of date, the trajectory of the texts to which I turn now evinces a retrenchment of these ideological structures in our cultural and critical imaginaries.

Love blind: Reading *On Beauty* and *Call Me by Your Name*

Zadie Smith's *On Beauty* famously satirizes early-twenty-first-century academia.[24] Like *Possession*, the academic plot is enmeshed with the intimate. But what is left ambiguous in Byatt's novel (does Maud know, or not know, that her love story is not an exception to the heteropatriarchy her research critiques?) is probed in Smith's attention to both the conditions of knowledge-making and academics' knowledge of those conditions. Elsewhere I have written about the heteropatriarchal scene, and negotiations of a black feminist subjectivity, at work in the novel's representations of academics' wives.[25] While revelations of infidelity make Kiki question the politicization with which she has viewed her gifts of love, her white husband Howard regrets only that he 'broke that splendid circle of Kiki's love ... a love (and it was to Howard's credit that he knew this) that had enabled everything else'.[26] Representing Howard's orientation to his wife's love as a relation to resource, the novel notices how the economy of affect within his domestic scene underwrites his academic one. In Howard's knowingness, it also apprehends a dissonance between the academic position he occupies, and the epistemic position of dispassion and disinterested aesthetics he professes. That dissonance is, of course, not a surprise given how academic labour structures assume there are no other cares for which academic bodies are responsible – not even their own.[27] But it is also, given the novel's attention to Howard's knowledge, wilful.

Howard's knowing orientation to the affective politics of his academic becoming scrutinizes how an ideology of social reproduction affirms, by depoliticizing, academic subjectivity. Briana Brickley points out that the epistemological foundations of Howard's aesthetics are 'thinly veiled racist and patriarchal requirements for subjectivity and citizenship'.[28] Brickley is hopeful about how the novel entangles the social and academic, arguing that official knowledge-making permeates the text, 'spilling over into the social world to mark the intimate, everyday, embodied and sensate', to produce 'unpredictable encounters of attachment'.[29] I read this in the reverse, however: the heteropatriarchal labour-logics of the university are actively *colonizing*, and the biopolitics of its encounters – including the idea that academia constitutes a discrete sphere whose 'spillage' into the social, intimate, personal, domestic, embodied or intimate represents a deconstructive radicality – entirely predictable. By scrutinizing Howard's perception of his intimate life, the novel reminds us that this permeation is actually a historically resilient structure distributing the work of knowledge-making across the range of labourers its work requires while disavowing that distribution to preserve the borders of officiation. The recalcitrant essentialism of that structure is tangible in the irony, given the very unoriginal labour conditions underpinning what he thinks, and the thought itself, when Howard espouses that academics 'produce new ways of thinking, then other people think it'.[30]

Importantly, these biopolitics are resilient to generational change. Consider how the novel, and critics, construe Zora, Kiki and Howard's daughter, a top-ranking student at the university where Howard works. Zora, acutely concerned with her academic career, is represented by critics as having a voracious zeal for acquiring the capital of academia and is branded with an instrumentalism and careerism that blinds her to her limitations. Ann Marie Adams, for example, describes Zora as 'devouring' culture; unaware 'that there may be more to such study than intellectual recall or abstraction', Zora is 'unable to distinguish her own mechanically produced writing from true artistic creativity'.[31] Although her attitude may seem instrumental ('as if we all had time to sit around reading whatever we fancied'[32]), Zora's scarcity discourse intimates a sense of impending precarity despite her grades, her socio-economic status or her father's connections. Brickley contends that the novel's vision of the neoliberal university shows how structures of race and gender are 'rerouted and expressed in new ways'.[33] But Zora's anxious attachments and the extent to which her abilities are so readily perceived to be limited suggest how easily the passion that would, in a different body, be lauded, is recuperated into the essentialist ideology of social reproduction that has already zoned her for the work of reproducing, rather than creating. 'Poor Zora', the novel laments, 'she lived through footnotes'.[34]

Reconstructing Zora's attachments as anxious also allows us to consider the affective politics of her conflict with poetry professor Claire Malcolm, whose class she wants to take. Claire perceives herself, and is perceived by others, to be disinterested in the 'tediously practical' concerns marking the ministrations of academics' wives.[35] Yet her tenure is also represented as indivisible from the erotic capital of the affairs she's had with other academics and her dedication to discovering and cultivating the next generation of poets. Social reproduction recuperates her, too, into the labours of love structuring the academic household. But it also engages her in administering its ideology. Consider the biopolitics of her outrage: '[Zora]'s simply untalented in this area ... My class rewards *talent* ... I'm trying to refine and polish a ... a *sensibility*. I'm telling you: she doesn't have one.'[36] Claire's recourse to the authority of her expertise in discerning another's viability for sensibility and refinement mobilizes the sentimental biopower of the colonial imagination. Kyla Schuller traces contemporary accounts of sensibility and affectability to the 'delicacy of feeling' theorized by nineteenth-century race theory, whose hierarchy of impressibility imagined the civilized mind to have an affective capacity for sensibility and refinement the primitive lacked.[37] It is the same language critics too often reproduce without examination when they attribute to Zora's appetites a distasteful excess that is bodily, or mechanistic. Also an anxious attachment, Claire's appeal to biopower seeks to de-legitimize Zora's viability within that hierarchy while asserting her own. Citing the biopolitics at work when we discern academic subjectivities, this scene registers how academia recruits white femininity with the promise of a sovereignty authorized by the willingness to police others' access to institutional scenes of social reproduction.

In *On Beauty*, the neoliberal university remains a resiliently heteropatriarchal and colonial institution consolidated through, rather than threatened by, academics' attachments. In its scrutiny of academics' knowledge of these economies, *On Beauty* calls to the future of academia: are we willing to relinquish our desires, or will we remain wilfully attached? I want to answer that call with my final love scene: Luca Guadagnino's *Call Me by Your Name* (2017), and the nostalgic ecology/economy of desire in both the film's epistemerotics and critical appraisals.[38] Set in the summer of 1983, 'somewhere in northern Italy',[39] the Perlman family holiday at their rural estate where seventeen-year-old musician and bibliophile Elio's summer-of-becoming takes shape through intellectual and sexual intimacy with Oliver, a PhD student assisting Elio's father, Samuel, an archaeology professor.

Discussing the origin of the film's creative direction, Guadagnino points to an Italian countryside where sensuous rurality allows you 'to let yourself go to the environment, to the landscape and to your feelings'.[40] Long shots linger over the sensuality of Elio and Oliver reading, swimming in and drinking from the fresh mountain spring that initiates their first kiss, and a ripe peach with flesh so yielding to pleasure that Elio is able to masturbate in a hole he fingers from it. We are intimates, here, with the affects of an ecology where the 'nothing happening' that initially embodies, for Elio, a time of boredom, is ripe with the potentiality of sensual re-attunement to the creativity of desire. This creativity is most visible, perhaps, in the moment when, after tasting peach juice on Elio's penis, Oliver dips his finger, and then his tongue, into the peach-well still holding Elio's semen. 'Ah, I see', says Oliver: 'You've moved onto the plant kingdom already, what's next, minerals? I suppose you've already given up animals, you know that's me.'[41] It's an erotic potential Elio didn't see coming, even in his own re-imagining of the peach flesh as sexual cleavage. Creative potential, however, is imbricated with coming-to-know: this is not only a sex scene, but a pedagogic one, and the sexual charge between Elio and Oliver is as enmeshed with their intellectual pursuits as it is their sensual. Oliver's tease tenders the sensuality of academic subjectivity by quipping taxonomy. Although not reducible to it, the creative potential of the feelings between them, and the goodness of a masculine intimacy not capturable by heteronormative affects of shame, as Elio's father later tells him, 'had everything and nothing to do with intelligence'.[42]

Reviewer Richard Brody bristles at the extent to which Elio and Oliver are represented as academics in love, indeed the extent to which their relationship *is* expressed through their love of themselves as academics. The result, he charges, is an 'empty, sanitized intimacy'.[43] But as Jaishikha Nautiyal points out, it is a mistake to read this as a dry orientation. In the ecological fecundity and lavish sensuality of ordinary living in this 'gorgeous summertime Italian context', Nautiyal locates a radically creative 'bloom-space' where 'ecology co-participates in nourishing queer aesthetics as part of the film's intersensory rhetoric'.[44] The film's attunement to the sensuality of shared academic passions should, for Nautiyal, be seen as a form of creative enmeshment whose potentiality is a radically artful queer blooming that exceeds heteromasculinity, unloosening the demands of heterocentrism: 'the warm lushness of Italian summer, fruit, vegetal life, sticky flies affirms the kinetic potentiality of desire over the cultural fixity of love objects'.[45] We can register, here, a claim to something like the critical potential Rebecca May Johnson locates in the vegetal, the 'slutty ingenuity of vegetables when it comes to desire and reproductive methods … that makes a mockery of conservative ideals of the natural'.[46] But can that kinetic potentiality, as Nautiyal contends, 'decouple sexuality from culturally determined reproductive economies'[47] in a scene that is, as Guadagnino draws our attention to, so highly cultivated? Elio and Oliver's is not a natural environment, but a highly aestheticized and curated one. If ecology is what unsticks sex, erotic becoming, and desire from heteronormativity, the economics of its tending does not.

The fertile conditions for this blooming intimacy of masculine epistemerotics is the estate that Anella, Elio's mother, has inherited. Yet in the film's first close attention to the ripeness of the environment, and the appetites it supplies, Oliver asks Samuel 'Is this your orchard?'[48] 'These are Anella's trees', Samuel replies: 'Pesche, ciliegi, albiococche.' Oliver is rapt, but only until Samuel finishes. When Anella adds 'Pomegranate. Melograno', Oliver turns his attention away and to his food. The physicality of Oliver's attitude registers an orientation of disinterest for Anella, and for her domain, other than as an experience these provide for him. Anella is, throughout the film, a background presence whose tending to men is so constant, and so unremarked, that her labours appear part of the natural world, and natural order. While Elio, Oliver and Samuel traverse the landscape with a lush freedom, Anella is never seen outside the estate except, near the end, when she and Samuel see Oliver and Elio off at the bus station. Even within the house – which Anella owns – her movements are tethered to the work of cultivation. Indeed it is notable how rarely she enters her husband's study. When Oliver arrives, Samuel welcomes him to the home by bringing him, and Elio, in while Anella hovers at the threshold.[49] As Elio and Oliver depart, Anella finally enters, but only when taken into Samuel's embrace as he calls after the boys, while holding Anella to him, 'You're very welcome here. Our home is your home.' The only other time she crosses the threshold is when she brings the men glasses of apricot juice. We can see her, as the men drink, orbiting in the background – indeed at one point the focus on Oliver makes all but the top of her head invisible. Although she stays, she does not participate in the academic exchange that follows when Samuel discourses on the etymology of 'apricot', only to be contested by Oliver's careful, but pleasurably combative, disagreement. Frisson culminates in Samuel's congratulation for Oliver's analysis, at which point Elio reveals it to be a familiar pedagogical scene: 'He does this every year'. What is Anella doing, here? Rather like the peripheral sofa on which she sits, she furnishes this encounter between academic men: while economics of class ensure her housekeeper and groundsman do the manual labour of pruning the apricot trees or pressing the juice, the hetero-economics of gender ensure Anella delivers ripe potentiality to the men in her husband's study. Feeding their senses, as well as their bodies, she cultivates the conditions in which they can encounter each other with pleasure, with passion and with the epistemic status that enables complex etymology to be modestly passed off as 'Philology 101'. If, in this scene, Oliver's intellectual intercourse with Samuel enables his becoming academically equal, its conditions are Anella's care. Yes, there is an ecology of blooming at work here, but its conditions are the ordinary economics of heteropatriarchy.

Conclusion: Love plots

These scenes from our cultural and critical imaginaries help us to see how critical attachments to love work as love plots – narrative structures that Berlant argues provide a 'seemingly non-ideological resolution to the fractures and contradictions of history'.[50] This desire for a non-ideological resolution is tangible in the intensification, as we move further into the twenty-first century, of critical desires for forms of academic love invulnerable to the neoliberal university. It is evident, too, in how often academics attribute the neoliberal university's economies of affect to its present and not to its marriage with the ideological institutions underwriting academia, and academic subjectivity, throughout our pasts. As Busso and Rivetti point out, our attraction to our passions is at its greatest intensity when 'workers cannot really come up with exit strategies nor threaten to implement them'.[51] In doing so, these arguments register the promise of an academic genre that indexes this crisis as impasse – a scene in which, Berlant writes, 'living beings [are] figuring out how to stay attached to life from within it, and to protect what optimism they have for that, at least'.[52] In tracing the economies of affect in our cultural and critical imagining of academic love, I have traced the conditions for that impasse: love can't transform our labour or its conditions because, regardless of how revitalizing or resistant it might feel, and regardless of the politicization underpinning it, no loving orientation is experienced by the institution as distinct, in any real way, from the economies of affect it already requires. Even if felt as resistance, these feelings are never beyond the heteropatriarchal and colonial biopolitics through which academia, as an institution, consolidates itself. When we imagine academic love as a source of (re)vitalization, we are recruiting the biopower of those institutions. What looks like repair is either purchase, recruitment or the perpetual promise of a return-yet-to-come.

Busso and Rivetti observe that academic love can also be attached to institutions: that includes the institution of academic subjectivity. *Let us imagine a scholar*. Yes, but let us, also, attend to the affective conditions that have made, and make, that imagining possible. Must we really relinquish love? Given the painfulness of the academic love scene in which I find myself, I understand why others may prolong their attachments in hopes of discovering an academic affection not enmeshed with injurious potential. But instead of passion I tender dispossession: I have no more time for love. Not now. I am not in the mood.

Notes

1 Jacques Derrida, 'Passions: "An Oblique Offering"', in *On the Name*, ed. Thomas Dutoit, trans. David Wood, John Leavey Jr. and Iain McLeod (Stanford: Stanford University Press, 1995), 3.
2 University of East Anglia (UEA) TEF submission, 5. https://apps.officeforstudents.org.uk/tefoutcomes2019/docs/submissions/Submission_10007789.pdf.
3 UEA TEF, 1. For TEF details see https://www.officeforstudents.org.uk/advice-and-guidance/teaching/about-the-tef/.
4 Ibid., 3.
5 Stefan Collini, *Speaking of Universities* (London: Verso, 2017), 31.
6 Definitions from *Oxford English Dictionary* online.
7 For academia's range of love feelings, see Caroline Clarke, David Knights and Carol Jarvis, 'A Labour of Love? Academics in Business Schools', *Management* 28, no. 1 (2012): 5–15.
8 Mona Mannevuo, 'Caught in a Bad Romance? Affective Attachments in Contemporary Academia', in *The Post-Fordist Sexual Contract: Working and Living in Contingency*, ed. Lisa Adkins and Maryanne Dever (Basingstoke: Palgrave Macmillan, 2015), 86.
9 Sandro Busso and Paola Rivetti, 'What's Love Got to Do with It? Precarious Academic Labour Forces and the Role of Passion in Italian Universities', *Recherches Sociologiques et Anthropologiques* 45, no. 2 (2014): 15–37.
10 Ibid., 16.
11 Rosalind Gill, 'Breaking the Silence: The Hidden Injuries of the Neoliberal University', in *Secrecy and Silence in the Research Process*, ed. Roisin Ryan-Flood and Rosalind Gill (London: Routledge, 2010), 241.
12 Millicent Churcher and Debra Talbot, 'Corporatisation of Education: Bureaucracy, Boredom, and Transformative Possibilities', *New Formations: Bureaucracy* 100, no. 1 (2020): 33.
13 R. Al-Mahmood et al., 'Love *Acts* and Revolutionary Praxis: Challenging the Neoliberal University through a Teaching Scholars Development Program', *Higher Education Research and Development* 39, no. 1 (2020): 83.
14 Emma Bell and Amanda Sinclair, 'Reclaiming Eroticism in the Academy', *Organization* 21, no. 2 (2014): 277.

15 Rebecca Lund and Janne Tienari, 'Passion, Care, and Eros in the Gendered Neoliberal University', *Organization,* 26, no. 1 (2019): 2.
16 Anna Jónasdóttir and Ann Ferguson, eds, *Love: A Question for Feminism in the Twenty-First Century* (London: Routledge, 2014), 2. Sara Ahmed discusses love and the maintenance of authority in 'In the Name of Love', *Borderlands* 2, no. 3 (2003): 1–41.
17 Churcher and Talbot, 'Corporatisation', 33–4.
18 Lauren Berlant, *Love/Desire* (New York: Punctum Books, 2012), 96.
19 Lauren Berlant, 'The Subject of True Feeling: Pain, Privacy, and Politics', in *Cultural Pluralism, Identity Politics, and the Law,* ed. Austin Sarat and Thomas R. Kearns (Ann Arbor: University of Michigan Press, 1999), 58.
20 Zeena Feldman and Marisol Sandoval, 'Metric Power and the Academic Self: Neoliberalism, Knowledge and Resistance in the British University', *tripleC: Journal for a Global Sustainable Information Society* 16, no. 1 (2018): 220.
21 Shiela Slaughter and Gary Rhoades, 'The Neo-Liberal University', *New Labor Forum*, no. 6 (Spring–Summer 2000): 73–39. See also Shiela Slaughter and Larry L. Leslie, *Academic Capitalism: Politics, Policies, and the Entrepreneurial University* (Baltimore: Johns Hopkins University Press, 1997); Gary Rhoades, *Managed Professionals: Unionized Faculty and Restructuring Academic Labor* (Albany: State University of New York Press, 1998).
22 Donna Tartt, *The Secret History* (New York: Penguin, 1992).
23 A. S. Byatt, *Possession: A Romance* (London: Chatto and Windus, 1990).
24 Zadie Smith, *On Beauty* (London: Penguin, 2005).
25 See Karen Schaller, 'Feminist Dwellings: Imagining the Domestic in the Twenty-First-century Literary Novel', in *The New Feminist Literary Studies*, ed. Jennifer Cooke (Cambridge University Press: Cambridge, 2020), 157–68.
26 Smith, *On Beauty*, 109.
27 For an elaboration of this expectation, see Martin Parker and Elke Weik, 'Free Spirits? The Academic on the Aeroplane', *Management Learning* 45, no. 2 (2014): 167–81.
28 Briana Brickley, '*On Beauty* and the Politics of Academic Institutionality', *Ariel: A Review of International English Literature* 48, no. 2 (2017): 73.
29 Ibid.
30 Smith, *On Beauty*, 120.
31 Ann Marie Adams, 'A Passage to Forster: Zadie Smith's Attempt to "Only Connect" to *Howards End*', *Critique: Studies in Contemporary Fiction* 52, no. 4 (2011): 385.
32 Ibid., 219.
33 Brickley, '*On Beauty*', 88.
34 Smith, *On Beauty*, 70.

35 Ibid., 57. See also 150.
36 Ibid., 158, italics in original.
37 Kyla Schuller, *The Biopolitics of Feeling: Race, Sex, and Science in the Nineteenth Century* (Durham: Duke University Press, 2017), 40.
38 Luca Guadagnino, Dir. *Call Me by Your Name* (USA: Sony Pictures Classics, 2017).
39 Ibid., 02:58.
40 Elisa Leonelli, 'Luca Guadagnino on Desire'. *Cultural Weekly,* 22 November 2017, https://www.culturalweekly.com/luca-guadagnino-desire/.
41 *Call Me by Your Name,* 1:39:00–1:39:05.
42 Ibid., 1:58:23.
43 Richard Brody, 'The Empty, Sanitized Intimacy of *Call Me by Your Name*', *New Yorker,* 28 November 2017, https://www.newyorker.com/culture/richard-brody/the-empty-sanitized-intimacy-of-call-me-by-your-name.
44 Jaishika Nautiyal, 'Queer Aesthetics, Playful Politics, and Ethical Masculinities in Luca Guadagnino's Filmic Adaptation of Andre Aciman's *Call Me by Your Name*', in *The Routledge Handbook of Gender and Communication*, ed. Marnel Niles Goins, Joan Faber McAlister and Bryant Keith Alexander (London: Routledge, 2020), 210.
45 Ibid., 14.
46 Rebecca M. Johnson, 'Qualities of Earth', *Granta: The Online Edition,* 13 May 2020. https://granta.com/qualities-of-earth/.
47 Nautiyal, 'Queer Aesthetics', 10.
48 *Call Me by Your Name,* 09:02–09:15.
49 Ibid., 04:02–04:20.
50 Berlant, *Love/Desire,* 96.
51 Busso and Rivetti, 'What's Love', 37.
52 Lauren Berlant, *Cruel Optimism* (Durham: Duke University Press, 2011), 10.

Bibliography

Adams, Ann Marie. 'A Passage to Forster: Zadie Smith's Attempt to "Only Connect" to *Howards End*'. *Critique: Studies in Contemporary Fiction* 52, no. 4 (2011): 377–99.
Ahmed, Sara. 'In the Name of Love'. *Borderlands* 2, no. 3 (2003): 1–41.
Al-Mahmood, Reem, Gerardo Papalia, Sinead Barry, Minh Nguyet Nguyen, Juliane Roemhild, Terri Meehan-Andrews, Brianna Julien et al. 'Love *Acts* and Revolutionary Praxis: Challenging the Neoliberal University through a Teaching Scholars Development Program'. *Higher Education Research and Development* 39, no. 1 (2020): 81–98.

Bell, Emma, and Amanda Sinclair. 'Reclaiming Eroticism in the Academy'. *Organization* 21, no. 2 (2014): 268–80.

Berlant, Lauren. 'The Subject of True Feeling: Pain, Privacy, and Politics'. In *Cultural Pluralism, Identity Politics, and the Law,* edited by Austin Sarat and Thomas R. Kearns, 49–84. Ann Arbor: University of Michigan Press, 1999.

Berlant, Lauren. *Cruel Optimism*. Durham: Duke University Press, 2011.

Berlant, Lauren. *Love/Desire*. New York: Punctum Books, 2012.

Brickley, Briana. '*On Beauty* and the Politics of Academic Institutionality'. *Ariel: A Review of International English Literature* 48, no. 2 (2017): 73–100.

Brody, Richard. 'The Empty, Sanitized Intimacy of *Call Me by Your Name*'. *New Yorker*, 28 November 2017. https://www.newyorker.com/culture/richard-brody/the-empty-sanitized-intimacy-of-call-me-by-your-name.

Busso, Sandro, and Paola Rivetti. 'What's Love Got to Do with It? Precarious Academic Labour Forces and the Role of Passion in Italian Universities'. *Recherches Sociologiques et Anthropologiques* 45, no. 2 (2014): 15–37.

Byatt, A. S. *Possession: A Romance*. London: Chatto and Windus, 1990.

Call Me by Your Name. Directed by Luca Guadagnino, USA: Sony Pictures Classics, 2017.

Churcher, Millicent, and Debra Talbot. 'Corporatisation of Education: Bureaucracy, Boredom, and Transformative Possibilities'. *New Formations: Bureaucracy* 100, no. 1 (2020): 28–42.

Clarke, Caroline, David Knights and Carol Jarvis. 'A Labour of Love? Academics in Business Schools'. *Management* 28, no. 1 (2012): 5–15.

Collini, Stefan. *Speaking of Universities*. London: Verso, 2017.

Derrida, Jacques. 'Passions: "An Oblique Offering" '. In *On the Name*, edited by Thomas Dutoit, 3–34. Translated by David Wood, John Leavey Jr. and Iain McLeod. Stanford: Stanford University Press, 1995.

Feldman, Zeena, and Marisol Sandoval. 'Metric Power and the Academic Self: Neoliberalism, Knowledge and Resistance in the British University'. *tripleC: Journal for a Global Sustainable Information Society* 16, no. 1 (2018): 214–33.

Gill, Rosalind. 'Beyond Individualism: The Psychosocial Life of the Neoliberal University'. In *Dissident Knowledge in Higher Education: Resisting Colonialism, Neoliberalism, and Audit Culture in the Academy*, edited by Marc Spooner and James McNinch, 193–216. Regina: University of Regina Press, 2017.

Gill, Rosalind. 'Breaking the Silence: The Hidden Injuries of the Neoliberal University'. In *Secrecy and Silence in the Research Process*, edited by Roisin Ryan-Flood and Rosalind Gill, 228–44. London: Routledge, 2010.

Johnson, Rebecca May. 'Qualities of Earth'. *Granta: The Online Edition,* 13 May 2020. https://granta.com/qualities-of-earth/.

Jónasdóttir, Anna, and Ann Ferguson, eds. *Love: A Question for Feminism in the Twenty-First Century*. London: Routledge, 2014.

Leonelli, Elisa. 'Luca Guadagnino on Desire'. *Cultural Weekly*, 22 November 2017. https://www.culturalweekly.com/luca-guadagnino-desire/.

Lund, Rebecca, and Janne Tienari. 'Passion, Care, and Eros in the Gendered Neoliberal University'. *Organization* 26, no. 1 (2019): 98–121.

Mannevuo, Mona. 'Caught in a Bad Romance? Affective Attachments in Contemporary Academia'. In *The Post-Fordist Sexual Contract: Working and Living in Contingency*, edited by Lisa Adkins and Maryanne Dever, 71–88. Basingstoke: Palgrave Macmillan, 2015.

Nautiyal, Jaishikha. 'Queer Aesthetics, Playful Politics, and Ethical Masculinities in Luca Guadagnino's Filmic Adaptation of Andre Aciman's *Call Me by Your Name*'. In *The Routledge Handbook of Gender and Communication*, edited by Marnel Niles Goins, Joan Faber McAlister and Bryant Keith Alexander, 206–22. London: Routledge, 2020.

Parker, Martin, and Elke Weik. 'Free Spirits? The Academic on the Aeroplane'. *Management Learning* 45, no. 2 (2014): 167–81.

Rhoades, Gary. *Managed Professionals: Unionized Faculty and Restructuring Academic Labor*. Albany: State University of New York Press, 1998.

Slaughter, Sheila, and Gary Rhoades. 'The Neo-Liberal University'. *New Labor Forum* 6 (2000): 73–39.

Slaughter, Sheila, and Larry L. Leslie. *Academic Capitalism: Politics, Policies, and the Entrepreneurial University*. Baltimore: Johns Hopkins University Press, 1997.

Schaller, Karen. 'Feminist Dwellings: Imagining the Domestic in the Twenty-First-Century Literary Novel'. In *The New Feminist Literary Studies*, edited by Jennifer Cooke, 157–68. Cambridge: Cambridge University Press, 2020.

Schuller, Kyla. *The Biopolitics of Feeling: Race, Sex, and Science in the Nineteenth Century*. Durham: Duke University Press, 2017.

Smith, Zadie. *On Beauty*. London: Penguin, 2005.

Tartt, Donna. *The Secret History*. New York: Penguin, 1992.

8

Should I be scared when you say that you love me? Youth work practice and the power of *professional love*

Martin E. Purcell

Introduction

This chapter contributes to an ongoing discourse on the importance of the relationship between practitioner and young person as a central and defining tenet of effective youth work practice.[1] Based on interpersonal ways of working in situations where young people's participation and engagement with the worker is voluntary, youth work is characterized as a process of relationship-building that allows the practitioner to provide both protection and challenge to the young person, while supporting them in fulfilling their potential. A key challenge for the practitioner in this relational form of practice is to recognize the vulnerabilities of the young people with whom they work, and ensure that they do not experience exploitative or otherwise inappropriate behaviour in their relationships with youth workers, who for many young people are the first adult with whom they have chosen to have a relationship. Practitioners are privileged in this regard, and are bound to ensure that relationships characterized by informality, intimacy and warmth foster space for reflection, growth and flourishing, and are used to provide meaningful support in times of difficulty.[2] This has become particularly important in the context of approaches to service delivery under the prevailing neoliberal hegemony, where the qualitative impact of youth work's person-centred, context-dependent and relational practice is perceived as problematic in managerialist approaches that distinguish 'clients' and 'providers' and fixate on procedure-led practice and quantitative monitoring.[3]

In examining the nature of this relationship, I explore in this chapter the idea that love should form a foundational basis of youth work practice, and report on my interpretation of the views of 100 youth work practitioners from across the globe who completed an online survey shortly before the emergence of the global Covid-19 pandemic. I sought the views of practitioners from a wide spectrum of settings to secure their perspectives on the need for this aspect of practice, and what *professional love* in youth work might look like. In my analysis, I build on Jools Page's work on the role of love in professional relationships between early years' workers and the children in their care to suggest what this might look like in practice with older young people.[4] My thinking is framed within bell hooks's advocacy for the place of love in society as a whole, and Paulo Freire's call to change the world through engaging the oppressed in dialogue informed by a profound love of humanity.[5] This radical approach recognizes the inherent worth of all humans, particularly the most marginalized and disenfranchised people, and it requires practitioners to demonstrate our love for those who we seek to serve in all aspects our practice.[6]

This chapter is structured to allow for an initial exploration of the relevant theoretical positions that have shaped my thinking, followed by discussion of the responses from the study. Throughout, attention is given to both the required components of *professional love* as an element of youth work practice and the challenges practitioners face when forming professionally loving relationships with the young people in their care.

If 'love' is the cure, what is the 'problem'?

The experience of being young should not by default be characterized as 'problematic', as the period of being a 'youth' (typically viewed as 13-19 years of age) is one of self-discovery and identity development, when new opportunities and adventures open up, and young people's personal biographies take new shapes.[7] Nevertheless, the lives of early-twenty-first-century global youths are impacted by (among other things) global economic changes, educational shifts and changing responses to relationships and household formation, affording greater freedoms and opportunities at the same time as increasing responsibility and competition between individuals.[8] As these trends influence how young people's lifelong outcomes are framed, their increasingly individualized experiences present structural challenges that are 'faced most acutely by the least resourced', reinforcing the impact of social, cultural and economic inequalities on generating unequal outcomes.[9]

Young people should not be seen as a homogenous group, and – while there are many common experiences – structural factors impact differently to affect the extent to which individual young people have choice and agency over their response to these. Youth work has a role precisely because many young people's autonomy is constrained as they struggle to negotiate the effects of these forces.[10] Moreover, as well as having to deal with issues related specifically to adolescence, the postmodern world presents young people with myriad challenges, the experience of which is particular to this era, and which combine uniquely to create a global crisis in young people's mental health and well-being.[11] Poverty, precarity, inequality, stress, competitive pressures to succeed and loneliness are undermining the life chances of large numbers of increasingly isolated and marginalized young people.[12]

All of these conditions have been exacerbated by the global Covid-19 pandemic: lockdowns, inactivity and self-isolation, and – in extreme cases – parental neglect/abuse have had especially adverse effects on young people, heightening the need for youth workers to enhance collective well-being over the coming years.[13]

Youth work and professionally loving practice

When these pressures are considered together, it is easy to understand why many young people might succumb to a depoliticized and passive form of learnt helplessness.[14] However, practitioners can mobilize love as the antidote to the destructive power of this sense of hopelessness, fuelling practice with 'critical optimism' by demonstrating their love of humanity to tackle oppressive and dehumanizing structures.[15] The all-encompassing power of loving practice inculcates radical hope about the possibility of an ethical, more humane future, in which individuals are able to imagine possibilities for life to flourish, beyond the constraints of their current circumstances.[16] This form of practice – imbued with love, humility, faith in and solidarity with others, hope and critical thinking – can help young people overcome the denigration they feel, moving them to a place of empowered resistance based on new understandings of their own oppression.

Youth work addresses the needs and interests articulated by young people themselves, promotes autonomy, self-reliance, self-esteem and empowerment while embracing diversity, challenging oppression and promoting social justice.[17] The relationship between the practitioner and young people is integral to this process, as – unlike other practitioners, who are required to maintain 'professional distance' from their 'clients' – youth workers are encouraged to overcome this distance to develop a partnership with the young person, characterized as '*a covenant ... in which Youth Worker and young person work together to heal hurts, to repair damage, to grow into responsibility, and to promote new ways of being*'.[18]

The importance of these relationships for helping young people navigate the new experiences and challenges of 'youth' cannot be overstated, especially where the young person has had a poor experience of or no meaningful familial relationship.[19] They are particularly important for the most vulnerable young people, who may be prone to heightened peer pressure and risky behaviour, by showing them how to develop feelings of self-worth. Their experience of attachments to practitioners helps young people to experiment with their affective responses to the challenges that relationships present. An empathic values-based practice can help sustain and contribute towards the overall flourishing and well-being of young people.[20]

My conceptualization of youth work *professional love* in practice builds on the view that early years practice should be informed by a 'pedagogy of love', ensuring that all children 'know and understand that they are worthy of being loved', providing a basis for their 'emotional resilience, learning and ultimately independence'.[21] Page further asserts that children require 'sensitive, skilled, loving, special adults with whom they have formed a deep and sustaining relationship'.[22] This is even more important for children who have experienced poorly attached relationships in their families, or when the professional caregiver's natural feelings towards an individual child are not instinctively warm and loving.

While youth work is not directly commensurate with early years work, practice can be enriched and becomes more valuable and impactful only when practitioners exhibit motivational displacement and attunement towards the young person they are working with, and are able to develop deep, sustaining, respectful and reciprocal relationships with them. Furthermore, by deliberately investing in a level of professional emotional intimacy as opposed to a level of professional distance, practitioners intellectualize their experience of the relationship as 'loving'.[23] Conceived as a form of 'love labour',[24] youth work should sustain people as 'emotionally and relationally engaged social beings' by being affect-driven and 'other-centred', and demonstrating that moral commitment, effort, time and energy have a place in emotional, mental, physical and cognitive work.[25] Hence, the practitioner must be able to actively demonstrate their love for the young person in all that they say and do, to develop and sustain purposive relationships that are genuine, trusting and respectful, and that are experienced as something similar to the compelling urge of care derived from pre-established (e.g. familial and friendship) relationships. A final aspect that should be present in sustained, relational-based practice is a degree of mutuality that is usually present in love labour.[26]

Ensuring ethically sound practice

This raises the potential for professionally loving practice to be misconstrued, or for strong emotional feelings to impair professional judgement and decision-making, particularly as youth work features many elements of friendship and the use of language codes familiar to young people which can potentially make them feel that the youth worker is their friend.[27] For instance, a young person may find the informal nature of the professional relationship confusing, meaning that the practitioner is responsible for ensuring clarity about the relationship, so that professionally loving practice does not cause confusion. Similarly, where a young person has not previously experienced a positive relationship with their parents, the practitioner must avoid being drawn into a relationship reflecting that of a surrogate parent/carer. Furthermore, as the young person may entrust the practitioner with deeply personal elements of their selves, they must make the young person feel that it is safe to be vulnerable.

As in all relational work, practitioners need to be aware of the potential impact of their positional power on the (re)actions of young people and the significance of 'choice' in relation to the young person's engagement in the relationship (if it does not meet their needs, the young person should be able to disengage from the process).[28] Power also features in the practitioner's multiple accountabilities (to the young person, their family, their employer, funders, etc.), with its potential impact being intensified when there is an affective or emotional dimension to the relationship.

Professionally loving practice comes with emotional and psychological costs for the practitioner, who – through excessive exposure to emotional labour – may lose touch with their authentic sense of personhood.[29] A blurring of the lines dividing professional and personal interactions places extra pressure on the practitioner who may become or appear less authentic in their work with young people, thereby undermining the potential their relational work offers.

Love and youth work: Listening to practitioners' voices

The rest of this chapter is informed by practitioners' contributions to an online survey, conducted shortly before the outbreak of Covid-19, and uses their voices to illuminate the themes addressed so far along with the practicalities of enacting professionally loving practice. Invitations and a link to the survey were emailed to 1,000 contacts on a professional networking site; I limited the sample to the first hundred responses to ensure the data set was manageable. Respondents live and work in disparate countries (including Australia, Bosnia, France, Ireland, Kenya, Sweden and Uganda), although the majority are UK-based (45 per cent England, 25 per cent Scotland, 10 per cent Northern Ireland and one from Wales). While only twelve respondents' current job title is *youth worker*, at least thirty-five have a professional qualification in youth work. A further twenty-eight respondents identify themselves as being in a management role in a range of youth work contexts. Of the rest, six respondents are employed as *support workers* and two as *social workers*, while three are employed in residential care; and other roles occupied by respondents include lecturer (three), foster carers (two), youth justice worker and the like.

Maintaining quality professional relationships

All respondents acknowledge the importance of the relationship between practitioner and young person, ascribing particular importance to being compassionate, acknowledging feelings and vulnerabilities, and demonstrating to young people that they are important to you. Allowing people to feel that they are worthy of love and that they are loved is felt to be 'essential/very important' by 87 per cent of respondents. As one respondent asserts: 'Young people's early experiences of positive, safe and caring people are crucial, and anything missing, lacking or negative can impact them into adulthood.'

A third of respondents identify consistency as key to ensuring the quality and impact of practitioners' relationships with young people, along with demonstrating genuine interest in their lives, concerns and aspirations. Typically, this involves for one practitioner 'finding out about the young person, their needs, perspective, ambitions. Being interested, friendly, welcoming, questioning.' For others, learning about the young person's personality, beliefs, environment and problems makes them 'feel seen' and demonstrates acceptance, especially when 'listening to their rants'.

Love features most in responses as a means of ensuring the *quality* of the relationship. One respondent asserts that practitioners should 'love them simply because they are human beings'; another suggesting that 'if people don't show love and respect with one another as adults, it will also be true of children they serve'.

Demonstrating love in professional relationships with young people

Respondents' views demonstrate the complexity of engaging in professionally loving relationships with young people. For many respondents, love is clearly something which they embrace as a driving force in their practice, as illustrated here:

> Love is at the centre of all that I do. I believe love is extremely important – it shows how genuine you are, enables you to be caring, helps a young person to develop and see what love is for themselves. If we don't show love how can we expect to see a loving response back from a young person? Love is interlinked with so many other important aspects and values too.

Typifying other responses, this comment highlights the conscious growth of love in practice:

> When I started out, I didn't expect to love my clients, but I do. It's a different kind of love than loving your own child or your friend or your partner, but, like those relationships, the love just comes across if it's genuine.

Presence and consistency

Over half of responses refer to the need to 'be there' and to be consistent in one's dealings with young people for them to feel loved. This reflects the impermanence of many key relationships in young people's lives, and the need to deliver on promises made to young people, 'too many of whom have been let down by adults too many times'.

Boundaries feature in comments on consistency, many highlighting their importance in helping young people feel safe. One residential worker emphasizes the importance of 'structure and routine' in the lives of the young people they work with, including eating meals together. Similarly, modelling and expecting appropriate behaviour features in several respondents' characterization of professionally loving practice, with one describing this as 'being considerate to young people's needs without indulging their whims'.

Responses also suggest that being present and consistent requires a carefully considered and crafted use of humour, warmth and any emotions (including anger) to show empathy ('definitely *not* sympathy'). Love demonstrated this way can allow for the emergence of a 'felt connection', something that 'cannot be forced, but is still within the professional boundary'. Similarly, several respondents identified forgiveness for previous 'transgressions' as a means of demonstrating your continued availability for the young person. One respondent linked forgiveness and love thus:

> Love is about attending to people: listening to them, seeing them for who they are despite some of their 'behaviours'. You have to see past this. I will accept them even when they mess up, without judgement and without anger.

Attentiveness

The importance of greeting each individual young person 'properly' every time you meet them features repeatedly, for instance to ensure 'they feel that my day is better now they have arrived'. Suggestions included welcoming them with a smile and a verbal greeting, using their name; making them cups of tea; maintaining eye contact when talking, thereby emphasizing that the young person is 'at the centre of your thoughts'.

Contributions linking communication to attentiveness include the suggestion that practitioners operate 'from a place of humility'. One French youth worker stressed that the relationship should not be 'about knowing more, or bestowing help. It's about drawing alongside and listening. Finding out what they need first and foremost.' Remembering the content of previous conversations, and being interested in what has happened about things you have discussed before also features in many responses. Similarly, incorporating elements of the individual stories of young people (such as 'the small things like what they like to eat or music they like') in plans for sessions and activities is another way respondents demonstrate love to young people.

Language and touch

Around two-thirds of respondents highlight the importance of language in conveying feeling and of bolstering young people's sense of identify and self-worth. Uniquely, one respondent's employer encourages staff to use the word 'love' in their interactions with young people as a form of 'affirmation of their place with us'. A quarter of respondents feel that overt physical expressions of love for young people (touch, kissing, cuddling, etc.) are deemed inappropriate. Nevertheless, another quarter advocated for the physical expression of *professional love*, including one therapist who acknowledged they are 'privileged to have the occasional hug', asserting that:

> The professional relationship in every circumstance is an intimate one, where young folk share experiences they would only share with people close to them. I fear with the lack of physical contact – that offers assurance and compassion – we've somehow thrown the baby out with the bath water.

One respondent gives equal prominence to 'sitting on the ground with them – less standing up' as to 'hugs, kisses, kind words, respectful listening and laughter together'. Other responses suggest that increasingly risk-averse and 'safeguarding-obsessed' settings and policies hamper their relationships with – and impede the development of – young people. Practitioners need to learn 'not to be afraid of appropriate contact', including 'rebuffing them if they pounce on you'.

Supervision is identified as a way to help practitioners navigate potential pitfalls (to avoid becoming too emotionally invested in relationships with young people; to manage boundaries effectively; to ensure 'courageous acts of love' are not misinterpreted as a precursor to intimacy; etc.). Respondents feel that this support should come from experienced practitioners who have managed the complexities of professionally loving relationships themselves.

Obstacles to professionally loving practice

Three respondents claim that there are no obstacles to professionally loving practice, as long as practitioners 'follow professional values and ethics', or/and 'start with the right motivation', or/and have sufficient time to commit to developing one-to-one relationships with young people. However, as summarized below, most respondents' practice is subject to at least one obstacle to professionally loving practice.[30]

Personal limitations of young people

The young person's prior experience of relationships with significant adults (parents, carers, social workers, teachers, etc.) may have been negative/abusive, undermining their ability to sustain rich relationships with practitioners. One respondent typically finds young people 'often reject love because they don't want to form meaningful relationships due to them constantly being let down by people who are supposed to care for them'. This may result in trust issues or low self-esteem, inability to receive or believe positive feedback from adults, or trauma-induced behavioural issues. One respondent finds 'young people I work with expect me to be angry and "shouty". They meet me with an expectation of conflict and the main obstacle is getting them to understand that I can be compassionate.' Practitioners need, therefore, to 'stick with the young people and continue to show them love even when they display behaviours that tell you they don't want to be loved'.

Several respondents recognize that young people may not 'understand loving and caring relationships in the way we might do', often confusing the distinction between youth work and friendship. In particular, many young people struggle to accept *professional love* as 'appropriate', while some 'don't know how to receive love, or interpret love as sexual or a power dynamic'. Crucially, the young person's expectation – based on prior experience – that the relationship will be curtailed can leave them feeling suspicious and fearful.

Other obstacles to professionally loving relationships experienced by respondents include peer or family pressure on the young person not to engage, and being expected to engage in environments where they struggle already (e.g. school or home). Similarly, their exposure to chaotic influences in their lives (drugs, violence, homelessness, etc.) can make it even more difficult to engage in such relationships.

Personal limitations of staff

Interestingly, the majority of respondents feel their own personal limitations outweigh those of the young people with whom they work, with several identifying the impact of professional development on their understanding of what is appropriate in relationships. One – having been 'taught in social work not to be attached to my clients' – self-limits their relationships with young people. For another, their fear of 'going anywhere near a topic that could lead to a crossing of a professional boundary' has been 'drilled into' them in their training. Others worry that their perception of the likely difficulty in resetting boundaries once loosened might limit their professionally loving practice.

The fear of being perceived as showing interest in the young person only because of being paid to do so is another recurring theme, while some respondents are also concerned about setting young people up to fail in relationships with other practitioners not committed to providing the same degree of love, care or positive regard. In addition, the fear of failure permeates and inhibits professionally loving practice for some, with one respondent evoking the darkness of the moment: 'when you can't spark even the smallest sense of hope or worth, and therefore they can't see the reason to try anything'.

Many respondents' initial route into youth work reflects their own stories of oppression, vulnerability and trauma. Some respondents are conscious that unresolved trauma may inhibit effective relationship-based practice, as young people's experiences might trigger their own emotional response. Furthermore, respondents worry about 'compassion fatigue', with one clarifying: 'If you experience, through love and compassion, the pain of all your clients – that's a lot of pain'. This relates to stress, an oft-cited obstacle to professionally loving practice emanating from practitioners or/and inadequate supervision, leaving many respondents feeling overtired or stretched.

Legal and organizational constraints

Over half of respondents feel that policies constrain their ability to engender supportive, caring or/and loving relationships with young people, with safeguarding legislation and policies seen as particularly problematic in this regard. All respondents accept that safeguarding rightly permeates all aspects of person-centred practice with young people, though many feel the implementation of safeguarding policy impedes relational practice, and the implementation of *professional love* in particular. For instance, one respondent feels that agencies and institutions 'have their hands tied by different approaches and protocols'. The requirement in safeguarding policy for staff to report anything that *might* indicate abuse inhibits respondents in their practice, as this requirement effectively 'betrays trust, and takes power away from the young person'.

In addition, around a third of respondents find policies requiring them to be physically distant from young people problematic, with many organizations proscribing physical contact altogether – something which several consider as potentially more damaging to the young person. One practitioner 'feel(s) the need to sometimes be guarded rather than open'; another is concerned that 'we aren't supposed to have physical contact, when sometimes they just need a hug'; while another 'would sometimes love to give a young person a hug, just because at that moment it's exactly what they need. I do not, however, as it would be viewed as crossing safeguarding boundaries'.

Practical considerations

The majority of respondents feel that their workload (specifically the numbers of young people with whom they are expected to work) mitigates against the development of profound relationships, undermining the potential to enact *professional love*. For one respondent 'making and sustaining loving relationships takes time plus commitment', and the lack of time is the main obstacle to effective relational practice.

Similarly, limitations in resources can result in practitioners not seeing young people often enough, or for too short a time, or in group sessions when what they need is personal attention. For several respondents, the demands of group work often mean that 'a young person in need may not get as much time as they should have'. Other respondents cite bureaucracy and the outcome-driven focus of funders as obstacles to relational practice, especially as it is 'hard to quantify care'.

Lack of understanding, support and trust among managers and colleagues inhibits professionally loving practice. In some cases, respondents' colleagues are simply 'uncomfortable' with their approach; in others, a lack of commitment and enthusiasm means colleagues fail to 'see the potential of young people and don't have empathy or understanding of their situation'.

A contested notion

Not all respondents accept the premise that there is a role for love in youth work practice, with seven contradicting the request to describe how they demonstrate love in their professional relationships with young people. Some are clear that they 'don't want to create loving relationships', with others clarifying that this relates to the use of the word 'love' in relation to their practice. For one respondent, the term is 'too intimate', though they acknowledge that love is 'manifested in myself (and others) when our work is not a *job* but considered a *vocation*'. Another feels that love is 'a deep personal connection, and I am not sure that it is realistic to expect that working with so many young people'.

A small number of respondents think that 'loving' practice could open young people up to potential harm if implemented by practitioners who do not have their best interests at heart: 'we know some adults will exploit trust and vulnerability. This means love and care in a boundaried and carefully supervised environment.' Similarly, some respondents are fearful that enacting *professional love* might open them up to allegations of abuse, particularly in their engagement with vulnerable young people where relational work must not be open to misinterpretation. Here, respondents see the pitfalls around the requirement to maintain boundaries and 'professional distance', which – if overstepped – can lead to 'fear of malpractice; fear of being perceived as abusive'. For one respondent, policing these perceived boundaries results in 'fear in forming relationships with young people, which is to their detriment'.

Three respondents feel more comfortable with the term 'care', which they describe variously as 'enthusiasm and passion for their safety and happiness'; 'doing what you say you will, giving young people time and space'; and 'a two-way thing, a relationship and stick with it good or bad'. Similarly, one respondent asserts, 'I demonstrate good support, not love'; while another prefers 'unconditional positive regard', a 'more spacious' term than *professional love*.

Conclusions

Notwithstanding the fact that different perspectives on the appropriateness of professionally loving practice are identified in this research, youth work practitioners should not be afraid of entering into the 'deep personal connections' that one wary respondent cautioned against. Indeed, I take encouragement from the fact that so many practitioners were prepared to engage in this research, and that the majority of them used the experience as an opportunity to reflect on making their practice more loving and ensuring the well-being of young people in different settings across the globe. The central message their contributions offer is that *professional love* is not only desirable as part of the youth work practitioner's 'toolkit', but that some practitioners have already devised sophisticated approaches to embodying love in practice and use it as a central tenet of their work with oppressed, marginalized or otherwise vulnerable young people.

My attempt to summarize the key elements of *professional love* in practice has identified three aspects which are compatible with the professional values and principles underpinning youth work: presence and consistency; attentiveness; and language/touch. These all feature in one practitioner's articulation of how they demonstrate love in their practice, which encapsulates my understanding of *professional love* perfectly:

> I smile with them, laugh with them, know them completely and demonstrate to them they can trust me. I comfort them when they are hurt or upset, I give them names for their emotions. I tell them I love them and make an effort to praise certain aspects of their character which make them unique. I'm always happy to see them and I think that demonstrates love. I am consistent in responding to their needs and similarly consistent in setting appropriate boundaries in terms of behaviour management.

The practitioner's willingness and ability to demonstrate that they know and are deeply interested in each young person with whom they work, remember what is important to them and stick with them is at the heart of a professionally loving practice. Crucially, given what we know about behavioural drivers, professionally loving practitioners must continue to show the young people they work with love even (or particularly) when they display behaviours that suggest they don't want to be loved. This is perhaps where the practitioner's conscious use of self comes to the fore, drawing on their own pool of experience to demonstrate empathy and understanding, and to nurture mutuality and reciprocity within the relationship. Indeed, it is the presence of these qualities in the relationship that I feel distinguishes professionally loving practice from care, which is nevertheless a component part of *professional love*.

I recognize that potential pitfalls exist, of which practitioners must be aware. Not least among these are concerns expressed by several respondents about the importance of safeguarding as a foundational aspect of practice, and the potential for genuine professionally loving practice to be misconstrued, or to impact on the necessarily flexible and sometimes porous boundaries of youth work practice.[31] Even worse, as in any profession, those determined to do harm could adapt this form of practice to suit their nefarious ends, with potentially catastrophic consequences. Nevertheless, as a form of humanistic practice, it is not unreasonable to seek out the best in people, and deterrents identified by this study can be built into practice management to bolster existing safeguarding measures. A focus on the role of supervision (seen as a cornerstone of youth work management[32]) was specifically foregrounded, suggesting that *professional love* can be critiqued and supported (and, potentially, modelled) in the relationship between the professionally loving practitioner and their supervisor. This offers the potential to enhance the benefits assigned to *professional love*, to augment measures to protect young people from unscrupulous practice and to protect against the recreation of young people's negative experiences of relationships with adults.

The different experiences and perspectives of the broad range of practitioners who participated in this research suggest that self-healing is a crucial part of the practitioner's preparation for professionally loving relational practice with young people: practitioners should only seek to enact *professional love* if and when they are psychologically and emotionally fit to do so, to obviate the potential for damage to them and to the young people under their care. Given our understanding of the emotional and psychological cost to practitioners of love labour, and the emerging interest in self-healing as preparation for community development and other forms of practice, this is perhaps the main area where my research will focus going forward.[33]

Notes

1 See Huw Blacker, 'Relationships, Friendship and Youth Work', in *Youth Work Practice*, ed. Tony Jeffs and Mark Smith (Basingstoke: Palgrave Macmillan, 2010), 15–30; Kate Sapin, *Essential Skills for Youth Work Practice*, 2nd edn (London: Sage, 2013), 57–72; Tania de St Croix, 'Youth Work, Performativity and the New Youth Impact Agenda: Getting Paid for Numbers?', *Journal of Education Policy* 33, no. 3 (2018): 414–38.

2 Peter Hart, 'The Reality of Relationships with Young People in Caring Professions: A Qualitative Approach to Professional Boundaries Rooted in Virtue Ethics', *Children and Youth Services Review* 83 (2017): 248–54; Jeffrey Jones and Nancy Deutsch, 'Relational Strategies in After-School Settings: How Staff-Youth Relationships Support Positive Development', *Youth & Society* 43, no. 4 (2011): 1381–406.

3 de St Croix, 'Youth Work and Performativity', 414–38; Hart, 'The Reality of Relationships', 248–54.

4 Jools Page, 'Characterising the Principles of *Professional Love* in Early Childhood Care and Education', *International Journal of Early Years Education* 26, no. 2 (2018): 125–41.
5 bell hooks, *All about Love: New Visions* (New York: Harper Perennial, 2020); Paulo Freire, *Pedagogy of the Oppressed* (New York: Herder & Herder, 1970).
6 For example, Page, 'Characterising the Principles of *Professional Love*', 125–41.
7 Alan France, Stephen Roberts, Julia Coffey and Catherine Waite, *Youth Sociology* (London: Red Globe Press, 2020).
8 Dan Woodman and Johanna Wyn, *Youth & Generation: Rethinking Change & Inequality in the Lives of Young People* (London: Sage, 2014).
9 Ibid., 6.
10 Simon Bradford, *Sociology, Youth & Youth Work Practice* (London: Palgrave Macmillan, 2012).
11 Martin E. Purcell, 'Investigating the Transformational Potential of "*Professional Love*" in Work with Young People', *Radical Community Work Journal* 3, no. 1 (2018); Martin E. Purcell, Jools Page and Jim Reid, 'Love in a Time of *Colic*: Mobilizing *Professional Love* in Relationships with Children and Young People to Promote Their Resilience and Wellbeing', *Child & Youth Services* 43, no. 1 (2022): 3–27.
12 Janet Batsleer and James Duggan, *Young and Lonely: The Social Conditions of Loneliness* (Bristol: Policy Press, 2020).
13 Liat Levita, *Initial Research Findings on the Impact of COVID-19 on the Well-Being of Young People Aged 13 to 24 in the UK* (Sheffield: University of Sheffield, 2020); Anant Kumar and K. Rajasekharan Nayar, 'COVID 19 and Its Mental Health Consequences', *Journal of Mental Health* 30, no. 1 (2020): 1–2.
14 Henry A. Giroux, 'War Culture and the Politics of Intolerable Violence', *Symplokē* 25, nos. 1–2 (2017): 191–218.
15 Paulo Freire, *The Politics of Education: Culture, Power and Liberation* (South Hadley, MA: Bergin & Garvey, 1985), 85.
16 David Robinson-Morris, 'Radical Love, (R)evolutionary Becoming: Creating an Ethic of Love in the Realm of Education through Buddhism and Ubuntu', *Urban Review* 51 (2019): 28–9.
17 Sapin, *Essential Skills*, 3–21.
18 Howard Sercombe, 'Youth Workers as Professionals: Managing Dual Relationships and Maintaining Boundaries', in *Ethical Issues in Youth Work*, ed. Sarah Banks (London: Routledge, 2010), 78, italics in original.
19 Nick Frost and Melanie Watts, 'Young People's Transition to Adulthood', in *Human Growth & Development in Children and Young People*, ed. Jonathan Parker and Sara Ashencaen Crabtree (Bristol: Policy Press, 2020), 153–70.

20. David Shemmings, *Attachment in Children and Young People* (Dartington: Research in Practice, 2016).
21. Page, 'Characterising the Principles of *Professional Love*', 134.
22. Jools Page, 'Developing *Professional Love* in Early Childhood Settings', in *Lived Spaces of Infant-Toddler Education and Care: Exploring Diverse Perspectives on Theory, Research and Practice,* ed. Linda Harrison and Jennifer Sumsion (London: Springer, 2014), 125.
23. Page, 'Characterising the Principles of *Professional Love*'.
24. Kathleen Lynch, 'Love Labour as a Distinct and Non-Commodifiable Form of Labour', *Sociological Review* 55, no. 3 (2007): 550–70.
25. Lynch, 'Love Labour', 553.
26. Ibid., 559.
27. Sercombe, 'Youth Workers as Professionals', 78–9.
28. Sapin, *Essential Skills*, 57–9.
29. Arlie Hochschild, *The Managed Heart: Commercialisation of Human Feeling* (Berkeley: University of California Press, 1983).
30. Or 'to engendering supportive, caring or/and loving relationships with children and young people in their care', as per the question.
31. Hart, 'The Reality of Relationships', 1381–1406.
32. Margo Herman, 'Reflective Practice Meets Youth Work Supervision', *Youth & Policy* 109 (2012): 118–28.
33. Hochschild, *Managed Heart*; Lynch, 'Love Labour'; Phia van der Watt, 'Prepared for a Journey into Wounded Communities – and into the Self', *Community Development Journal* 55, no. 4 (2020): 662–79.

Bibliography

Batsleer, Janet, and James Duggan. *Young and Lonely: The Social Conditions of Loneliness.* Bristol: Policy Press, 2020.

Blacker, Huw. 'Relationships, Friendship and Youth Work'. In *Youth Work Practice*, edited by Tony Jeffs and Mark Smith, 15–30. Basingstoke: Palgrave Macmillan, 2010.

Bradford, Simon. *Sociology, Youth & Youth Work Practice.* London: Palgrave Macmillan, 2012.

de St Croix, Tania. 'Youth Work, Performativity and the New Youth Impact Agenda: Getting Paid for Numbers?'. *Journal of Education Policy* 33, no. 3 (2018): 414–38.

France, Alan, Stephen Roberts, Julia Coffey and Catherine Waite. *Youth Sociology.* London: Red Globe Press, 2020.

Freire, Paulo. *Pedagogy of the Oppressed*. New York: Herder & Herder, 1970.
Freire, Paulo. *The Politics of Education: Culture, Power and Liberation*. South Hadley, MA: Bergin & Garvey, 1985.
Frost, Nick, and Melanie Watts. 'Young People's Transition to Adulthood'. In *Human Growth & Development in Children and Young People*, edited by Jonathan Parker and Sara Ashencaen Crabtree, 153–70. Bristol: Policy Press, 2020.
Giroux, Henry. 'War Culture and the Politics of Intolerable Violence'. *Symplokē* 25, nos. 1–2 (2017): 191–218.
Hart, Peter. 'The Reality of Relationships with Young People in Caring Professions: A Qualitative Approach to Professional Boundaries Rooted in Virtue Ethics'. *Children and Youth Services Review* 83 (2017): 248–54.
Herman, Margo. 'Reflective Practice Meets Youth Work Supervision'. *Youth & Policy* 109 (2012): 118–28.
Hochschild, Arlie Russell. *The Managed Heart: Commercialisation of Human Feeling*. Berkeley: University of California Press, 1983.
hooks, bell. *All about Love: New Visions*. New York: Harper Perennial, 2020.
Jones, Jeffrey, and Nancy Deutsch. 'Relational Strategies in After-School Settings: How Staff-Youth Relationships Support Positive Development'. *Youth & Society* 43, no. 4 (2011): 1381–1406.
Kumar, Anant, and K. Rajasekharan Nayar. 'COVID 19 and Its Mental Health Consequences'. *Journal of Mental Health* 30, no. 1 (2020): 1–2.
Levita, Liat. *Initial Research Findings on the Impact of COVID-19 on the Well-Being of Young People Aged 13 to 24 in the UK*. Sheffield: University of Sheffield, 2020.
Lynch, Kathleen. 'Love Labour as a Distinct and Non-Commodifiable Form of Labour'. *Sociological Review* 55, no. 3 (2007): 550–70.
Page, Jools. 'Characterising the Principles of *Professional Love* in Early Childhood Care and Education'. *International Journal of Early Years Education* 26, no. 2 (2018): 125–41.
Page, Jools. 'Developing *Professional Love* in Early Childhood Settings'. In *Lived Spaces of Infant-Toddler Education and Care: Exploring Diverse Perspectives on Theory, Research and Practice*, edited by Linda Harrison and Jennifer Sumsion, 119–30. London: Springer, 2014.
Purcell, Martin E. 'Investigating the Transformational Potential of *Professional Love* in Work with Young People'. *Radical Community Work Journal* 3, no. 1 (2018).
Purcell, Martin E., Jools Page and Jim Reid. 'Love in a Time of *Colic*: Mobilizing *Professional Love* in Relationships with Children and Young People to Promote Their Resilience and Wellbeing'. *Child & Youth Services* 43, no. 1 (2022): 3–27.
Robinson-Morris, David. 'Radical Love, (R)evolutionary Becoming: Creating an Ethic of Love in the Realm of Education through Buddhism and Ubuntu'. *Urban Review* 51 (2019): 26–45.
Sapin, Kate. *Essential Skills for Youth Work Practice*. 2nd edn. London: Sage, 2013.

Sercombe, Howard. 'Youth Workers as Professionals: Managing Dual Relationships and Maintaining Boundaries'. In *Ethical Issues in Youth Work*, edited by Sarah Banks, 77–91. London: Routledge, 2010.

Shemmings, David. *Attachment in Children and Young People*. Dartington: Research in Practice, 2016.

van der Watt, Phia. 'Prepared for a Journey into Wounded Communities – and Into the Self'. *Community Development Journal* 55, no. 4 (2020): 662–79.

Woodman, Dan, and Johanna Wyn. *Youth & Generation: Rethinking Change & Inequality in the Lives of Young People*. London: Sage, 2014.

9

Reciprocity, love and market in Brazilian care work for the elderly

Anna Bárbara Araujo

Introduction

What is the place of love in care work? In a deeply unequal society like Brazil, what forms has love taken as part of care work? Love has been discussed by several care theorists. Arlie Hochschild (2003), for instance, characterizes love as a commodity that is being extracted from poor countries.[1] She investigates how women in these countries migrate to the Global North to do care work, and start to direct their motherly love to the children of their employers, leaving their own family behind. Viviana Zelizer points out the importance of negotiation in establishing the appropriate interplay of love and money in intimate relations, including care work, so that money does not necessarily contaminate personal bonds.[2] These theoretical insights come in response to the significant growth in occupations related to the care domain in developed countries. This growth results from sociodemographic changes such as population aging and the entry of a higher proportion of women into the labour market. Such changes are especially prevalent in Brazil, which has seen a rise in the number of elderly needing care and an increasingly strong presence of women in the workforce since the 1960s, which reduces their availability for providing unpaid family care.[3] At the same time, the prevalence of ineffective and narrow public policies aimed at elderly care turns it into a private problem to be solved by individuals. In these conditions, privileged Brazilian families tend to contract out their care needs.

Several authors have insisted on the effects of emotions and affections on care work. In Hochschild's famous analysis, for example, in the evocatively titled essay 'Love and Gold', she argues that paid and professional care would replace that performed by families, especially by mothers.[4] This transformation of care, defined as a 'heart transplant', will include an emotional dimension and will have global reach with the growth of female migration related to care jobs.[5] The tension between work relationships and emotions is also discussed by Gutiérrez Rodríguez who, in her research on migrant care workers, cites the case of a professional who established such deep emotional dependence with her employer that she simply did not see how she could leave her job.[6] In these cases, intimacy can act as a kind of trap that limits care workers' choice in relation to making decisions about their own work.

Part of this literature, especially the studies inspired by Hochschild, is anchored in a paradigm which England calls 'prisoners of love' – that is, the idea that the presence of emotions would contaminate work relationships, making it difficult to exercise utilitarian rationality and workers' bargaining capacity.[7] However, authors such as Tronto insist that the emotions of care, and sometimes domestic work, can be understood as a subaltern ethics, potentially disruptive to market relations.[8] In a recent article, I discussed the analytical weaknesses of this position, suggesting that the 'ethics of care' paradigm produces a normative and idealized vision of care.[9] By taking care as a practical ethics that should be valued, these studies end up minimizing class and race hierarchies that are reproduced and renovated in care relations.

How, then, to frame love in care work? I argue that it is essential to focus the analysis on inequalities related to income, gender and race, and the way they are mobilized as part of the work. It is also fundamental to regard how care workers negotiate and resist definitions of love offered by their employers. This becomes clear when considering the Brazilian context, as I will show below.

This research took place in an employment agency located in the city of Rio de Janeiro, the second largest and richest city in Brazil. The agency had more than 6,000 care workers registered at the time of research and was responsible for training care workers and placing them on the job market. I observed the company's routine for a month and conducted forty-five interviews with care workers. In this context, the company operates as a disciplining agent of work in which the very insertion in the labour market is the currency of negotiation.[10] That means that care workers who appear to be non-ideal workers can simply be left out from the database and never be invited to job interviews.

This chapter focuses on the work performed by care workers who have their services offered on the labour market through a private enterprise. It addresses the tension between, on the one hand, the requirements for formalization and professionalization of care and, on the other, the active character, on part of the enterprise, in building an image of care workers as entrepreneurs of values associated with reciprocity and family, especially love.[11] I show how love is transformed in a moral and emotional demand for care workers and how they exercise agency in the way they understand love, reflecting on its gendered and racialized aspects.

Care inequalities in Brazil

In Brazil, most care workers (*cuidadoras* in Portuguese) are domestic workers by law. The majority of them do not have access to health training courses of long duration or a formal certification. Some have a background in nursing, but they tend to identify themselves as nurse aides, instead of care workers.

In 2018, there were approximately 210 million inhabitants in Brazil, of which 6.6 million were domestic workers, according to official sources.[12] This means that almost 15 per cent of the female labour force in the country is engaged in domestic work.[13] In the previous decade, about 16 per cent of Brazilian households, most of which were headed by white people, hired at least one domestic worker (Guerra 2017).[14] Today Brazil has the largest number of domestic workers in the world.[15] This deep national dependence on domestic workers can be understood as a reflection of racial and income inequalities. Brazil was the last country to abolish slavery, and it left strong marks on our sociability:

> Slavery left very deep marks on the imaginary and later social practices … Around it, an ethics of degraded work was built, a disparaging image of the people, or of the national element, a moral indifference of the elites in relation to the needs of the majority, and a social hierarchy of great rigidity and leaked by enormous inequalities.[16]

Domestic work is a socially devalued job – as reflected in low wages – which on average fall below the national minimum wage, long hours and high rates of informality.[17] In 2018, black women made up 63 per cent of domestic workers in the country.[18] The formalization of employment links, which gives access to labour rights as paid vacations, retirement pensions and sick leave, reached only about 28.6 per cent of the category of domestic workers in general.[19]

The recent International Labour Organization (ILO) report on care work worldwide[20] shows that Brazil, Uruguay, Argentina and Venezuela stand out, in Latin America, as countries that solve their demand for care by hiring housekeepers, nannies and care workers for the elderly. The high presence of domestic service indicates both the lack of adequate or sufficient care policies and the income inequality prevalent in these countries. Indeed, it demonstrates that the greater the income inequality, the greater the likelihood that paid domestic employment would make up a large proportion of the total employment.[21] Brazil, then, becomes an especially interesting case as a privileged locus for understanding the chains that bind care work and love in a deeply unequal society.

In the next section, I show how emotions are stratified, echoing Eduardo Bonilla-Silva, who discusses race, class and gender as categories that affect the circulation of emotions in our societies.[22] To this end, I analyse love as a moral and emotional demand in care work, considering that the majority of care workers are black and poor women providing services to white and wealthy families. I also highlight their agency in modulating these demands.

Rather than discussing whether affections and emotions have a pre-discursive origin, whether they are mere bodily responses or whether they are the fruit of the individual psyche, I am interested, inspired by feminist theorist Sara Ahmed, in discussing the sociality of affections and emotions. I argue that affections and emotions are thought of as cultural and social practices.[23] In this sense, affections and emotions have a performative dimension, insofar as they adjust different types of action.

Reciprocity as an icon: The production of moral and emotional demands in care work

My research suggests that the femininity norms that guide family care are shifted to the dynamics of paid care, and that the ideals of female reciprocity and solidarity are operated and transformed by the market, becoming moral and emotional demands to care workers. They also connect to historical stereotypes that construct black women as servants.[24] I analyse the power relations that end up defining and entangling the practice of care through the production – and management – of the ambivalence between what I call here reciprocity and the market.

The analysis of moral and emotional demands of work can be useful to capture this tension between reciprocity and market in its various possible arrangements, but, for the purposes of this chapter, I will deal exclusively with the case of care workers. It is worth stating that the moral and emotional demands of care are more related to an idealization of female roles in unpaid care, consolidated through the ideals of altruism, affection and attention, than to the concrete relationships and practical situations where care activities happen, in the family and in the market.

It is important to understand that paid care work does not only reproduce gender hierarchies, but also reflects race and class hierarchies, as working-class women, migrants and racial minorities tend to be overrepresented among care workers.[25]

The racial axis of care work is particularly visible in analyses of the relationship between care work and migration. When analysing the working relationships established between elderly and migrant care workers in southern Italy, Lena Näre shows how certain nationalities (and ethnicities) were identified as a synonym for honesty and cleanliness by employers, and at the same time, how they expected the care workers to show gratitude, familial feeling and affection in their work.[26] Romero and Pérez, on the however, discuss how in the United States, non-white women, including immigrants, experience having their skills treated as 'natural' or 'cultural' qualities that frame them as 'ideal' babysitters, care workers or domestic workers.[27] Thus, American employers continue to express preferences for certain ethnic-racial groups based on their supposedly natural skills for care and domestic work.

In Brazil, where international immigration is generally not a significant factor in care work, gender and racial axes are visible through the cultural construction of reciprocity as a value. Reciprocity, according to Eric Sabourin's argument, can be understood as a feeling or an impulse of concern for the other that tends to translate into obligations towards him or her.[28] Reciprocity can take place through gifts between people or groups, but it can also manifest itself indirectly, through the circulation of (material and symbolic) goods between generations.

The notion of indirect reciprocity underlies unpaid and paid care work. Care would be animated by intergenerational reciprocities whose model is the family. Nevertheless, it is important to consider that the indirect reciprocity of care is gendered. It is mostly women who provide care, and the activity of these women as professional and family care workers is presupposed in the narratives about the importance of care for maintaining solidarity between different age groups.

Care often involves heavy, difficult and emotionally demanding work. Care workers tend to justify their work alluding to the idea of reciprocity: they care well because they expect to be taken care of in the future. Sometimes, they equate care with the construction of positive emotional bonds in family relationships. As one care worker stated: 'I want a treatment like what I give them [elderly people]. I ask God that my children will take good care of me. Because I take good care of them and I take care of other people too.'[29] In other words, I propose that the notion of reciprocity, as present in care workers' narratives, can be understood as part of an ideological construction that has the effect of justifying the sexual and racial division of labour. This implies considering that reciprocity operates, in this case, primarily at the representational level. This discursive construction on family relationships that privileges the notion of reciprocity guides care workers, insofar as it promotes the valuation and prescription of certain feelings and types of relationships, as I will show next.

Love as a work demand

I interviewed the director of the care agency where I conducted the research. When I asked her 'what does it take to be a good care worker?', this is what she answered:

> So, the first thing is that the person *loves serving*, right, *loves caring*, and has a lot of patience. And we try to evaluate at the time of the interview, we try to scrutinize it to see if she has the ideal profile or not. But we have no way of knowing, we always look for her last work reference. The checking department calls to see if she was a good employee, if she was patient, you know, all of that. *I think the main thing is that she loves and knows* [how to care]. Not everyone can be a care worker, there are a lot of people taking the course here and we see that they don't have the ideal profile, you know.

Love appears as an important notion in her discourse. It is possible to say that love is more than just one quality of good care workers; it constitutes a work demand, in that: (1) care workers are expected to have such quality; (2) this quality becomes part of the work and, as such, participates in the process of (de) valuing it; and (3) it is subject to employers' control.

The following section discusses three different narratives that touch on the importance of love for care workers. I treat them as modulations or variants of the same matrix, that is, love as a moral and emotional demand in the work performed by care workers. Each, however, represents a different level of professionalization. By professionalization I mean the different processes that have the effect of giving more autonomy and more control to the members of a particular professional occupation with reference to the contents and technical aspects of the work. In the case of care workers, professionalization is developed especially through training courses. The distribution, duration and price of these courses varies widely, as well as adherence to them, since participation in the courses is not an indispensable condition for exercising the occupation. What these courses have in common is the effect of producing standardized and formalized content on work and its procedures. They cover topics that go beyond technical knowledge and also discuss how the relationship between care worker and the elderly should be conducted.

Family love

Family love was a common theme among care workers. One of the interviewees, reminiscing about the time she spent caring for an eighty-year-old woman who had dementia, stated thus:

> The last one that I took care of, she called me mom. The last time she spoke, she called me her mother. And that, wow ... for me. Six months working with her, do you understand? She did all kinds of 'arts' [mess] in the world. The day she called me mom she never spoke again. But she recognized me as a mother until the last moment ... So, I was everything to her. When the other care worker arrived, she wouldn't take a shower for three days ... She was dirty. I went there, cleaned it all up, so I started to treat her like my daughter.

This excerpt clearly alludes to family care, as it evokes a fictitious kinship bond between the care worker and the elderly woman. This would be considered as the highest standard of professional care, understood as a deriving from and recreating the care women provided in the family, and it appears especially in the accounts of older care workers. They generally speak proudly of the ways in which they were called by the elderly people they cared for, as if family vocatives were a symbol of their good work. Mentioning the kinship bond, in this case, at the same time explains and justifies the caregivers' work. Driven by the notion of family love, and more than that, by the bonds of reciprocity and solidarity that are destined – or ideally would be destined – for those who are part of the family, these women accept to perform the dirty work that constitutes a significant part of care work, thus accepting the 'arts' of the elderly they care for.

Dirty work is a term developed by Everett Hughes to qualify jobs whose activities consist of engaging in issues that society, in general, does not know or does not want to deal with, because they are morally difficult.[30] The term was initially developed to address the work of Germans in concentration camps, but I understand that it can be used to analyse a variety of jobs and occupations, as it helps to clarify the mechanisms of social distribution which operate in morally condemnable or devalued practices.

Julia Twigg argues that care work requires dealing with bodily impurities, which also involves handling dirt and disgust.[31] Having to manipulate impurities always involves the risk of contamination – be it physical or moral. What matters, in this case, is that there are people – generally women, often black and poor women – that are subjected to these contaminations most frequently, people who deal with what many would not like to deal with or say they cannot handle.

For such care workers, who are often middle aged and less educated, the affective connection developed with the elderly they care for is treated as something very significant in their lives, and dirty work is less of a taboo than for other care workers. It is as if the affective bond acted against the sense of transgression attributed to the crossing of bodily boundaries, allowing the naturalness of acting on the other's body. In this way, this bond – crystallized in the imperative of love and affection – operates for as a kind of propellant of care, insofar as it is the condition that justifies and explains care work, as explained above.

What defines this type of narrative is precisely the erasure of boundaries, insofar as the emotional and physical approach between care worker and elderly person is valued and that this becomes symbolized as someone to whom everything is given and, in return, affection and admiration are received.

Humanitarian love

Love also appears in care workers' accounts in a more widespread way:

> So, first you have to love. Love the human being. Why? Because there are many elderly people ... their whole lives they carry characteristics that are only theirs.

So, some get crankier, others don't. And if you love, you learn to respect the limits of the elderly. Where I work, for example, there are elderly people who are difficult to deal with. So, if you don't have love, don't even try it. Another thing, if you're going to do it for the money, don't even try it. Because seeing the human being simply as a financial exchange, there is no way, you have to love.

The excerpt evokes love for others as a factor that guides care work. Here, there is a certain distance from family care models. Alternatively, it could be seen as its expansion, since the idea that morally commands it is that everyone is part of the same human family or community and deserves to be treated with care and respect as a result. There is the exaltation of a type of love that arises from the valorization of humanity, which, at least ideally, should extend to all its members.

This type of account is recurrent among religious care workers, especially Catholics and Evangelical Protestants. It is common for these care workers to mention that they choose not to know or not to take into account the past of the elderly they care for so that they can provide care regardless of moral judgements about their past lives. Their work is thus animated by the Christian principles of absolution, mercy and compassion. Despite the relative ideological departure from care based on the family model, it is clear that this type of account is built on a foundation of love and is rooted in a strong sense of selflessness and altruism.

These care workers express a negative moral judgement of care done 'only' in exchange for material goods. Instead, they value sacrifice. It is the sacrifice made in the name of love – moral and emotional demands of work, but also demands arising from the naturalization of female roles in the family and racial hierarchies that tend to construct 'natural servants' – that legitimizes care work. Without love there is no sacrifice and only money remains. This is treated as a profane thing, which has the potential to pollute the true sense of care. This sense of obligation attributed to care falls more heavily on black and poor women in Brazil. In contrast, white and educated women have more power to delegate care tasks to others.

Some authors think that economic interest 'contaminates' the care relationship and puts the care workers' good intentions in check. This is the position adopted by the Canadian economist Anthony Heyes, for example. He argues that care workers – he mentions specifically the case of nurses – ideally should receive low wages, as a way to protect patients from workers whose main motivation is earning money.[32] Evidently this thesis has been contested by feminist theorists who have questioned the opposition established between love and money – or economic interest and personal motivations – as mutually exclusive terms.[33] On the contrary, Zelizer shows that commercial exchanges and intimate personal relationships are profoundly interlinked whether emotionally, physically or psychologically.[34] Marriage, for example, usually involves some form of income and property sharing. Similarly, paid care work often includes emotional and economic exchanges.

Professional love

Some care workers, alternatively, mention love as part of the knowledges and practices related to care:

> Most of my patients, they don't speak anymore. They express themselves very little. So, my love comes down – comes down is a figure of speech – it's taking care of them: Always keep them clean, they peed, we change them soon. They pooped, we change them soon … Try to sit them down to rest because the elderly person lying down has accumulation of fluid in the lung and then there may be pneumonia … We give them the right food. We give good food, most of which are all mixed in a blender, right? But we try to give fresh food, cooked in the same day … This is our love, this is our care, this is our affection.

This account represents a greater departure from the previously presented family model of care. Here, love does not necessarily concern the establishment of emotional bonds with the elderly, but the application of techniques and knowledge aimed at their well-being. This narrative articulates the specialized, professionalized knowledge and the gendered moral and emotional grammar, which dictates reciprocity and solidarity with the other.

Although care workers who share this position experience the imperative of love in their daily work as an organizing principle of care, they do so by distancing themselves, albeit in a limited way, from the models of reciprocity and solidarity associated with family care. In this way, it is as if they strategically sought to secure their position in the paid labour market through the renunciation of the precepts considered to be proper to women, and specially, black women. They are the ones that most strongly embrace the professionalization model of care that is disseminated by enterprises like the one in which I conducted my research, even though this model is partially disseminated and is also partial in its contents, that is, it does not neutralize gender and race.

For care workers of this group, care is more of a technique than an undifferentiated gift or know-how that comes from their family socialization. Thus, it is not enough to be a woman, it is necessary that they specialize and qualify themselves through short courses, in addition to assuming a professional attitude – namely, among other things, that they distance themselves from the intimacy of the family.

It is not by chance that these care workers emphasize the control of feelings as a fundamental component of their work. That is, they understand that, although emotions and affections are part of their work, they need to be managed so that they do not interfere with their professional posture, as is clear in this statement:

> Sometimes you realize that you like your patient just as you like someone in your family. So you have to know how to separate things. We have to keep our professional place because we are not their family. We are professionals. We can like them, whatever, but in the patient's home, even in the middle of their family, we have to put ourselves as professionals. But liking [them] is inevitable.

Thus, care workers of this group elaborate strategies of distancing from the elderly: they avoid treating them in terms that resemble a family relationship and choose not to express an opinion on matters that they consider to be the responsibility of the family such as the frequency of visits by relatives.

For most professional care workers, emotions and feelings are always at stake, always in dispute. And, in most cases, hiding them, or consciously seeking to separate themselves from roles closer to the family, in favour of adopting a professional, formal posture represents a kind of protection against the difficulties of the work.

Since the path of affections and emotions is often translated as the path of favours, of the unbalanced exchange of gifts, of requests that are not denied by appreciation or consideration, of service and abuse, the path of professionalization seems the most strategic for these women. Alexandre Barbosa Fraga comments that it is common for Brazilian Domestic Workers Unions to value and seek to encourage the creation of more rational and contractual work relationships, since, when work relations are confused with family relations, workers' rights are more easily violated.[35] What is sought, in the cases of the care and domestic workers surveyed by Fraga, is a departure from the total benefits model, which is based on gift exchange, in the name of the supposed greater justice governed by the market exchange. The latter, however, implies, as is clear in the care worker's account quoted above, a tireless mediation of feelings and emotions, which here translates into the establishment of limits, the creation of boundaries between what is or is not the responsibility of the care worker, and between what you are allowed or not to hear, feel and say. According to Sara Ahmed, emotions can mediate the relationship between the psychic and the social and between the individual and the collective.[36] In the care workers' case, this becomes explicitly clear. As shown above, in their daily work, emotions circulate; love gives meaning to their practices and informs their interactions in distinct ways.

Concluding remarks

I started the text by discussing how the idea of family care and intergenerational reciprocities represents an idealized scenario that informs the moral and emotional demands of the work performed by care workers. Subsequently, I showed how the idea of professionalization implies a distancing from family care models, which can be seen, for example, in the emphasis given to distance – including affective – in the relationship between care worker and the elderly.

It was found that gendered and racialized morality, understood here in terms of reciprocity and family solidarity, is a hindrance to the appreciation of care workers and operates as a mechanism for maintaining subordinations. It is precisely the removal of this subjectivity that becomes a strategy of resistance against certain forms of exploitation in care work.

This chapter has considered love's significant role in constructing and deconstructing supposed natural hierarchies and analysed how the meanings it holds should be scrutinized to understand care work and its inequalities. As pointed out by several feminists, gender inequality has the capacity to transfer itself, repeatedly, from the family sphere – here understood as the sphere of reciprocities – to the sphere of the market, and vice versa. This chapter also brings attention to the importance of highlighting the racial division of labour that continues to inform care work.

Notes

1 Arlie Hochschild, 'Love and Gold', in *Global Women: Nannies, Maids, and Sex Workers in the New Economy,* ed. Arlie Hochschild and Barbara Ehrenreich (Berkeley: University of California Press, 2003), 15–30.

2   Viviana Zelizer, 'L'économie du care', *Revue Francaise de Socio-Économie* 2, no. 2 (2008): 13–25.
3   See Lycia Tramujas Vasconcellos Neumann and Steven M. Albert, 'Aging in Brazil', *Gerontologist* 58, no. 4 (2008): 611–17 and Nadya Araujo Guimarães, 'Casa e mercado, amor e trabalho, natureza e profissão: controvérsias sobre o processo de mercantilização do trabalho de cuidado', *Cadernos Pagu*, no. 46 (2016): 59–77.
4   Hochschild, 'Love and Gold', 15–30.
5   Ibid., 22.
6   Encarnation Gutiérrez-Rodríguez, 'The "Hidden Side" of the New Economy: On Transnational Migration, Domestic Work, and Unprecedented Intimacy', *Frontiers: A Journal of Women Studies* 28, no. 3 (2007): 71.
7   Paula England, 'Emerging Theories of Care Work', *Annual Review of Sociology* 31, no. 1 (2005): 389.
8   Joan Tronto, *Moral Boundaries: A Political Argument for an Ethic of Care* (New York: Routledge, 1993).
9   Anna Bárbara Araujo, 'Da ética do cuidado à interseccionalidade: caminhos e desafios para a compreensão do trabalho de cuidado', *Mediações – Revista De Ciências Sociais* 23, no. 3 (2018): 43–69.
10 The research was carried out as part of a master's thesis in sociology at the Federal University of Rio de Janeiro, Brazil. The study was conducted in 2014 and was financed by the Coordenação de Aperfeiçoamento de Pessoal de Nível Superior – CAPES (Coordination of Superior Level Staff Improvement).
11 Howard Becker, *Outsiders: Studies in the Sociology of Deviance* (New York: Free Press Glencoe, 1963). Becker uses the term 'moral entrepreneurs' to describe individuals or groups that try to enforce or change moral norms. Here I use the term 'entrepreneurs' to show how care workers cement family values.
12 Luana Pinheiro, Fernanda Lira, Marcela Rezende and Natália Fontoura, 'Os desafios do passado no trabalho doméstico do século XXI: reflexões para o caso brasileiro a partir dos dados da PNAD continua', *Textos para discussão*, no. 2528 (2019): 1–52
13 See Guimarães, 'Casa', 59–77. Domestic work statistics in Brazil encompasses many occupations, including cleaners, cooks, care workers, nannies and personal drivers.
14 Maria de Fátima Lage Guerra, 'Trabalhadoras domésticas no Brasil: coortes, formas de contratação e famílias contratantes', PhD diss., Federal University of Minas Gerais, Brazil, 2017, 128.
15 International Labour Office (ILO), *Care Work and Care Jobs for the Future of Decent Work* (Geneva: ILO, 2018), 190.
16 Adalberto Cardoso, *A Construção da Sociedade do Trabalho no Brasil: Uma investigação sobre a persistência secular das desigualdades*, 2nd edn (Rio de Janeiro: Amazon, 2019); my translation.

17 Bila Sorj, 'Socialização do cuidado e desigualdades sociais', *Tempo Social* 26, no. 1 (2014): 123–8.
18 Pinheiro et al., 'Os desafios', 12.
19 Ibid., 25.
20 Cf. ILO, *Care Work and Care Jobs*.
21 Ibid., 190.
22 Eduardo Bonilla-Silva, 'Feeling Race: Theorizing the Racial Economy of Emotions', *American Sociological Review* 84, no. 1 (2019): 1–25.
23 Sara Ahmed, *The Cultural Politics of Emotion* (Edinburgh: Edinburgh University Press, 2014), 9.
24 Lelia Gonzalez, 'Racismo e sexismo na cultura brasileira', *Ciências Sociais Hoje* 2 (1984): 223–44.
25 Evelyn Nakano Glenn, 'Creating a Care Society', *Contemporary Sociology* 29, no. 1 (2000): 84–94; Rosemary Crompton, *Employment and the Family: The Reconfiguration of Work and Family Life in Contemporary Societies* (Cambridge: Cambridge University Press, 2006); Eileen Boris and Jennifer Klein, 'Organizing Home Care: Low-Waged Workers in the Welfare State', *Politics & Society* 34, no. 1 (2006): 81–107.
26 Lena Näre, 'The Moral Economy of Domestic and Care Labour: Migrant Workers in Naples, Italy', *Sociology* 45, no. 3 (2011): 396–412.
27 Mary Romero and Nancy Pérez, 'Conceptualizing the Foundation of Inequalities in Care Work', *American Behavioral Scientist* 60, no. 2 (2016): 172–88.
28 Eric Sabourin, 'Marcel Mauss: da dádiva à questão da reciprocidade', *Revista Brasileira de Ciências Sociais* 23, no. 66 (2008): 131–8.
29 All care workers' names have been removed to protect their identity from publication. All the participants agreed to take part in the study and provided verbal informed consent.
30 Everett Hughes, 'Good People and Dirty Work', in *The Sociological Eye: Selected Papers*, ed. Everett Hughes (New Brunswick: Transaction Publishers, [1962] 1993), 87–97.
31 Julia Twigg, 'Carework as a Form of Bodywork', *Ageing and Society* 20, no. 4 (2000): 389–411.
32 Anthony Heyes, 'The Economics of Vocation *or* "Why Is a Badly Paid Nurse a Good Nurse"?', *Journal of Health Economics* 24, no. 3 (2005): 561–9.
33 See, England, 'Emerging Theories of Care Work', 381–99; Nancy Folbre, 'Demanding Quality: Worker/Consumer Coalitions and "High Road" Strategies in the Care Sector', *Politics and Society* 34, no. 1 (2006): 11–31; Viviana Zelizer, *The Purchase of Intimacy* (Princeton, NJ: Princeton University Press, 2005).
34 Zelizer, *Purchase of Intimacy*, 35–41.

35 Alexandre Barbosa Fraga, *De empregada a diarista: as novas configurações do trabalho doméstico remunerado* (Rio de Janeiro: Editora Multifoco, 2013), 160–1.
36 Sara Ahmed, 'Affective Economies', *Social Text* 22, no. 2 (2004): 17–39.

Bibliography

Ahmed, Sara. 'Affective Economies'. *Social Text* 22, no. 2 (2004): 17–39.

Ahmed, Sara. *The Cultural Politics of Emotion*. Edinburgh: Edinburgh University Press, 2014.

Araujo, Anna Bárbara. 'Da ética do cuidado à interseccionalidade: caminhos e desafios para a compreensão do trabalho de cuidado'. *Mediações – Revista De Ciências Sociais* 23, no. 3 (2018): 43–69.

Becker, Howard S. *Outsiders: Studies in the Sociology of Deviance*. New York: Free Press Glencoe, 1963.

Bonilla-Silva, Eduardo. 'Feeling Race: Theorizing the Racial Economy of Emotions'. *American Sociological Review* 84, no. 1 (2019): 1–25.

Boris, Eileen, and Jennifer Klein. 'Organizing Home Care: Low-Waged Workers in the Welfare State'. *Politics & Society* 34, no. 1 (2006): 81–107.

Cardoso, Adalberto. *A Construção da Sociedade do Trabalho no Brasil: Uma investigação sobre a persistência secular das desigualdades*. 2nd edn. Rio de Janeiro: Amazon, 2019.

Crompton, Rosemary. *Employment and the Family: The Reconfiguration of Work and Family Life in Contemporary Societies*. Cambridge: Cambridge University Press, 2006.

England, Paula. 'Emerging Theories of Care Work'. *Annual Review of Sociology* 31, no. 1 (2005): 381–99.

Folbre, Nancy. 'Demanding Quality: Worker/Consumer Coalitions and "High Road" Strategies in the Care Sector'. *Politics & Society* 34, no. 1 (2006): 11–31.

Fraga, Alexandre Barbosa. *De empregada a diarista: as novas configurações do trabalho doméstico remunerado*. Rio de Janeiro: Editora Multifoco, 2013.

Glenn, Evelyn Nakano. 'Creating a Care Society'. *Contemporary Sociology* 29, no. 1 (2000): 84–94.

Gonzalez, Lelia. 'Racismo e sexismo na cultura brasileira'. *Ciências Sociais Hoje* 2 (1984): 223–44.

Guerra, Maria de Fátima Lage. 'Trabalhadoras domésticas no Brasil: coortes, formas de contratação e famílias contratantes'. PhD diss., Federal University of Minas Gerais, Brazil, 2017.

Guimarães, Nadya Araujo. 'Casa e mercado, amor e trabalho, natureza e profissão: controvérsias sobre o processo de mercantilização do trabalho de cuidado'. *Cadernos Pagu*, no. 46 (2016): 59–77.

Gutiérrez-Rodríguez, Encarnation. 'The "Hidden Side" of the New Economy: On Transnational Migration, Domestic Work, and Unprecedented Intimacy'. *Frontiers: A Journal of Women Studies* 28, no. 3 (2007): 60–83.

Heyes, Anthony. 'The Economics of Vocation *or* "Why Is a Badly Paid Nurse a Good Nurse"?'. *Journal of Health Economics* 24, no. 3 (2005): 561–9.

Hochschild, Arlie. 'Love and Gold'. In *Global Women: Nannies, Maids, and Sex Workers in the New Economy*, edited by Arlie Hochschild and Barbara Ehrenreich, 15–30. Berkeley: University of California Press, 2003.

Hughes, Everett. 'Good People and Dirty Work'. In *The Sociological Eye: Selected Papers*, edited by Everett Hughes, 87–97. New Brunswick: Transaction Publishers, [1962] 1993.

International Labour Office (ILO). *Care Work and Care Jobs for the Future of Decent Work*. Geneva: ILO, 2018.

Näre, Lena. 'The Moral Economy of Domestic and Care Labour: Migrant Workers in Naples, Italy'. *Sociology* 45, no. 3 (2011): 396–412.

Neumann, Lycia Tramujas Vasconcellos and Steven M. Albert. 'Aging in Brazil'. *Gerontologist* 58, no. 4 (2018): 611–17.

Pinheiro, Luana, Fernanda Lira, Marcela Rezende and Natália Fontoura. 'Os desafios do passado no trabalho doméstico do século XXI: reflexões para o caso brasileiro a partir dos dados da PNAD contínua'. *Textos para discussão*, no. 2528 (2019): 1–52.

Romero, Mary, and Nancy Pérez. 'Conceptualizing the Foundation of Inequalities in Care Work'. *American Behavioral Scientist* 60, no. 2 (2016): 172–88.

Sabourin, Eric. 'Marcel Mauss: da dádiva à questão da reciprocidade'. *Revista Brasileira de Ciências Sociais* 23, no. 66 (2008): 131–8.

Sorj, Bila. 'Socialização do cuidado e desigualdades sociais'. *Tempo Social* 26, no. 1 (2014): 123–8.

Tronto, Joan. *Moral Boundaries: A Political Argument for an Ethic of Care*. New York: Routledge, 1993.

Twigg, Julia. 'Carework as a Form of Bodywork'. *Ageing and Society* 20, no. 4 (2000): 389–411.

Zelizer, Viviana. *The Purchase of Intimacy*. Princeton, NJ: Princeton University Press, 2005.

Zelizer, Viviana. 'L'économie du care'. *Revue Francaise de Socio-Économie* 2, no. 2 (2008): 13–25.

10

Love, power and justice in the shadow of the contemporary English prison

Christina Straub

Introduction: Theoretical and methodological underpinning

Love matters greatly in human life. As a connective and protective element in the neurobiological predisposition of human beings and as a major interrelational factor, love can influence human development and human behaviour.[1] As attachment and basic human need, love can act protectively against dysfunctional psychological coping strategies and in favour of human resilience and growth.[2] Its absence can induce states of psychological and physiological pain and illness.[3] As a cultural construct, love can structure not only individual but also social relationships.[4] In its ideal form, love acquires knowledge about the innermost truth of another and can ultimately lead to greater mutual understanding and social cohesion.[5] As a philosophical concept, love plays a major role in ethically motivated life choices.[6] As a virtue, it is said to promote valuing of the other as well as self-transcendence to further another's well-being.[7] To act with love represents the choice of a moral agent to pursue the 'good life'.[8] Greek philosophy describes four ideal types of love: *eros*, *philia*, *storge* and *agape*. *Eros* most commonly refers to love as romantic and sexual desire. *Philia* refers to love between friends, based on shared interests, purposes and truths. *Storge* has been described as 'affection, especially between parents and their children', similar to psychological attachment,[9] whereas *agape* is mostly referred to as an unconditional love for mankind.

These qualities of love have been distilled during a multidisciplinary concept analysis[10] conducted for my PhD. It delivered themes that structured my exploration of the effects of the absence and presence of love as human virtue and human need on the lives of a small sample (*n*=16) of long-term male prisoners in a low-security English prison. On its basis, this chapter critically questions whether love deprivation can be regarded as a just or unjust part of imprisonment.[11]

In line with much criminological research on the pains of imprisonment,[12] prisoners of my sample felt the absence of love to be one of the most negative factors pervading their long-term prison experience. They inhabited an environment devoid of opportunities to experience or express love along with other, more vulnerable, emotions such as sadness or weakness. This represented a source of emotional pain and could prompt some prisoners to deploy harmful coping mechanisms such as self-harm, suicide (attempts), numbing through drug use, or to externalize inner suffering through violent or hypermasculine behaviour towards others.[13]

These harmful effects caused by deprivations encountered in many English prisons have been well documented, and recent statistics on safety and deaths in custody (e.g. Ministry of Justice) illustrate their practical manifestation: self-harm and suicide (attempts), prisoner-on-prisoner assaults, as well as assaults on staff have been rising consistently over the years.[14] This development not only points towards persistent concerns for staff and prisoner safety, but similarly towards questions about the moral legitimacy of the institution itself. As Alison Liebling has noted: 'If prisons are to be more rather than less legitimate, they should not be places that prisoners cannot endure'.[15] Similarly, Anthony E. Bottoms and Richard Sparks have emphasized that a prison's legitimacy could be judged predominantly on the grounds of its procedural and relational dimensions, that is, the extent to which they recognized 'prisoners in terms both of their citizenship and their ordinary humanity'.[16] Scholars such as Bottoms and Sparks, Liebling, or Eamonn Carrabine therefore challenged the notion that 'legitimate prisons can be characterized by ... maintaining a largely consensual prison environment' only, suggesting that their legitimate execution of state power is connected to larger humanitarian imperatives.[17]

In line with the above discussion, this chapter interrogates the ways in which the prison's failure as a state institution to consider the effects of the deprivation of human needs and human virtues – such as love – affect those exposed to its environment. It further asks what the absence of love in institutional structures can tell us about the legitimacy of state power and justice. In doing so, it departs from Martin Luther King Jr.'s proposition that 'power at its best is love implementing the demands of justice, and justice at its best is power correcting everything that stands against love'.[18] It suggests that a closer look at institutional power and justice in relation to love can illustrate broader moral commitments practised by the state and its institutions in their treatment of human beings. Relatedly, it also considers the potential pitfalls of reformist, humanitarian intentions to introduce their relational framework of *sympathy* into penal justice.

Yet, this chapter argues neither that the practice of punishment or penal justice itself is illegitimate due to current limitations on loving practices it imposes, nor that these should be administered as a dose of 'coercive caring'.[19] Rather, an inclusion of love within the penal system such as argued for here should be regarded as a critical thinking exercise aimed at reforming practices of the prison as an agent of state power avoiding the pitfalls of those that came before. I venture to propose alternative frames of reference when thinking about justice in relation to *love*, such as Paul Tillich's concept of *creative justice*. To account for the multi-layered interrelations between moral and practical implications of my contemplation, this chapter adopts a multidisciplinary philosophical, criminological and socio-historical perspective.

Background: Historical and political developments in English penal culture

Over the past 200 years, a penal culture has been created that provides a 'set of instructions as to how we should think about good and evil, legitimate and illegitimate, order and disorder'.[20] When it comes to imprisonment, this may mean that 'the intensity of punishments ... and the forms of suffering which are allowed in penal institutions are determined not just by considerations of expediency but also by reference to current mores and sensibilities'.[21] Throughout their existence in England, prisons have served to convey a certain set of images, emotions and meanings which 'have by now become embedded in ... culture'.[22] Some of these can be traced back to the original set-up of prisons in the Victorian era and have been described by Drake as 'including the notion of exile, the importance of punishment, the principle of ... austerity and the belief that prisoners require moral, spiritual or other personal ... reshaping or reform'.[23] When reforms of capital punishment were gaining a foothold in the nineteenth century, prisons were established with a view to punish offenders by removing them from society, without transporting them to the colonies.

Today's prison estate in England represents a distinct move away from the infliction of grievous physical pain practised in the nineteenth century through capital punishment. It could be argued that this represents 'moral progress and a liberation from past abuses'.[24] As Nils Christie exclaims, 'From slaveries and workhouses with their uncontrolled abuses, to well-ordered penitentiaries, is that not progress? From whipping for disobedience to loss of privileges? From the old smelling stone castles to single rooms with hot and cold water – does that not exemplify reduction in pain?'[25]

Be that as it may, critics such as Christie or Mill warned that it was 'chimerical … to suppose that whatever has absolute power over men's bodies will not arrogate it over their minds; will not seek to control'.[26] According to McGowen, it is important to not fall prey to the assumption that this new form of punishment was generally more beneficial and ignore the possibility that it too represented a form of coercion. Now, the criminal had to be separated from his outside life in order to 'experience isolation' and 'suffer from his own otherness'.[27]

Although prison was seen as a more life-affirming alternative to capital punishment, its purpose was still geared towards destruction, albeit in a different sense. It was aimed at changing the 'anti-social' personality attributed to offenders in order to 'render them good neighbors and citizens'.[28] This value orientation represented one specific governing rationality of the state, namely penal welfarism. Its notion was that state law and sovereignty can wield power over citizens' 'bare life' – to borrow Giorgio Agamben's term – to transform it into the 'good life'.[29] Michel Foucault has come to define this kind of power as 'biopower' and identifies it as one of the greatest transformations taking place in the nineteenth century.[30] 'Sovereignty's old right – to take life or let live – was replaced … by a new right', he writes.[31] This new form of power took control of both body and life, using devices and institutions such as prisons 'to ensure the spatial distribution of individuals' bodies (their separation, their alignment … and their surveillance)'.[32]

The underlying condition of 'biopower', of keeping prisoners against their will and exercising coercive power over their bodies and lives, represents an ongoing matter of concern and scrutiny. Drawing on David Beetham's view that any form of power exerting physical coercion on individuals 'supremely stands in need of legitimation yet is also uniquely able to breach all legitimacy',[33] Bottoms and Sparks also acknowledge the persisting need to monitor penal and especially prison practice as a form of state power in their critical discussion of *Legitimacy and Order in Prisons*.

The moral legitimacy of prison as an expression of state power (without love)

The question of whether and how prisons can be legitimated, especially, if prison is regarded as a means for the state to protect the public has been a topic of scholarly discussion for more than twenty-five years. As Foucault warns, 'when the stakes are life itself anything can be justified.'[34] Making those identified as a potential threat to life or safety suffer and separating them from society may be seen as wholly justified. Great care has to be taken, however, when superior power, such as that of a state institution, is directed towards those in an inferior position, such as the state's own subjects. Tillich warns that injustice may occur if a 'superior power uses its power for the reduction or destruction of the inferior power.'[35]

This risk of injustice brings us back to love's qualities as human virtue and the related question of prison as moral practice. Deprivation of love as an inherent feature of the prison experience can not only lead to pain, but also to a dispossession of a human virtue and a reduction of power (i.e. self-affirmation) in a moral agent.[36] If prison deprives prisoners of love as human virtue, can it still be seen as legitimate in so far as it fulfils the criteria discussed by Bottoms and Sparks, namely recognizing prisoners in terms of citizenship, humanity and moral agency? If we depart from moral philosophy's notion that 'acknowledgment of someone as fully human is an act of justice', we must consider the consequences of not doing so, especially when a 'superior power' such as the state and its agents are involved.[37] It becomes necessary to ask whether the exclusion of love from the set-up of prison as institutional expression of state power and penal justice can indeed be regarded as just considering the implications for its subjects?

Delivering love through (penal) justice and the pitfalls of reformist views

Similar to King, existential philosopher Paul Tillich, in his deliberation on *Love, Power, and Justice* (1954), asserts love as the ultimate principle of justice. 'Justice', he writes, 'is the form in which and through which love performs its work.'[38] This view stands in opposition to ideas of justice as a means of separation, such as retributive justice delivered through prison, which deprives individuals of their connection to community as a punishment. In doing so, it physically and psychologically prevents prisoners from expressing human agency through practicing human virtues such as love.

When it comes to the punishment of crime, however, justice must contain an element of the offender being 'reduced in his power of being', though not entirely cut off from his own agency.[39] Tillich explicitly opposes the idea of false leniency when it comes to treating an injustice committed against the self or the community, since it would violate the legitimate demands made by love and justice:

> A man may say to another: 'I know your criminal deed and, according to the demand of justice, I should bring you to trial, but because of my Christian love I let you go.' Through this leniency, which is wrongly identified with love, a person may be driven towards a thoroughly criminal career. This means he has received neither justice nor love, but injustice, covered by sentimentality.[40]

Just as power without love can become reckless and abusive, so love without power can become 'sentimental and anaemic' and, in turn, unjust.[41] This becomes a substantial argument when thinking about prison reform in terms of implementing love. A similar line of reasoning has been previously taken up by the humanitarian reform movement in early-nineteenth-century Britain. In developing their rehabilitative ethic, they posited that there was something lacking in the (predominantly violent) offender that had to be (re-)installed: *sympathy*. This concept became the focal point of their reformist efforts. Seen as 'a new way of ... connection with other people based on feeling and concern', the ability to cultivate *sympathy* within one's self 'belonged potentially to all humans'.[42]

The association of *sympathy* with the cultivation of 'a common humanity' chimes with a sociological view of love as a sense of community or 'social affection'.[43] It also strongly resembles the moral philosophical idea of *agape* – a selfless love for mankind. Although the concept of *sympathy* takes up some qualities of love, it is important to note the reformists' underlying assumption that *potentially* all humans were regarded as able to experience or exhibit *sympathy*. It prepared a fertile ground for a division into those that already possessed this quality and *the others* who had to be supplied with it. Consequently, 'the reformers desired to promote a union with the outcast, but on their own terms'.[44]

Sympathy could thus be used to reinforce structures of power, albeit 'soft power', or, as McGowen described it, moral power, which required that 'the social other' would 'come to feel at one with the possessor of humanitarian feelings'.[45] McGowen and Bottoms both point out the potentially problematic nature of this rehabilitative ethic as an 'ethic of coercive caring'.[46] It is therefore important to differentiate between the concept of *love* and related concepts such as *care*, *sympathy* or *pity* as a means for change in the prison set-up. According to Georges Bernanos, pity can even be antithetical to love, since

> we never find people who love pitiful souls for themselves. The more fortunate put up with or tolerate the wretched out of pity. And by pitying them, they exclude them from love, for love obeys the law of reciprocity and pity makes reciprocity impossible.[47]

Equating love with pity would disregard the quality of love as a human virtue, as a human power that is inherent in a moral agent, who acts with love as a motivating force. Implementing a loving practice in the prison set-up would therefore have to be rooted in reciprocity, in human agency, instead of approaching its organization with the assumption that prisoners do not possess the ability to know love and its qualities.

Implementing love as *creative justice* into penal culture

Carving out an alternative approach is by no means a straightforward task. The idea of and push towards prison reform has been relevant since the introduction of this institution, yet it still represents an area of conflict often caused by opposing political and moral commitments. Fassin, for example, identifies a tension 'between the penal state and the welfare state' which stems from blurred lines 'between those destined for repression and those who inspire compassion'.[48] Yet, as moral philosopher Raimond Gaita asserts, it is one of society's duties to express a concern for institutions that are 'responsive to the full humanity in each of our fellow human beings'.[49] Gaita's argument for the delivery of state justice shares some similarities with Liebling's call for endurable (i.e. survivable) prisons. He understands state justice 'as a virtue that consists in the creation of institutions which … should not be the cause of such suffering in our fellow citizens that we should be ashamed of ourselves if compassion were fully to reveal it to us'.[50]

How, then, could love be (re-)introduced into the prison system? What impact would this have on understanding it as a legitimate expression of penal justice and state power? Tillich, for example, puts forward the idea of *creative justice*. This concept differs from retributive justice in that it does not exclude a criminal offender per se, but that it accepts those who are unacceptable. In *creative justice*, love is implemented within personal encounters through the acts of 'listening, giving, forgiving'.[51] In his view, justice can be delivered 'only through the love which listens ... penetrat[ing] in the dark places of the motives and inhibitions'.[52] He identifies therapeutic methods deployed by depth psychology as practical means to shine a light on the inner life and 'intrinsic claims of a human being'.[53]

Creative justice gathers knowledge by striving to understand the individual. According to sociologist Sal Restive, this could benefit not only the individual, but also society itself since it raises the aggregate level of knowledge. It allows us to gain 'a perspective on the sociocultural ... settings of self and others'.[54] When criminal offending is concerned, utilizing this concept could therefore support a holistic understanding of individual and larger environmental and social factors influencing criminal acts.

Another function of *creative justice* is giving, since 'it belongs to the right of everyone whom we encounter ... that ... the other one is acknowledged as a person'.[55] If denied, it could lead to the person's resistance to a perceived injustice, for

> the 'thou' demands by his very existence to be acknowledged ... as an 'ego' for himself ... Man can refuse to listen to the intrinsic claim of the other one. He can disregard his demand for justice. He can remove or use him. He can try to transform him into a manageable object ... But in doing so he meets the resistance of him who has the claim to be acknowledged as an ego.[56]

If, therefore, justice failed to regard an offender as a person with human needs and agency but treated him instead mainly as a risk to be managed, it could provoke resistance in those at its receiving end.[57] Herein, we re-encounter one of the criteria for prison legitimacy as stated by Bottoms and Sparks, namely recognizing prisoners in terms of their personhood. If lacking, prison as a form of state power could lose its claim to being perceived as legitimate or just.

The final component of *creative justice* is represented by forgiveness as 'the only way of reuniting those who are estranged by guilt'.[58] *Creative justice* incorporates the quality of love as a connective element in building community and belonging.[59] Reconciliation and forgiveness serve to (re-)include into a community those who have been expelled (or have expelled themselves) from it by causing damage. *Creative justice* as forgiveness exemplifies love as a form of justice that reinstates power to all parties involved by treating them as accountable, moral agents.[60] Weaving love as an expression and practice of justice into the fabric of the English prison system may thus undergird its role as legitimate state power. To accord those inside English prisons the moral agency to practise and receive love as human virtue and human need could – in light of above discussion – be perceived as a just act by a morally legitimate institution.

Concluding outlook: Potential contributions of love research to penal reform and social sciences

I would like to suggest that the theoretical aim for *love, power* and *justice* to work in unison, as set out by Tillich and King, could, indeed be implemented practically into the set-up and purpose of the contemporary English prison. The following recommendations are by no means complete but rather offer starting points for professional discussion. The human costs of pain caused by the absence of love as human need could be addressed, for example, by creating prison environments that adopt a (mental and physical) health- and resilience-centred approach. It could include the provision of psychotherapy to those incarcerated (on a voluntary basis to avoid coercive caring) as the love that *listens* and as part of *creative justice*. Best-practice examples could be taken from Therapeutic Communities[61] or PIPE units (Psychologically Informed Planned Environments).[62] To enable love in personal encounters, conjugal or extended visits, offering privacy and intimacy with loved ones, could be considered. Best-practice examples could be taken from European and US jurisdictions.[63]

Working towards a realistic shift in the prison set-up must take into consideration that some cultural values and frameworks are deeply ingrained and have remained unchallenged for a long time. To expose and challenge the current culture of penology and to develop a less humanly costly and more legitimate one, Garland advocates a research method within the sociology of punishment that exhibits and analyses contemporary sensibilities and structures of the affects that lie at the heart of penal culture.[64] Looking at the functions of affects in prisons might contribute to a change from a punitive culture towards a more holistic perception of the offender as an emotional human being and of prison as a corresponding moral practice. There is scope for more research to be conducted on the effects the absence or presence of emotions (like love) can have within the prison context and how this may challenge the moral legitimacy of this institution's power.

What this serves to show is the necessity to expand criminological research in this regard, in addition to a larger scale challenge to current disciplinary boundaries within the social sciences. As it stands, social sciences continue to 'neglect love relations, concentrating instead on the political relations of the state, the economic relations of the market, and the cultural relations' as the governing forces of social and human life.[65] Some re-evaluation of this has been initiated by feminist scholars such as Martha Nussbaum, Selma Sevenhuijsen, Eva Kittay, bell hooks and Martha Fineman.[66] Their work takes love out of the private sphere, drawing attention to its salience 'as public good, and … as a human capability meeting a basic human need'.[67] Feminism denotes love as a political matter, demanding that the state creates infrastructures of love to produce 'the nurturing capital that enables people to flourish' and for public policy 'to be directed by norms of love'.[68] Further research on love as a significant factor of social and legal relations could continue to build on this work and include love in the analysis of relations between individuals and institutions as well as within society itself. Multidisciplinary research cooperations could examine love and its intersections with power and justice as parameters for social justice and social ethics, especially when it comes to questioning implicit agreements held within social and political systems about the moral architecture of state institutions.

Notes

1 See Barbara Fredrickson, *Love 2.0* (New York: Hudson Street Press, 2013); Gerald Hüther, *The Compassionate Brain* (Boston: Shambala Publications, 2006); Thomas Lewis, Fari Amini and Richard Lannon, *A General Theory of Love* (New York: Vintage Books, 2000).

2 See Abraham Maslow, *Motivation and Personality* (London: HarperCollins Publishers, 1987); Sue Gerhardt, *Why Love Matters. How Affection Shapes a Baby's Brain* (East Sussex: Brunner-Routledge, 2004).

3 See Felicity De Zulueta, *From Pain to Violence: The Traumatic Roots of Destructiveness* (London: Whurr Publishers, 1993); Edward L. Deci and Richard M. Ryan, 'The "What" and "Why" of Goal Pursuits: Human Needs and the Self-Determination of Behavior', *Psychological Enquiry* 11 (2000): 227–68.

4 See Jennifer S. Hirsch and Holly Wardlow, *Modern Loves: The Anthropology of Romantic Courtship and Companionate Marriage* (Michigan: University of Michigan Press, 2006); Eva Illouz, *Why Love Hurts* (Cambridge: Polity Press, 2012).

5   See Sal P. Restive, 'An Evolutionary Sociology of Love', *International Journal of Sociology of the Family* 7 (1977): 233–45.
6   See Christian Smith, *What Is a Person?* (Chicago: University of Chicago Press, 2010).
7   See also Bennett W. Helm, *Love, Friendship, and the Self: Intimacy, Identification, and the Social Nature of Persons* (Oxford: Oxford University Press, 2010).
8   See also, Plato, *Symposium*, ed. C. J. Rowe (Warminster: Aris & Phillips, 1998).
9   Clive S. Lewis, *The Four Loves* (London: Geoffrey Bles, 1960), 42.
10 See Lorraine O. Walker and Kay C. Avant, *Strategies for Theory Construction in Nursing* (New Jersey: Pearson Prentice Hall, 1994).
11 Ethical approval for this research has been obtained from the University of Leeds's ESSL, Environment and LUBS (AREA) Faculty Research Ethics Committee on 20/12/2016, ID: AREA 16-041. See Christina Straub, *Love as Human Virtue and Human Need and Its Role in the Lives of Long-Term Prisoners – A Multidisciplinary Exploration* (Wilmington: Vernon Press, 2020).
12 See Barry Richards, 'The Experience of Long-Term Imprisonment: An Exploratory Investigation', *British Journal of Criminology* 18, no. 2 (1978): 162–9; Timothy J. Flanagan, 'The Pains of Long-Term Imprisonment: A Comparison of British and American Perspectives', *British Journal of Criminology* 20, no. 2 (1980): 148–60; Hans Toch, 'Studying and Reducing Stress', in *The Pains of Imprisonment*, ed. Robert Johnson and Hans Toch (Beverly Hills: Sage, 1982), 25–44; Ben Crewe, Susie Hulley and Serena Wright, *Life Imprisonment from Young Adulthood: Adaptation, Identity and Time* (Basingstoke: Palgrave Macmillan, 2020).
13 See Ian Brunton-Smith and Daniel J. McCarthy, 'Prison Legitimacy and Procedural Fairness: A Multilevel Examination of Prisoners in England and Wales', *Justice Quarterly* 33, no. 6 (2016): 1029–54; Ben Crewe and Ben Laws, 'Emotion Regulation among Male Prisoners', *Theoretical Criminology* 20, no. 4 (2015): 529–47; Martha Morey and Ben Crewe, 'Work, Intimacy and Prison Masculinities', in *New Perspectives on Prison Masculinities*, ed. Matthew Maycock and Kate Hunt (London: Palgrave Macmillan, 2018), 17–41.
14 See Ministry of Justice, *Safety in Custody Statistics Quarterly January 2018* (London: Ministry of Justice, 2018).
15 Alison Liebling, 'Prison Suicide and Its Prevention', in *Handbook on Prisons*, ed. Yvonne Jewkes (Devon: Willan Publishing, 2007), 443.
16 Anthony E. Bottoms and Richard Sparks, 'Legitimacy and Order in Prisons', *British Journal of Sociology* 46, no. 1 (1995): 59.
17 Brunton-Smith and McCarthy, 'Prison Legitimacy and Procedural Fairness', 1032. See also Eamonn Carrabine, *Power, Discourse and Resistance: A Genealogy of the Strangeways Prison Riot* (Aldershot: Ashgate Publishing, 2004).

18 Martin Luther King Jr., *Where Do We Go from Here? Chaos or Community?* (Boston: Beacon Press, 1968), 37.
19 Anthony E. Bottoms, 'An Introduction to the Coming Crisis', in *The Coming Penal Crisis: A Criminological and Theological Exploration*, ed. Anthony E. Bottoms and Ronald H. Preston (Edinburgh: Scottish Academic Press, 1980), 1–24.
20 David Garland, *Punishment and Modern Society – A Study in Social Theory* (Oxford: Clarendon Press, 1990), 252.
21 Ibid., 195.
22 Ibid., 26.
23 Deborah Drake, *Prisons, Punishment and the Pursuit of Security* (Basingstoke: Palgrave Macmillan, 2012), 20.
24 Randall McGowen, 'A Powerful Sympathy: Terror, the Prison, and Humanitarian Reform in Early Nineteenth-Century Britain', *Journal of British Studies* 25, no. 3 (1986): 312.
25 Nils Christie, *Limits to Pain* (Oxford: Martin Robertson, 1981), 2.
26 John Stuart Mill, *Dissertations and Discussions. Political, Philosophical, and Historical* (London: John W. Parker and Son, 1859), 378.
27 McGowen, 'A Powerful Sympathy', 312.
28 Ibid., 326.
29 See Giorgio Agamben, *Homo Sacer* (Stanford: Stanford University Press, 1998).
30 See Michel Foucault, *Society Must Be Defended: Lectures at the Collège de France, 1975–1976* (London: Penguin, 2003).
31 Ibid., 245.
32 Ibid.
33 David Beetham, *The Legitimation of Power* (London: Palgrave Macmillan, 1991), 40.
34 Michel Foucault, *The History of Sexuality, Volume I: The Will to Knowledge* (London: Penguin, 1998), 137.
35 Paul Tillich, *Love, Power, and Justice* (Oxford: Oxford University Press, 1954), 88.
36 Ibid., 37. See also, Plato, *Symposium* and Helm, *Love, Friendship, and the Self*.
37 Raymond Gaita, *A Common Humanity: Thinking about Love and Truth and Justice* (London: Routledge, 2002), 81; see also Didier Fassin, *At the Heart of the State: The Moral World of Institutions* (London: Pluto Press, 2015).
38 Tillich, *Love, Power, and Justice*, 71.
39 Ibid., 67.
40 Ibid., 14.
41 King, *Where Do We Go from Here?*, 37
42 See McGowen, 'A Powerful Sympathy', 314.
43 John Ruskin, *Unto This Last and Other Writings by John Ruskin* (London: Penguin, 1985), 169.

44 McGowen, 'A Powerful Sympathy', 329.
45 Ibid., 333.
46 Bottoms, 'An Introduction', 20.
47 Georges Bernanos, *Nous autres Francais* (Paris: Editions du Seuil, 1984), 205.
48 Fassin, *At the Heart of the State*, 2.
49 Gaita, *A Common Humanity*, 84.
50 Ibid.
51 Tillich, *Love, Power, and Justice*, 84.
52 Ibid.
53 Ibid., 85.
54 Sal P. Restive, 'An Evolutionary Sociology of Love', *International Journal of Sociology and the Family* 7 (1977): 241.
55 Tillich, *Love, Power, and Justice*, 85.
56 Ibid., 78.
57 See David Garland, *The Culture of Control. Crime and Social Order in Contemporary Society* (Oxford: Oxford University Press, 2001).
58 Tillich, *Love, Power, and Justice*, 86.
59 See Restive, 'An Evolutionary Sociology of Love', 233–45.
60 This approach bears strong resemblance to the concept of Restorative Justice which 'aims to restore the harm caused by crime and rebuild the relationship between all the parties concerned' (see Masahiro Suzuki and Xiaoyu Yuan, 'How Does Restorative Justice Work? A Qualitative Metasynthesis', *Criminal Justice and Behavior* 48, no. 10 (2021): 1347).
61 Prison-based therapeutic communities (TCs) promote psychological well-being and welfarist 'values such as trust, hope, meaning and affirmation' (see Jamie Bennett and Richard Shuker, 'The Potential of Prison-Based Democratic Therapeutic Communities', *International Journal of Prisoner Health* 13, no. 1 [2017], 21).
62 PIPEs as contained environments operate as separate units within conventional prison establishments, aiming to facilitate self-development and 'actively recognize the importance and quality of relationships' (Caroline Turley, Colin Payne and Stephen Webster, *Enabling Features of Psychologically Informed Planned Environments*, NatCen Social Research, Ministry of Justice Analytical Series [2013], 2).
63 See Helen Fair and Jessica Jacobson, *Family Connections: A Review of Learning from the Winston Churchill Memorial Trust Prison Reform Fellowships – Part II* (London: Institute of Criminal Policy Research, Birkbeck, University of London, 2016).
64 See Garland, *Punishment and Modern Society*.

65 Sara Cantillon and Kathleen Lynch, 'Affective Equality: Love Matters', *Hypatia* 32, no. 1 (2017): 172.
66 Martha Nussbaum, 'Emotions and Women's Capabilities', in *Women, Culture, and Development: A Study of Human Capabilities*, ed. Martha Nussbaum and Jonathan Glover (Oxford: Oxford University Press, 1995), 360–95; Selma Sevenhuijsen, *Citizenship and Ethics of Care: Feminist Consideration on Justice, Morality, and Politics* (London: Routledge, 1998); Eva Kittay, *Love's Labor* (New York: Routledge, 1999); bell hooks, *All about Love* (New York: William Morrow, 2000); Martha Fineman, *The Autonomy Myth: A Theory of Dependency* (New York: Free Press, 2004).
67 Cantillon and Lynch, 'Affective Equality', 171.
68 Ibid., 178, 169.

Bibliography

Agamben, Giorgio. *Homo Sacer*. Stanford: Stanford University Press, 1998.
Beetham, David. *The Legitimation of Power*. London: Palgrave Macmillan, 1991.
Bennett, Jamie, and Richard Shuker. 'The Potential of Prison-Based Democratic Therapeutic Communities'. *International Journal of Prisoner Health* 13, no. 1 (2017): 19–24.
Bernanos, Georges. *Nous autres Francais*. Paris: Editions du Seuil, 1984.
Bottoms, Anthony. E. 'An Introduction to the Coming Crisis'. In *The Coming Penal Crisis: A Criminological and Theological Exploration*, edited by Anthony E. Bottoms and Ronald H.Preston, 1–24. Edinburgh: Scottish Academic Press, 1980.
Bottoms, Anthony. E., and Richard Sparks. 'Legitimacy and Order in Prisons'. *British Journal of Sociology* 46, no. 1 (1995): 45–62.
Brunton-Smith, Ian, and Daniel J. McCarthy. 'Prison Legitimacy and Procedural Fairness: A Multilevel Examination of Prisoners in England and Wales'. *Justice Quarterly* 33, no. 6 (2016): 1029–54.
Cantillon, Sara, and Kathleen Lynch. 'Affective Equality: Love Matters'. *Hypatia* 32, no. 1 (2017): 169–86.
Carrabine, Eamonn. *Power, Discourse and Resistance. A Genealogy of the Strangeways Prison Riot*. Aldershot: Ashgate Publishing, 2004.
Christie, Nils. *Limits to Pain*. Oxford: Martin Robertson, 1981.
Crewe, Ben, and Ben Laws. 'Emotion Regulation among Male Prisoners'. *Theoretical Criminology* 20, no. 4 (2015): 529–47.
Crewe, Ben, Susie Hulley and Serena Wright. *Life Imprisonment from Young Adulthood. Adaptation, Identity and Time*. Basingstoke: Palgrave Macmillan, 2020.
De Zulueta, Felicity. *From Pain to Violence. The Traumatic Roots of Destructiveness*. London: Whurr Publishers, 1993.

Deci, Edward L. and Richard M. Ryan. 'The 'What' and 'Why' of Goal Pursuits: Human Needs and the Self-Determination of Behavior'. *Psychological Enquiry* 11 (2000): 227–68.

Drake, Deborah. *Prisons, Punishment and the Pursuit of Security*. Basingstoke: Palgrave Macmillan, 2012.

Fair, Helen, and Jessica Jacobson. *Family Connections: A Review of Learning from the Winston Churchill Memorial Trust Prison Reform Fellowships – Part II*. London: Institute for Criminal Policy Research, Birkbeck, University of London, 2016.

Fassin, Didier. *At the Heart of the State. The Moral World of Institutions*. London: Pluto Press, 2015.

Fineman, Martha. *The Autonomy Myth: A Theory of Dependency*. New York: Free Press, 2004.

Flanagan, Timothy J. 'The Pains of Long-Term Imprisonment: A Comparison of British and American Perspectives'. *British Journal of Criminology* 20, no. 2 (1980): 148–60.

Foucault, Michel. *Society Must Be Defended: Lectures at the Collège de France, 1975–1976*. London: Penguin, 2003.

Foucault, Michel. *The History of Sexuality Volume I: The Will to Knowledge*. London: Penguin, 1998.

Fredrickson, Barbara. *Love 2.0*. New York: Hudson Street Press, 2013.

Gaita, Raimond. *A Common Humanity. Thinking about Love and Truth and Justice*. London: Routledge, 2002.

Garland, David. *Punishment and Modern Society – A Study in Social Theory*. Oxford: Clarendon Press, 1990.

Garland, David. *The Culture of Control. Crime and Social Order in Contemporary Society*. Oxford: Oxford University Press, 2001.

Gerhardt, Sue. *Why Love Matters. How Affection Shapes a Baby's Brain*. East Sussex: Brunner-Routledge, 2004.

Helm, Bennett W. *Love, Friendship, and the Self. Intimacy, Identification, and the Social Nature of Persons*. Oxford: Oxford University Press, 2010.

Hirsch, Jennifer S. and Wardlow, Holly. *Modern Loves. The Anthropology of Romantic Courtship and Companionate Marriage*. Michigan: University of Michigan Press, 2006.

hooks, bell. *All about Love*. New York: William Morrow, 2000.

Hüther, Gerald. *The Compassionate Brain*. Boston: Shambala Publications, 2006.

Illouz, Eva. *Why Love Hurts*. Cambridge: Polity Press, 2012.

King Jr., Martin Luther. *Where Do We Go from Here? Chaos or Community?* Boston: Beacon Press, 1968.

Kittay, Eva. *Love's Labor*. New York: Routledge, 1999.

Lewis, Clive S. *The Four Loves*. London: Geoffrey Bles, 1960.

Lewis, Thomas, Fari Amini and Richard Lannon. *A General Theory of Love*. New York: Vintage Books, 2000.

Liebling, Alison. 'Prison Suicide and Its Prevention'. In *Handbook on Prisons*, edited by Yvonne Jewkes, 423–46. Devon: Willan Publishing, 2007.

Maslow, Abraham. *Motivation and Personality*. London: Harper Collins, 1987.

McGowen, Randall. 1986. 'A Powerful Sympathy: Terror, the Prison, and Humanitarian Reform in Early Nineteenth-Century Britain'. *Journal of British Studies* 25, no. 3 (1986): 312–34.

Mill, John Stuart. *Dissertations and Discussions. Political, Philosophical, and Historical*. London: John W. Parker and Son, 1859.

Ministry of Justice. *Safety in Custody Statistics Quarterly January 2018*. London: Ministry of Justice, 2018.

Morey, Martha, and Ben Crewe. 'Work, Intimacy and Prisoner Masculinities'. In *New Perspectives on Prison Masculinities*, edited by Matthew Maycock and Kate Hunt, 17–41. London: Palgrave Macmillan, 2018.

Nussbaum, Martha. 'Emotions and Women's Capabilities'. In *Women, Culture and Development: A Study of Human Capabilities*, edited by Martha Nussbaum and Jonathan Glover, 360–95. Oxford: Oxford University Press, 1995.

Plato. *Symposium*, edited by C. J. Rowe. Warminster: Aris & Phillips, 1998.

Restive, Sal P. 'An Evolutionary Sociology of Love'. *International Journal of Sociology of the Family* 7 (1977): 233–45.

Richards, Barry. 'The Experience of Long-Term Imprisonment: An Exploratory Investigation'. *British Journal of Criminology* 18, no. 2 (1978): 162–9.

Ruskin, John. *Unto This Last and Other Writings by John Ruskin*. London: Penguin, 1985.

Sevenhuijsen, Selma. *Citizenship and the Ethics of Care: Feminist Considerations on Justice, Morality and Politics*. London: Routledge, 1998.

Smith, Christian. *What Is a Person?* Chicago: University of Chicago Press, 2010.

Straub, Christina. *Love as Human Virtue and Human Need and Its Role in the Lives of Long-Term Prisoners – A Multidisciplinary Exploration*. Wilmington: Vernon Press, 2020.

Suzuki, Masahiro, and Xiaoyu Yuan. 'How Does Restorative Justice Work? A Qualitative Metasynthesis'. *Criminal Justice and Behavior* 48, no. 10 (2021): 1347–65.

Tillich, Paul. *Love, Power, and Justice*. Oxford: Oxford University Press, 1954.

Toch, Hans. 'Studying and Reducing Stress'. In *The Pains of Imprisonment*, edited by Robert Johnson and Hans Toch, 25–44. Beverly Hills: Sage, 1982.

Turley, Caroline, Colin Payne and Stephen Webster. *Enabling Features of Psychologically Informed Planned Environments*. NatCen Social Research, Ministry of Justice Analytical Series, 2013, https://assets.publishing.service.gov.uk/government/uplo

ads/system/uploads/attachment_data/file/211730/enabling-pipe-research-report.pdf.
Walker, Lorraine and Avant, Kay. *Strategies for Theory Construction in Nursing*. New Jersey: Pearson Prentice Hall, 1994.

Index

abuse 1, 19, 73, 74, 97, 100, 134 (*See also* inter-racial love)
   care work 159, 161, 179
   child 76
   parental 151
   physical 92
   prison abuse(s) 188
   verbal 76
academia 130, 133–9, 142–3 (*See also* institutions and labour)
adolescence 151
adoption 76, 78
Agamben, Giorgio 188
affect 7, 129–33, 140–2, 172, 186, 193 (*See also* critical love studies)
   economy of 136–7
affection 143, 173, 176, 178, 185, 190
   platonic affection 64
   romantic affection 21, 25, 54, 63
affections 58, 169, 172, 179
affective 129
   capital 176
   politics 133, 137–8
   response 152
African National Congress 73
Afrikaner 75
Ahmed, Sara 25, 172, 180
Amyotrophic Lateral Sclerosis (ALS) 73
Anarkali 15, 20, 23–4, 26
apartheid 6, 46, 73, 75–7, 80–5
   post-apartheid 73, 74–5, 83–5
attachment 130–9, 142–3, 152, 185
audio 121–2
   audio-description 107–9, 116–18
austerity 187
autonomy 37, 40, 151, 175

Berlant, Lauren 132–3, 142
Bhabha, Homi 74
bhajans 17

biopolitics 139
boundaries 2, 92, 194
   between self and other 17
   in care work 155, 157, 159, 161–2, 176, 180
   marriage 18
   safeguarding 160
Bourdieu, Pierre 23
Brazil 3, 169–73, 177
bureaucracy 26, 131–3, 160
Byatt, A. S. 7, 130, 135, 137
   Possession: A Romance 7, 130, 133, 135–7
body 7, 28, 118, 120, 176, 188
   ageing 67
   civic 23
   of text 109
   social body 42
   'ugly' bodies 6, 54, 60
   women's bodies 60, 61, 64, 138
Bollywood 15–17, 24

capital 3, 6, 131, 133–4
   academic 138
   affective 129, 194
   cultural 22, 133, 136
   erotic 138
   human 2, 3
   women's 136
capitalism 19, 132–3
   academic capitalism 131
care 1–8, 82, 89–90, 108–9, 115–16, 191
   caring *with* 112–13, 119, 121–2
   crisis of 2
   for elderly 3, 8, 169, 172–80
   family 175, 178
   industry 3
   neoliberal 7, 131
   parental 77, 96
   philosophical definitions 4

professional 8, 160–2, 169
residential 154
services 2, 8
work 2–3, 169–70, 172–3, 176–7, 180
workers 170–80 (*See also* domestic worker)
spousal 6, 141
The Care Manifesto 2
in youth work 150, 153, 158–9, 160–1, 163
caregiver 152, 175
Carline, Hilda 6, 53
children 7, 80, 89–91, 92, 95, 101, 185
care work's impact on 169, 174
and marriage 45–6, 62, 77
parenting and 90–2, 96–103
socialization of 29
Christian 39, 177, 190
citizenship 137, 186, 189
clients 149, 152, 155, 159
coercion 2, 38, 44, 48, 83, 100
physical 188
self-coercion 36, 38, 44, 48
Cohen, Rob 134
Skulls 134
Collini, Stefan 129
colonial 18, 25, 139, 142
anti-colonial 40
colonialism 36
commodification 5, 108, 114
Covid-19 8, 109, 112, 150–1, 154
creative justice 187, 191–3 (*See also* Paul Tillich)
crime 190
graffiti and 23–4
criminal 188–92
acts 192
critical 35, 188, 42, 140, 142
consciousness 90, 93, 95–100, 102 (*See also* Freire, Paulo)
imaginaries 133, 137, 142
love studies 7, 130–2, 136 (*See also* affect)
optimism 151
reading 36, 74, 139
thinking 97, 100–1, 151, 187
Crumble, Roger 134
Cruel Intentions 134

de Beauvoir, Simone 19
devotion 47, 58, 62, 129–31, 134
domination 1, 7, 76, 89–91, 94
love and 95–6, 101–3
over another 78, 39
parental 99–100
systems of 3, 35, 91–2, 98
white 42
Dutch 73

economic 2, 28, 132–3, 136, 140, 194
of class 141
development 21
global economic changes 20, 45, 150
hetero-economics 141–2
inequality 150
interests in care work 177–8
solutions 113
socio-economic contexts 3, 114, 138
education 2, 4, 7, 77, 90
concept of 98
in fiction 135
immigrant 38
as parental practice 95, 97 (*See also* parenting and children)
prison 8
problem-posing education 100 (*See also* Freire, Paulo)
for women 21
Eidsheim, Nina Sun 120
elderly 171 (*See also* care for elderly)
empowerment 43, 151
eros 17, 26, 131, 185
erosic 17–8, 20, 23, 29
erotic 1 (*See also* Lorde, Audre), 6, 23, 53, 136 (*See also* erotic capital), 140
epistemerotic fantasy 134, 139, 141
ethics 4, 134, 157, 194
of appropriation 136
of care 170
degraded 171
of love 7, 131 (*See also* love)
subaltern 170
ethnicity 42, 173
ethnic subjects 43

family 2, 7, 20, 57, 112
and care work 8, 169, 171–4, 179–80

children's contributions to 99
and domination 89 (*See also* hooks, bell), 98
and love 100–2, 171, 175
and marriage 16, 18, 21, 37, 44
model of care 177–8
nuclear family 5
patriarchal family 90–2, 95–7, 103
representation in fiction 6, 74, 80, 139
and youth work 153, 158
fantasy 16, 38, 40, 45, 56, 134
femininity 139, 172
feminism 194
black feminist tradition 89, 137
feminist politics 91–2, 194
feminist theory 4–5, 43, 172, 177
liberal feminist tradition 2
non-Western feminist tradition 20
postcolonial 35–6
Foucault, Michel 35, 188–9
freedom 8, 81, 98–9 (*See also* Freire, Paulo), 102, 141
access to 8, 23
collective 94
desire for 100
and equality 42–3, 74
liberal freedom 25, 27
and love 95
Freire, Paulo 7, 90, 92, 93–5, 97, 99–101, 150
Pedagogy of the Oppressed 7, 90, 92, 97
friendship 153, 158
Fromm, Erich 6, 74, 76–9, 80, 84–5
The Art of Loving 76

gender 6, 91–2, 118, 138
a-gendered 118
gendered care work 170–3, 178
inequality 42–3, 180
norms 19, 131, 136, 141,
performance 89, 91, 99, 116
Giorgione 61
Sleeping Venus 61
Global North 169
graffiti 24 (*See also* public space; wall painting)
gratitude 6, 35–42
(*See also* coercion and self-coercion) 44–8, 59, 79, 173

grotesque 6, 134
Guadagnino, Luca 8, 130, 139–40
Call Me By Your Name 8, 130, 137

health 171, 193
healthcare 38
mental 58, 151
hegemony 149
Hepworth, Dorothy 63
heterocentrism 140
heteromasculinity 140
heteropatriarchy 137, 142 (*See also* patriarchy)
Hill Collins, Patricia 89
(*See also* black feminist tradition)
history 47
art 4–5, 53
cultural 5
home 3, 28, 141, 158, 82
and belonging 59
family 2, 5, 7
homeless 22, 158
and marriage 42–3, 57, 66
patient's 179
hooks, bell 1, 7, 19, 89, 91–2, 95, 98, 150 (*See also* black feminist tradition)
'Understanding Patriarchy' 91
hope 76, 93, 100–3, 137, 159
hopeless 137, 151
radical 97, 151
human 18, 78, 97, 189
agency 4, 190–1
being 17, 41, 76, 176–7, 185, 187, 191–3
capital 2–3
desire 26 (*See also* desire)
flourishing 8
life 185, 194
nature 54
need 1, 185–6, 192–4
relations 74 (*See also* Fromm, Erich), 89, 91, 93, 95
rights 73
virtue 186, 189, 190–1, 193
humanity 85, 100–2, 150–1, 177, 186, 189–91
recognition of 90, 93 (*See also* Freire, Paulo)

ideology 7, 137–9
  essentialist 138
  patriarchal 18
immigrant 173
immigration 6, 173
imperialism 36, 38–40, 42, 44
individualism 21, 135–6
individualization 39, 131
inequality 5–6, 151, 172, 180 (*See also* gender)
institutions 5, 131, 136, 142, 159, 191
  neoliberal 7
  penal 187, 188
  state 187, 194
interpersonal 4, 82, 84, 149
isolation 188
  self-isolation 151

justice 179, 185, 187–93
  creative 187, 191–3
  Ministry of 186
  penal 8, 187, 189
  retributive 191
  social 151, 194
  state 186, 191
  youth worker 154

King, Martin Luther 186, 189, 193
Klein, Melanie 37

labour 4, 129–30, 141
  academic labour 131, 137
  conditions 138
  division of 174, 180
  domestic 2
  emotional 153
  female 171
  International Labour Organization (ILO) 172
  and love 114, 131, 133, 142, 152–3, 163
  market 169–70
  paid/unpaid 109, 114, 178
  rights 171
language 15, 82–3, 121, 129, 157, 162
  abusive 80
  artistic 110
  codes 153
  critics 139

of love 131
  performative 107–8, 116
legal 159, 194
legitimacy 186, 188, 192
  moral 8, 186, 192 (*See also* justice)
loneliness 37, 75, 83, 151
Lorde, Audre 1 (*See also* black feminist tradition)
love 3–8, 21, 54, 84
  absence of 186–7, 189, 193
  academic 130–6, 139–40, 142
  anti-capitalist 132
  binding love 108
  in care work 169–72, 174–5, 180
  children and 96–7, 99–100, 102–3
  Christian love 190
  and class 28
  critical study of 132
  democratisation of 19
  erosic love 17–18, 20, 23, 29
  ethic of 90, 95, 98, 131
  family 175 (*See also* love in care work)
  feminist critique of 25–6, 194 (*See also* Ahmed, Sara)
  and forgiveness 73
  forms of 107–9, 116, 121
  Freire's theory of 90, 92–4 (*See also* Freire, Paulo)
  Fromm's theory of 6, 76–7, 82 (*See also* Fromm, Erich)
  Hindu 24–5
  as human virtue 186–7, 189, 193
  humanitarian 176 (*See also* love in care work), 185
  genuine 82–4, 133
  and illness 83
  interracial love 37, 39–45, 74–6 (*See also* post-apartheid)
  language of 110, 131
  letters 135
  making 59, 62, 64
  marketization of 22,
  nature of 53–4
  neoliberal 7
  objects 140
  patriarchal 24
  performing 112, 117–19, 121
  physical 65

plots 136, 142
as practice 1, 8, 100–2, 149
professional 150, 152–4, 157–63, 178
   (*See also* love in care work)
pseudo 74, 84–5
reciprocated 54
right to 26
romantic 5–6, 17–19, 21–3, 54, 59, 64
sadistic 77, 79, 82 (*See also*
   Fromm, Erich)
scenes 130, 139, 142
secret 15
social justice 194
stories 15, 23, 36, 137
tactile 61–2
Tillich's theory of 189–92 (*See also*
   creative justice)
unrequited 54, 134
utopian 19
wife's 137
and work 114, 133
lovers 55–6, 60–2, 64–7, 111

management 39, 42, 163, 172
   behaviour 162
   multicultural 40
   role 154
managerialist 139, 141
Mandela, Nelson 73
Marcuse, Herbert 27
marginalization 3
marginalized 24, 35–6, 47, 150–1, 162
market 3, 8, 26, 136, 172–3, 180
   labour 169–70, 178
   Middle Eastern 42
   place 135
   relations 170, 194
marketization 3, 5, 22, 135
   hyper 20, 23
marriage 15–18, 24, 28, 75, 142, 178
   arranged 16, 18, 21
   dysfunctional 6, 43, 55, 57, 62–6, 84
   heterosexual 6, 135–6
   ideological 130
   as institution 5
   interfaith 18
   interracial 6, 73
   traditional 6

masochism 74, 79 (*See also*
   sadomasochism)
meritocracy 129
Middle East 20
migrant 36, 38, 41–3, 170, 173
migration 6, 8, 170, 173
money 37, 43, 45, 169, 177
   -oriented 37–8
monitoring 118, 134, 149
mother 21, 31, 74, 79, 81, 90, 102, 141,
   170, 175
   -daughter 6
motherhood 74–5, 84
Mughal 15
Mughal-e-Azam 15

National Party 73
nationalist 75
Nautiyal, Jaishikha 140
neoliberal 1–2, 119, 134, 149 (*See also*
   neoliberal work; neoliberal care;
   neoliberal university)
   economy 3
   university 7, 129–36, 138–9, 142
neoliberalism 1–2, 7, 21, 131–2, 135–6
norms 5, 20, 22–6, 103, 133, 194
   gender 131, 136, 172
   patriarchal 29, 89 (*See also*
      heteronormative)
   subverting 26, 28
normative 7, 24, 170
   heteronormative 7
   ideals 23
Nussbaum, Martha 194

oppression 1–3, 5–6, 83, 90–2, 101
   situation of 90–1, 94, 97 (*See also*
      patriarchal family)
   youth 151, 159
organization 159–60, 191
   capitalist 29
   family 97
   neoliberal 5
   prison 8
   social 74

pain 54–5, 63, 159, 185–6, 189, 193
   physical 82, 188

painful 55, 66, 76, 90, 102, 142
painting 6, 56, 58–60, 63
  wall painting 15–16, 20, 23–4, 26–7, 29 (*See also* Anarkali)
Pan Africanist Congress (PAC) 73
pandemic 8, 54, 65, 112, 150–1 (*See also* Covid-19)
parent 65, 78, 81, 84 (*See also* pedagogy; parental practice), 153, 185
  -child 76, 90
  in context of care 153, 158
  neglect 151
patriarchy 91–2, 96, 98, 103
  women under 91–2 (*See also* patriarchal family)
pedagogy 93–5, 97 (*See also* Freire, Paulo), 134
  of love 152
  political 7, 96–7, 102–3
performance 5, 7, 26–7, 130
  culture 131
  gendered 99
  of love 21
  of resistance 28
  space 109, 112
  theatre 107–9, 112–15, 117, 119–21 (*See also* theatre)
personal 6–7, 35, 58, 138, 150, 187
  attention 160
  connection 16, 169
  correspondence 63
  encounters 192–3
  feeling 132
  histories 122
  interactions 95, 116, 153
  limitations 158
  lives 7, 107
  personalization 129
  personality 154, 188
  relationships 91–2, 95, 97, 178
philia 185
postcolonial 5, 35–6, 38, 40–2, 45, 74
  subject 35–6, 38, 42, 48
postmodern 39, 151
poverty 6, 25, 46, 151
power 1, 7, 20, 38–44 (*See also* Foucault, Michel), 76, 153
  abuse of 97, 100, 134

biopower 4, 139, 142, 188
  coercive 188
  creative 59
  critical 115
  destructive 151
  dynamic 158
  human 114, 191
  institutional 187
  justice and 190, 193–4
  maintaining 132
  parental 90, 96, 98, 100, 102–3
  pastoral 39
  political 90
  racialized 43
  regulatory 35–6, 48, 92, 95
  relations 113, 172, 177
  state 186–7, 189, 192–3
  transformative 131
  workings of 36, 74
practice 3, 18, 93–4, 97–8, 150, 155
  artistic 58, 112–15 (*See also* artistic work; collaborative/collective work)
  of care 1–3, 5 (*See also* The Care Manifesto), 108–10, 113, 178, 180
  creative 7
  cultural 21
  devalued 176
  gifting 21
  of justice 192
  liberatory 100
  loving 8, 84–5, 95, 99, 102, 151, 155–63 (*See also* professional love), 191
  malpractice 161
  moral 189, 193
  parenting 90, 95–7, 98–103
  prison 188 (*See also* prison)
  relational 149 (*See also* youth work)
  social 171–2
  of spousal care 6 (*See also* marriage)
  of subjugation 92 (*See also* hooks, bell)
  of teaching 130
practitioner 8
  theatre practitioner 108
  youth work practitioner 149–63
praxis 17, 93–102
precarious 113–14 (*See also* precarious worker)
  academics 131 (*See also* academic)

employment 8
precarity 112, 131, 138, 151
   financial 112
prison 2, 186-9, 191-3
   English 186, 193
   reform 190-1, 193 (*See also* reform)
   system 3, 8, 193
prisoner 186, 188-92
production 2, 118, 172
   social production 22, 90
professional 2, 4 (*See also* professional care; professional love) 108, 131, 170, 193
   boundaries 156, 159, 161
   development 158
   qualification 154
   relationships 92, 150, 153-5, 157-8, 160
professionalism 7
professionalization 108, 113, 135-6, 171, 175, 178-80
provider 149
psychoanalysis 74 (*See also* Fromm, Erich)
Psychologically Informed Planned Environments (PIPE) 193
public 6, 56, 116, 189
   art 20, 24 (*See also* graffiti)
   consumption 20-1, 35
   good 134, 194
   hearings 73 (*See also* apartheid)
   in 116
   policy 169, 194
   romance 17, 20-1, 29
   space 5, 21-6, 28-9, 47
   sphere 21, 136
punishment 78, 187-90
   capital punishment 8, 187-8
   sociology of 193

queer 5, 140
   queer platonics 7, 108, 120

race 8, 43-4, 73, 138-9, 170, 172-3, 178
reciprocity 44, 113, 162, 171-5, 178-80, 191
reform 187, 189-90, 193
reproduction 2, 21
   social 137-9
resilience 152, 185, 193

resistance 19-20, 24, 26, 29, 115, 142
   aesthetic-based 23
   empowered 151
   intentional 90
   performing 23, 28, 132
   provoking 192
   resistance to 40, 109
   strategy of 180

sadomasochism 74, 84
sadism 74-81, 83-4
   (*See also* Fromm, Erich)
Schulman, Tom 134
   Dead Poet's Society 134
service 64, 99, 130, 149, 179
   care 2, 170 (*See also* care work)
   domestic 172 (*See also* domestic work; domestic worker)
   healthcare 38
   state 3
sexuality 21, 26, 140
   heterosexuality 18
   homosexuality 24
   women's 19, 20
sexual 17-18, 55, 59, 62, 134, 158
   bisexual 18
   desire 18, 61, 185
   division of labour 174
   (*See also* labour)
   heterosexual 6, 21, 24, 136
   (*See also* heterosexuality)
   homosexual 18, 22, 139-40
   (*See also* homosexuality)
   identity 18
   nonsexual 76
   rejection 63
She Goat 7, 107-11, 119, 122
   The Undefinable 7, 107-11, 112-18, 120-2
Shuddhikaran 24,
singing 18, 108, 118-19, 121
   (*See also* voice)
Smith, Zadie 8, 130, 137
   On Beauty 8, 130, 137, 139
song 17, 82, 116-17, 122
   Bollywood 17, 24
South Africa 6, 73-80, 84
   (*See also* apartheid)

Spencer, Stanley 6, 53-9, 61-7
  Apple Gatherers 61
  At the Chest of Drawers 64
  Beatitudes of Love 55-9, 63-4
  Desire 64
  Neighbours 64
  On the Landing 64
  Parents Resurrecting 65
  Resurrection of the Soldiers 64
  The Resurrection, Cookham 65
  Toasting 65
  Worship 64
storge 185
Sufi 17, 18
Sweden 36-7, 40-4, 46, 154
Swedish 6, 36-44, 46-8
symbiosis 74 (*See also* Fromm, Erich)
sympathy 156, 187, 190-1

Tartt, Donna 7, 130, 133, 134
  The Secret History 7, 130, 133, 134, 136
Teaching Excellence Framework (TEF) 129
theatre 2, 7, 107, 110, 121
  Camden People's Theatre 107
  Little Bulb Theatre 111
  multiplex/movie theatres 21, 28
  practitioners 108
therapeutic 192-3
Tillich, Paul 187, 189-91, 193
  Love, Power, and Justice 189

university 42, 109, 129-31, 134, 135, 138
  contemporary 7, 130

van Niekerk, Marlene 6, 73-4, 83-4
  Agaat 6, 73-4, 84
Vietnam 36-8, 41
Vietnamese 36-7, 40-2, 45, 48 (*See also* Vietnamese women)
  diaspora 36
violence 26, 81, 135, 158
  against couples 22, 25
  complicity with 44
  patriarchal 38, 91-2 (*See also* hooks, bell)
  physical 91
  post-apartheid 73, 84 (*See also* apartheid; post-apartheid)

postcolonial 36, 38, 47
sexual 15, 74, 79
racial 42
virtue 47, 58, 185-6, 189-91, 193
visually impaired audiences 107-8
Voice 107-9, 112, 116-21
  of children 92, 100, 103 (*See also* children)
  poetic 84
  scholarship on 109
  of women 74, 82

women 19, 21, 24, 28, 42, 179
  black 171-2, 176-8
  and care work 2, 169, 175
  migrant 6, 36, 173
  non-white 173
  poor 172, 176-7
  representation of 56, 74-5, 83, 135-6
  subaltern 74
  subordination of 1, 63
  under Apartheid 6
  Vietnamese 6, 36, 41, 47
  white 36, 47, 78, 139, 177
  working-class 173
work 1, 4 (*See also* care work; youth work), 26, 109 (*See also* paid/unpaid labour), 138,
  academic 130 (*See also* academia), 132-3, 138
  art 6, 24, 54-7, 59-61, 63-7
  artistic 108, 112-18
  and children 95, 150, 152, 155
  collaborative/collective 7, 101, 109, 114-15, 121
  contractual 179
  of cultivation 141
  daily 28, 178, 180
  definitions of 114
  diplomatic 46
  dirty 176
  ethic 27
  feminist 4, 194
  immigrant 39-42, 45
  neoliberal 4
  of love (*See also* Fromm, Erich), 189, 193
  and marriage 37, 39

of parenting 98–100
of power 74
racialized 171
radical 95 (*See also* Freire, Paulo), 97, 100, 102–3, 193
relational 161
reproductive 2
social 8, 159
voluntary 46
workload 160
worker 8, 142, 149 (*See also* youth worker; care worker)
  Brazilian Domestic Workers Union 179
  domestic 170–1, 173
  precarious 2
  sex 23
  social 45, 158
  working-class 43, 173

youth 55, 66, 74, 150, 152, 162
  work 3, 8, 149–54, 158–60, 161–3
  worker 3, 8, 149, 151–4 (*See also* justice) 155

Zulu 75
  Battle of Blood River 75